RV LIVING in the 21st Century

The Essential Reference Guide for ALL RVers

All the great helpful hints and tips from the best-selling publication – *Spirit of the Open Road* plus a vast amount of new information based on seven years of updates.

The first RV!

Written by *Peggi McDonald*

ISBN: 1-4140-5213-8 (e-book)
ISBN: 1-4184-4315-8 (Paperback)
ISBN: 1-4184-4314-X (Dust Jacket)

This book is printed on acid-free paper.

Cover Photo
The mural on the back of our motorhome – photo taken along the picturesque Highway 11 between Rocky Mountain House and The Crossroads, a midway stop *en route* from Banff to Jasper, Alberta.

First published by AuthorHouse 04/19/04

To John, the love of my life…

*John enjoys a luscious strawberry shortcake
at the Strawberry Festival in Plant City, Florida.*

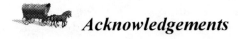 *Acknowledgements*

When John and I retired, a friend gave us a card with the words,

*"The future belongs to those who believe
in the beauty of their dreams."*

Our first book *Spirit of the Open Road* began as a dream early into our third year of life on the road – a dream that become a reality eight years later thanks to the support and encouragement from family, friends and my publisher, Canada's Explorer RV Club. Now seven years later *Spirit*, with its many revisions, additions and information updates, has emerged as *RV Living in the 21ˢᵗ Century.*

I could not have done this without the loving support of my best friend, my travel partner and my husband John. He has been with me from the beginning through all the traumas, late night and early morning writing and putting his plans on hold when I had 'just one more thing' to finish. I appreciate all the times he went where he didn't want to be – all in the name of research. John – your editing help, your suggestions to make it better and re-reading numerous drafts was an enormous help.

Thanks for edging me over the occasional roadblocks. Without your love and support *Spirit* would never have been a reality and now you have repeated this unending support a second time. You never once lost faith! Thanks so much for being there. I couldn't have done it without you. I love you, babe.

Di and me July 2002

Thanks also to my good friend Diane Batten from MAS Media Publications and editor of *Spirit of the Open Road* and Canada's foremost RV magazine – the *RV gazette*, for her help in launching this new edition. She found time between her extensive chemo treatments to read and re-read my manuscript again and again – incorporating her valued suggestions added a unique professional touch to *RV Living in the 21ˢᵗ Century*. Thanks so much for your patience with me as I try to comprehend the rules of grammar and punctuation. I owe you so much Diane.

A great team of readers assisted with the editing of *RV Living in the 21st Century*, and to those friends I send a special thank you: Trudy Rickard and Rodney Pickles (fulltimers); Suzanne White, part-timer and extensive traveller; Kathie Oriente, a fellow camper at our park during the summer and new to the RV world; Les Doll, my mentor for writing e-books and website maintenance and web host of www.rverscorner.com, and to Judie Riblett from Recreation U.S.A., one of the foremost discount camping clubs (www.campingandcampgrounds.com) who verified my American input. They each read my final manuscript for errors and suggested ways to make it easier to understand. I sure appreciate your input everyone.

This upgrade may never have happened without the help of John and Liz Plaxton, authors of *RVing in Canada's Arctic* and *RVing in Mexico, Central America and Panama*. Several years ago John scanned each page of *Spirit* to a 'word' file. Thanks for the effort John (and Liz), it made writing *RV Living in the 21st Century* so much easier.

I also have to say thank you for the numerous kind words and extensive praise that we received from so many readers of *Spirit of the Open Road* these words of encouragement gave me the inspiration to write *RV Living in the 21st Century*.

Our family and home!

John and I will soon be celebrating two decades of our life on the road and although *Spirit of the Open Road* hit the bestseller status with over 10,000 copies sold, it was time to update the content and add numerous new informative tips we have learned over the past seven years.

I dedicate this book to you John, sent with love…

— Peggi McDonald

TABLE OF CONTENTS

THE BEGINNING

Cover photo from Spirit of the Open Road.

 *Introduction*

RV Living in the 21 Century is an upgrade of ***Spirit of the Open Road.***
It is not a completely new book, but an amended version to reflect current
price structures plus seven years of fresh ideas and updates as we continue
to RV into the future. Our original two years of proposed travel has
gradually increased to nearly two decades of fulltiming where we called a
home-on-wheels our only home. Even though we sometimes talk of hanging
up the keys a few years down the road it seems there is always one more trip
we want to take before we settle into a 'home' that doesn't move.

My husband John and I bought our first RV in 1985 one year before our
retirement from the Canadian military. I was nearing the completion of 26
years in the Air Force and John was ending 33 years in the Navy. In May
1986, we sold our house, placed some furniture and keepsakes in storage
and sold everything else at colossal garage sales. Three months later we said
goodbye to our military life and jobs and hit the road on the way to our new
lifestyle.

At that time I was 44 and John was 48. We were also newlyweds (four
years) and thought the world was our oyster. Every place we explored was a
new adventure and every person we met became a new friend. Our
expectations were high and our experience was limited but, somehow, we
managed to balance the two even though some of the lessons we learned
were not only expensive but also extremely frustrating. Nevertheless, we
were free to enjoy ourselves and follow our dreams and two decades later
our journey continues.

Since a posting from one base to another is common in the military, we
had excellent training for the nomadic lifestyle of RV travelling. But, unlike
being transferred to another base and meeting up with others with a common
background, living on the road is a whole new ballgame. Usually the only
thing you have in common with your campground neighbour is the fact that
your home is on wheels.

Over the years I have had many opportunities to share our experience of
the RV lifestyle (or as RVers say, "the good life") by talking to others and
conducting seminars at RV shows, dealerships and rallies. We continued to
relay the joys of this great way of life as guests on CBC radio and several
daytime TV news-talk shows. The original draft of *Spirit* began early in our
travels simply because it seemed that everyone we met was hungry for
information. Presenting seminars led to our participation as crewmembers

and field reporters for the first 13 weeks of a Canadian RV television series, *RV Vacation Adventures* (now *Distant Roads*) – an experience that went beyond my wildest dreams. This opened the door to writing columns for several Canadian and American RV publications and later for Internet RV newsletters. I continue to present many seminars and share info at a variety of RV gatherings.

In 2000 Diane Batten, editor of **Spirit of the Open Road** and the **RV gazette** presented us with www.rvliving.net as a Christmas gift. Diane served as primary webmaster for two years until I finally took over most of the duties. The **RV Living website** has evolved into a comprehensive compendium of facts, tips, hints and general information that every RVer needs to know to enjoy this fantastic lifestyle to the fullest.

Two decades later and we are still travelling. We look for different southern hot spots to enjoy each winter but, by early spring, we head north to our home base in Ontario and spend the glorious Canadian spring, summer and fall sightseeing and visiting family and friends.

In 1998/99 we spent the winter in our motorhome in southern Ontario. *Spirit* was one year old and we took the opportunity to promote our comprehensive book at every opportunity during the RV shows, TV/radio interviews and more. It was a very interesting winter and challenging at times but the experience added one more facet to this outstanding way of life.

RVing offers such a sense of freedom and can be adapted to accommodate any form of living on the go. And, it doesn't matter if you're fulltiming or simply experiencing the joys of frequent weekend getaways, all RVers face the same experiences and learn how to cope – usually by trial and error.

Shortly after we bought our Kruisin' Kastle we camped several months in a campground 20 minutes from work. When looking back, this was one of our smartest moves because our super neighbours, Jack and Eunice, were seasoned RVers who patiently explained the ins-and-outs of the RV lifestyle. In my writing I try to be as helpful as these wonderful teaching neighbours.

No matter where we are or what we are doing, numerous people are enthralled with our interesting nomad life and many are eager to take to the open road themselves. Unfortunately, the majority of these folks are hesitant and money is the main reason. We have received letters – some polite and some not so polite – saying that they, too, wish they had the money so they could just travel around in an RV.

Well, guess what? Neither John nor I are rich, nor are we famous. Although (because of our promotion of the RV life) we are well-known, John and I live on a pension and yes, we must follow a budget but we manage quite nicely. RVing is not an inexpensive way to live but when you have a strong desire to follow a dream you will find a way to make it possible. Numerous RVers supplement their income by working on the road. These concerns are addressed in upcoming chapters. ***RV Living in the 21st Century*** is a necessity for all RVers who are just like us and want to join the good life but the entire experience seems overwhelming. It is also loaded with information and tips for experienced RVers as well.

To make your transition to the RV lifestyle as easy as possible, I've grouped related subjects into easy-to-find sections, ending with a handy reference directory. Actual dollar quotes will only be approximate because this is one area that changes constantly. (At the time of printing, $1.00 U.S. was worth about 75 cents Canadian.) Buying this book is your first step to joining this fabulous lifestyle and I know that you're impatient to hit the road. But, wait, before you sell the house and put your furniture and dog in storage, sit back and take a deep breath.

You can't join the RV life without – you guessed it – an RV. Unless you've inherited a fortune or won the lottery, you just can't walk out the door into a fully-equipped RV custom-made for you. Of course, if you have acquired a fortune or already have your dream-home-on-wheels skip 'The Beginning' and go directly to the next section.

4

To RV Or Not To RV

Taking each step slow and steady is the key to maximizing your RV enjoyment. John and I began our search for our dream home-on-wheels three years before retirement. We knew nothing about RVs (and little about the camping lifestyle) but, as we passed a motorhome on the highway one day, we both screamed, "That's what we should do for our retirement!"

Deciding what we wanted to do was easy. Finding a motorhome to do it in was definitely a challenge – we didn't even know a motorhome was called an RV. John and I were both extremely naive and inexperienced about what we wanted, what we needed and where to buy it.

These days with the advance of the Internet, TV shows and RV magazines on the newsstands, etc., information is fairly easy to come by. We studied the yellow pages for motorhomes and Winnebagos (we thought all motorhomes were called Winnebagos). At that time we had no idea that the phone book listed the entire scope of mobile travelling homes under recreational vehicles – at least in Ontario. Later on, when we started travelling, we found listings under the categories of travel trailers, vacation homes, mobile homes and trailers. Once we knew where to look, we found dealers with a wide range of inventory located everywhere throughout Canada and the U.S.A.

Our first motorhome – Kastle #1.

The First Step

What set us on the right road was an outdated magazine that John found at work. Although it was 10 years old, the magazine answered some of our questions but not enough to get us started. When I sent away for a subscription I discovered that publication was no longer in print but they directed me to others. By reading those publications we found dealers, information on various models and a schedule of upcoming RV events in our area.

Until then, we didn't even know there were shows designed to solely promote recreational vehicles and we quickly decided that this was one event we didn't want to miss. Announcements for upcoming RV shows are advertised on both radio and TV, in newspapers and magazines and on our website www.rvliving.net. These events take place year-round but more frequently between January and April, even in southern states where snowbirds gather. They are such a great place to meet RV dealers, talk to other RVers and visit vendors promoting RV products. In general, RV shows are the place to be to see what the market offers.

Neither John nor I will forget our first RV show. We were awestruck by the extensive variety of RVs. There were so many styles, types and models and, surprisingly, some were even within our planned budget. Finally we found a place to start us on our way.

That day so many models beckoned us to take a look and the experience was overwhelming. We entered the show with a hundred questions and left with a thousand more. Although shows are an excellent venue for RV shopping, some research before you get there helps sort through the maze. Be sure to take notes and pick up numerous brochures. FYI – it took us three years to find our first dream machine but several years ago I overheard one comment at one of my seminars that says it all... "I am so confused, we have been looking three weeks and I do not know what I want". Three weeks is nothing – take your time; buying an RV is a huge investment.

First, look for local RV dealers in the yellow pages and jot down their names. When attending the show, search for their displays and see first-hand what they have to offer. In some shows the dealers work with a manufacturer so you might find a grouping from that manufacturer in one area. Chances are you'll also find representatives from a specific manufacturer as well as from the dealership.

Scan local newspapers for dealer promotions – if a big show is being held in your area, the newspaper will probably devote a special section towards the event and dealers will advertise. Also, take a look at the used classified section for private sales. Again, jot down prices so that you will have some comparison price reference when you are at the show.

Most shows have a used RV section featuring pre-owned units from various dealerships. Even though there are good deals to be had when buying privately, first-time buyers should concentrate their search around established dealers. Whether buying a new or pre-owned RV the dealer's policy of follow-up maintenance plus the availability of experienced personnel to explain the workings of your new acquisition may be worth paying a slightly higher price.

After the show visit as many dealers as possible and familiarize yourself with market availability. If the show was your first, or if you haven't compared prices and makes and models before attending, don't be in a hurry to sign up for your 'dream machine' because of a special show price. Most dealers will allow the special show price to stand for at least a week after the show. Talk to the dealer and ask. If you really think that you've found 'the one', have a representative write down the make, model, year and type of RV. Record the show price and, this is very important, what features that price includes. Also have the rep note when the price offer expires. Make sure you get the rep's name and call the same person when you are ready to buy.

Dealer Open Houses

Most RV dealers host similar shows at their dealership several times a year. This show is as much an extravaganza as the larger RV shows but all specials are limited to the hosting dealership. Visitors will find low prices, good deals and new units of all types along with many used ones open and ready for you to explore and dream about.

Check the local newspapers for dates, locations and special features. For instance quite a few product reps attend these three-day events so they can answer questions from the source. I also present seminars at several dealers, as do many other seasoned RVers. Food tents, music, kids' events and more are part of the schedule.

 ## *The ABCs of RVing*

Years ago a non-RVing friend remarked that he and his wife wanted to buy "one of those kinds of motorhomes that look like a bus". He stated he didn't want the type that looks like it's built on a truck. "We want a motorhome," he insisted.

As a matter of fact, both units he described are motorhomes. The bus-style is a Class A and, the one built on a truck, is a Class C. The difference is the design, available storage space and cost.

Don't be fooled by the designation of campers or mobiles or trailers and so on. In actual fact these words all describe recreational vehicles or RVs. If it has wheels and you can eat and sleep in your unit, it is an RV. Knowing the different types of RVs makes it easier to determine the style suitable to your lifestyle. Frequently, owners of one type can't understand why someone would choose another. Any RV that fits your budget and your present and future lifestyle expectations is the right RV for you. The time you plan to spend on the road is another consideration in the style you select. An RV is not expected to last a lifetime and your first RV will most likely not be your last. As your needs change, switching from one style to another is also possible[1].

Always keep in mind that there are only **two categories of RVs – towable and motorized**. Decide what you want and make your choice from there. Towables include everything from a pop-up camper (tent trailer) to the more elaborate fifth wheel. Although the sizes and appointments vary, these models are all pulled by a separate vehicle and require proper hitch devices.

Motorized RVs are self-propelled vehicles. In the motorized category there are four classes: Class A (these look like big buses), Class B (van conversions or those built on a van chassis), Class C (the living quarters are built right on to a truck chassis with an extension over the cab) and bus

---

1 Two websites designed to provide information about what is happening in the RV industry are www.gorving.com (U.S.A) and www.gorving.ca (Canada). The Go RVing phone will be answered by staff in the country from where you are calling...
1-888-GORVING (or 1-888-467 8464).

conversion (diesel bus shells are transformed into classy units by do-it-yourself handymen; some businesses also offer this service).

To make the choice easier for you, I've listed a brief description of each class, starting with the towables.

Towables

> ### *Travel Trailers*

Travel trailers are what most people think of when they hear the term 'mobile home'. (They aren't. In reality a mobile home sits semi-permanently in a park; it can only be moved by a specialty-designed truck). Towable RVs have been popular since the 1920s. Travel trailers come in many different lengths and styles. Travel trailer styles range from the long, rectangular look to rounded, aerodynamic shapes. Interior designs and appointments vary from model to model but, on the whole, these units are fitted with every amenity found in your home.

In the last few years, travel trailers have undergone many changes and are now available in lightweight sizes (designed to be towed by the family car or van), hybrids (a body of a travel trailer with extendible soft-sided sleeping "wings" like a pop-up camper) and telescoping or low-profile units. Telescoping units have a hard body, usually constructed of fibreglass, with a hard roof. The unique design of these units allows the top to drop down over the base for travelling. When extended for camping, there is usually about 6-1/2 feet to 7 feet of interior headspace.

Some models of travel trailers (and fifth wheels) are available with a 'garage' – an open space that can house ATVs, small boats and other 'toys".

> ### *Fifth Wheels*

These models are the elite of all the towable RVs. Built with a split-level design, these sumptuous units can make camping in the wilderness seem like a stay in a luxury hotel – without maid service, of course.

Divided into two sections, fifth wheels traditionally feature the kitchen, dining area and living room on the lower level and, the second level (built over the fifth wheel hitch) contains a bedroom and bathroom. Like the other classes of RVs, fifth wheels are available with different floorplans.

The vehicle (truck) needed to pull a fifth wheel can cost the same as the unit itself, raising the total overall price. Because of the size of some 'fivers' (like the larger travel trailer and motorized units), travel to out-of-the-way spots may be limited. This design should not be considered if anyone in your family has difficulty climbing stairs.

➤ *Pop-Up Camping Trailers (Tent Trailers)*

Pop-up camping trailers or tent trailers are the popular choice of first time buyers, especially for those with young families who want a weekend and holiday getaway unit. The less costly pop-ups combine all the comforts of home with the thrill of open-air tent camping – without having to sleep on the ground.

These collapsible units are constructed on a trailer chassis with the bottom and roof usually made from fibreglass. The collapsible sides can be canvas or a lightweight, waterproof and durable synthetic material. For travelling, the whole unit folds down into itself with the roof acting as a cover.

These units can be easily towed by the family car or van and set-up takes only a few minutes. Fold-downs are suitable for late spring summer and early fall.

➤ *Truck Campers*

Although truck campers aren't towed behind a vehicle, they do fit on the bed of a pickup truck. Truck campers have evolved from utility units to well-appointed RVs featuring many of the amenities of a larger RV. These units are now available with full three-piece washrooms, stoves, microwaves and air conditioning. With the growing popularity of truck campers, most manufacturers are insulating the units and installing a furnace for year-round use.

Truck campers are available in sizes to fit most pickup boxes and, depending on size, these units can comfortably sleep from two to six people. There's very little (or no) campsite set-up time involved and, when not in use or on an extended stay in a campground, the camper can be removed from the pickup and stored away.

Extra Info

Most towable units include conveniences such as washrooms and kitchen facilities ranging from a full-scale bathroom and complete kitchen to a porta-potti and a two-burner camping stove. However, no matter how elaborate the facilities, when travelling none of these are accessible as they can only be reached from outside of the unit. It is also illegal for passengers to be in the unit when travelling on the road.

Major benefits of having a towable are that these units have a very slow rate of depreciation and command a good re-sale value. There's very little mechanical maintenance required and, whenever your trailer is set up in a campsite, you can unhitch the tow vehicle to use for sightseeing.

Motorized

All other RVs fall under the category of motorized units and, again, the types and styles are numerous. Motorized RVs are simply those that you can drive and are available with either a gas or diesel engine. Styles range from the small compact models to luxurious diesel-powered buses.

One advantage of using a motorized RV is that all facilities are easily accessible. If you can move from the driving/passenger seats to the living quarters without going outside, your unit is a motorized unit. However, moving around must be done with extreme caution and, in areas where seat belt laws are in effect, walking inside your unit when the vehicle is moving is illegal.

Although setting up is extremely easy at a campsite (just connect water, electric and sewer), a minor drawback with a motorized RV is the lack of a getaway vehicle for sightseeing and running errands. Many RVers choose to tow a small car behind their unit for this purpose.

Motorized RVs are also the most costly – both in initial cash outlay, replacement upgrade and maintenance. Remember, though, that if you have to purchase a tow vehicle to pull a towable unit, the cost between motorized and non-motorized is comparable. However, unlike towables, you don't have the luxury of replacing the tow vehicle one year and the unit the next. Also, because the unit is all-in-one, the depreciation value is greater than that of a towable.

Something to keep in mind if you decide on a motorized RV is that, unlike towables, when the engine of the motorhome develops mechanical problems, the whole unit must go in for repair. Living in your unit in the parking lot of the repair facility does not make for a memorable vacation.

➤ *Class A*

Class A motorhomes are the cream of the crop, the top of the motorhome line and, with the elaborate interiors and varied floor plans; it's easy to find your dream home. Along with the fifth wheel, these RVs seem to be the main choice for fulltimers.

In the beginning storage pod doors were very small but now Class As have huge basement storage compartments. This is because manufacturers raised the inside floor of the units and the space between the floor of the unit and the chassis is transformed into a fairly substantial storage area. Usually accessible from the outside, this area is the perfect place to pack items that 'you can't live without'.

Most of these spacious compartments contain slide-through areas for skis, ladders, hoses and even an inflatable boat and motor. There is also a model that offers a rear storage compartment large enough to stow a small car (about the size of a Mini) for travelling. Some of these compartments even include slide-out trays for easy access to your treasures. Another advantage to the basement model is that the driver, co-pilot and passengers all travel at the same height level. (However, in non-basement models the driver and co-pilot sit higher than travelling passengers). These high-level basement units are more prone to wind gusts but steering stabilizer systems for the front axle are available to ease side-to-side motion. You do have to watch for tunnel heights and overhead clearance at gas stations and bridges, especially on secondary roads.

➤ *Class B*

Another member of the motorized group of RVs is the Class B motorhome. The Class B (or camper vans or van conversions) looks similar to the family van but they are taller. With the raised roof and sunken (lowered) floor, these units have about six-and-a-half feet of interior headspace.

The interiors are more spacious than they appear from the outside. These units are equipped with a comfortable galley, living area and sleeping/dining area. Most Class Bs also include a toilet and shower, ranging from a full bathroom to a closet that quickly converts into a bathroom with scaled-down amenities. Some manufacturers offer slide-outs designed to increase interior space.

The compact size of the Class B offers maximum mobility and can be easily parked almost anywhere. Basic models of this dual-purpose vehicle are available for a moderate cost, but those with more elaborate styles can carry a fairly high price tag.

Although a Class B can double as a family car and sightseeing vehicle, you must break camp before leaving the campground and set up again on return. The limited storage and living space in a Class B may also discourage extensive long-term travel, especially in poor weather conditions. This, however, is not always the case. An RV friend, living in her Class B, proudly described her home-on-wheels this way,

"I have every room in my house but I only have one room at a time. I simply must decide which room I wish to use at the moment". Incidentally, my friend and her husband travelled extensively in their Class B for many years – their journeys took them to interesting out-of-the-way places in Europe, Mexico, the U.S. and Canada.

Several companies specialize in van conversions. However, unless the finished product is high enough to stand in, a converted van may be too uncomfortable for prolonged travel. (See Class C for an important fact regarding overloading.)

➢ *Class C*

Last, but not least, in the motorized group is the Class C. These motorhomes are a smaller version Class A built onto a truck chassis, complete with an overhead cab. The main sleeping area is usually in the cab-over bunk, although there are models with bedroom configurations.

Class C models and floorplans vary from the extremely basic to a more elaborate and comfortable home-on-wheels. Smaller units may be low in height with compact designs but larger units are more spacious. These units can do double duty as both a vacation home and a touring vehicle. If using this RV as a tour vehicle, you must break camp (up awnings, disconnect water, electric and sewer before moving) and set-up again when you return to your campsite. A Class C, depending on size, is functional for short vacation jaunts and for fulltime living.

Since the Class C and Class B have a smaller engine and chassis than a Class A, overloading takes on a stronger importance. Storage space is limited. Be aware of your recommended GVWR (Gross Vehicle Weight Rating) set by the chassis and engine manufacturer. Weigh your RV after it is fully loaded with luggage, passengers, fuel and water. Carrying too much weight reduces the handling ability plus adds stress to the chassis springs, tires and vehicle components. While this is true for any type of RV, it is more critical in both the Class C and Class B.

➢ *Converted Buses*

Many do-it yourself RVers prefer to purchase a diesel bus shell and remove everything back to the walls. These can also be converted by businesses specializing in RV upgrades. Before insulation, special electric and plumbing modifications are added. As bus conversions have interiors built from 'scratch', RVers can build and create the motorcoach of their dreams. These units present an awesome sight and since they are designed with the owner's needs in mind, they are a very personalized unit[2].

---

2 Helpful websites covering all facets of the RV lifestyle can be found in various sections of the RV WebLink *page of www.rvliving.net.*

For Your Information

➢ *Park Models*

A park model trailer is in a class of its own and is perfect for those who are looking for a permanent set-up in a trailer park. People who buy park models rent land space at designated seasonal campgrounds and use this type of RV in lieu of a cottage.

Usually the unit is placed on a concrete pad and many owners add rooms and porches to extend the living space of this compact unit. You will occasionally see many of these 'permanent' RVs in a landscaped setting with fences around the lots and driveways with covered parking areas.

➢ *Slide-outs*

Numerous models of RVs now include room extenders or, as they are more commonly called, 'slide-outs'. These slide-outs are available in varying lengths and are frequently considered standard equipment on many towables and motorized units. The latest room extender promotes double the space with the push of a button.

Even though these extensions add tremendously to the living, dining and bedroom space, they also add weight with the slide in travel mode. Occasionally campsites are narrow and slide-outs can't be extended when camping. For some models, this makes the interior living space very limited.

➢ *Rental Units*

If you have done your research, attended the shows or open houses but are still not sure what type of RV will suit your lifestyle, consider taking a vacation in a rental unit similar to the one you think you might like to buy.

With a rental unit it's easy to experience RV living before putting out purchase money. Renting not only introduces you to the advantages of the RV life, it is also a wonderful way to add variety to your family vacation.

Renting during prime camping season can be quite expensive but during fringe seasons (spring and fall) they are more affordable. Frequently, vacations in a rental unit are more economical than staying in a hotel or motel and eating all meals in restaurants.

Campground rates cost less than a night in a motel and you can cook and eat your meals in the unit, saving on the expense of restaurants. You can also use the entertainment facilities at most campgrounds and save your money for extra sightseeing jaunts.

In some areas, RV rentals are listed in the telephone book with RV dealers and, in others, under automotive rentals[3].

If finding a local rental office is a problem, call a dealership. Quite a few dealers keep rental units on hand and, if not, they can tell you where to find an RV rental office.

Designs Keep Changing

When we began our on-the-road adventure, RVs were pretty basic, these days built-in computer stations, multiple slide-outs, fireplaces and many other features are added to enhance your living comfort. Each year new designs appear in the line-up of both towables and motorized units. Some motorhome models features a roof-top patio, another boasts of an extended ceiling (plus sunken floor). Murphy beds that lower from the ceiling are very popular – some have computer stations below. At the last dealer open house we attended, a fifth wheel featured an extendable back patio complete with awning and screen room. New features are only limited by the imagination of the manufacturer. However remember that all these extras do add additional weight to the unit and may limit your payload.

Your Choice

With so many different classes, types and models to choose from, the hardest part of joining the RV life is deciding which RV is right for you. Determine what you want your RV for – occasional camping or full-time living quarters. Make a list of comforts that you simply cannot do without before shopping for your dream home-on-wheels.

If you are planning to live fulltime in your unit (or at least 50 percent of the time), travel trailers, fifth wheels, Class A or C motorhomes and bus conversions are more comfortable; anything smaller could turn your dream into a nightmare.

Start Small

If you are nearing retirement, it may be wise to buy a small 'almost new' version of your chosen home-on-wheels just to try out the lifestyle. Use it for a few years to become familiar with the pros and cons of the RV lifestyle. Most of the 'bugs' are usually worked out in the first years of use

---

3 *Many RV dealers and RV rental places are also listed on the* RV WebLink *page of www.rvliving.net.*

(in other words, the previous owner dealt with them) and you will not get hit so much with the high depreciation of a new RV during trade-in. If you decide that RVing is the life for you, then trade your smaller unit in for a larger one of your dreams. FYI – new motorized units depreciate faster than those a few years old; but new towable RVs depreciate at a slower rate. Your trade-in price can give you a good start on a larger unit. (For more info on this subject see the chapter on *How to Buy a Pre-Owned or New RV.*)

Before You Sign

Whether attending an RV show or a dealer open house, you'll always find an RV that will dazzle you. Look beyond the glitz and glitter; you want the construction to last longer than the 'like new' shine.

Most RVs in the same model line and class are fairly equal in looks and features and carry about the same price tag. Floorplans and colour schemes do differ, but, if you see two similar models with an outrageous price difference, stop and ask why the one is so much lower.

There's a good chance that the one selling at a rock bottom price is exactly that – rock bottom. It may be missing some standard options. Construction costs and materials might have been skimped on and, if the price is that much lower, you'll probably end up paying for extras to make it liveable such as a generator or awning. Paying for options is fine, if the item is really an option.

Make an appointment to see the unit after the show or open house. The sales rep will be able to spend more time with you.

Hint: Many dealers will add options such as a washer/dryer and window awnings at wholesale cost if you negotiate their addition before the final price is determined. Knowing what you want before your negotiations are complete could save you many thousands of dollars.

Look beyond price and appearance; do not assume that what you see in the unit you are looking at is what you will get. When you contract to buy, have every single thing written on the bill of sale. If a condition of your purchase is the inclusion of an air conditioner or a pair of roof vents or a complete maintenance check at six months or whatever you and your sales rep decide on – make sure that the salesperson writes it down and initials the additions. Unless you have the proof on paper, you might find yourself, once again, digging into your wallet and starting to actively resent your new RV.

RV Shopping List

You've found your dream machine, the price and all the features are right and everything seems to be a go. Hold on a minute – before signing, ask yourself if you can live in the RV of your choice. If everything is not exactly as you hope, find out if you will be able to modify things with ease.

Have your sales rep leave you (and your spouse) alone for a time with the unit. Go inside the RV, shut the door and sit down on the sofa and close your eyes. At the count of 10, open your eyes and take a good, slow look around. Take out your checklist and mentally ask these questions, making notes of the answers.

Can you live with the layout of the floorplan? If you answered yes, get up and walk around. Open every drawer and every cupboard to see if the space is easily accessible. Make sure that nothing interferes with the ease of opening.

Check out the location of the bathroom and open the door. Nothing in the way? Great. Now picture the dinette folded down into a bed. Can you still get to the bathroom without climbing over sleeping bodies with the bed down? Or just as bad, will the bathroom door even open if the bed is down? If you are absolutely sure that it will only be yourself and your partner in the RV at all times, then maybe you could live with that 'little' inconvenience.

Go right inside the bathroom. Shut the door and sit on the toilet (with the lid down). Is there enough room to move without smacking your funny bone? Can you reach the toilet paper without being a trained contortionist? No problem? Okay, now stand up and pretend you are taking a shower. Is the towel rack located in an area where it will stay dry? Is the bathroom big enough to dry yourself and for you to get dressed without hopping from one leg to another? Look for a vent in the bathroom or at least a window that can be opened. Without either of these, the bathroom could stay damp and eventually mould will become a problem.

If the bathroom passed the test, go into the bedroom. Lie down on the bed – yes, both of you – to see if it is wide enough and long enough for sleeping comfort (good way to check the firmness of the mattress, too). Make sure that any cupboards hanging on the wall over the bed aren't so low that you'll bang your head every time you sit up and that at least three sides of the bed have walk-around space. Do you have an area to stand to dress? Crawling around a bed to tuck in sheets can become awfully wearing after a while. Check to see how much storage space you have under the bed or the couch.

Once the bedroom has passed inspection, go back to the galley, or kitchen. Stand at the sink and check the height and width of the counter. If the counter is too low you could develop a persistent backache. If it's too high, you will be straining to reach the faucets. The counter top should be wide enough for a dish-draining rack with a bit of room to spare. Anything smaller will eventually make meal preparation a real chore. In some cases adding extras such as a fold-down shelf can make a lot of difference. Check to see if the kitchen includes a filter-style water purifier.

The sink should be wide enough and deep enough to hold the required amount of water to wash dishes. If you plan on living in your RV for longer than one week at a time, a double stainless-steel sink is more functional to clean up after meals. Most RVs come with a fitted sink cover (to match the counter) that creates additional counter space – a necessity in an RV.

Does your kitchen have everything you need?

Make sure the stove and fridge doors can be easily opened without banging into a wall and that the fridge door opens wide enough to remove the shelves and crisper drawers. Be sure the lock works as well. If your RV includes an oven, stand in front of it and fully open the door. It can be a hassle hauling out the roast pan while bending over the side of the door. Another thing, make sure there is a range hood and fan to remove cooking steam and odours.

If the dinette is a bench-style and the seats do not pull out or push in, try it out for sitting comfort. If your dinette does fold into a bed, ask your sales rep to show you how to do it and practise a few times when he or she is present.

Examine all cupboards, closets and additional storage space. Check that all doors and drawers have proper latches to prevent them from opening when the RV is in motion. Look for suitably placed electrical receptacles, phone jack; ask the dealer to add more if required – before you settle on the final price. Is there space for extra appliances or will they have to be stored outside between use? Don't forget about the fridge, air conditioner and furnace, etc.

> **If your 'Dream Unit' is equipped with a generator, is it large enough to accommodate the style of RVing you have in mind? For short stops at rustic, no-hookup campgrounds, a small 'genny' is sufficient. But, if you like to dry camp (boondocking) for long periods of time, you may need a large auxiliary power unit. FYI – for every hour a generator operates; it uses approximately three litres (one gallon) of gas/fuel/propane. Considering these costs, will you really save money dry camping?**

Finally, go back to the sofa or easy chair and relax. Pretend you are reading or watching TV. Is there enough lighting for comfort? Can you watch television without lying down or craning your neck?

When you finish your interior inspection, walk around the outside of the RV. Examine all outside storage to locate all valves and holding tanks as well as electrical and hose connections. If you do not understand your electric system (12-volts and 120-volts – AC/DC system inverters, generators, etc.), ask for an explanation at least once. It is easy to be overloaded with info. If you have an abundance of storage space, it adds comfort to RV living. If you plan on winter camping, make sure the unit has proper insulation as well as one or more standard furnace.

If you choose a motorized RV take a good look at the engine. Since most of us know only the basics when it comes to engines, it is recommended that you have an independent mechanic take a look at your prospective buy to verify if it is in good working condition. A qualified mechanic can also tell you if the engine has sufficient power for mountain driving and if all systems are functioning.

Have your mechanic test drive the unit to ensure that it is in top condition at the time of purchase. If your purchase is new from a dealer, ask (and get in writing) what mechanical follow-up is standard. Those considering a pre-owned unit, should obtain the past maintenance records if possible, and let your mechanic go over them.

Investing in an RV is not an impulse purchase so, take your time and do your research. Buying an RV is just the same as buying a house or car – you have to be able to live with your decision.

> **Solar panels and inverters also help to offset power costs when camping without hookups. If extensive dry camping is in your plans, do your homework. Installing a few solar panels plus extra 6 or 12-volt 'house' batteries may provide a quiet alternative.**

Ask other RVers what they like about their unit, make a list of what you want and, by all means, shop around[4]. Your satisfaction is the key to enjoying the good life. Above all, do not become discouraged; eventually, everything will fall into place. After our three-year search for our dream RV we were only 90 percent satisfied with our first purchase. In the nearly two decades we've enjoyed fulltiming travels, many things changed for the better.

Finally, we're confident that, although we're not experts, we are able to handle most of what's going on. As the saying goes, "We've come a long way, babe!"

---

4 To determine approximate pricing (U.S.$) of pre-owned units, Internet users can check retail prices on *www.nadaguide.com*. Others sources are listed on the RV Weblink page, under RV Info at *www.rvliving.net*. The prices should also be listed in Kelley's Blue Book from your dealer or the public library.

 ***How To Buy A Pre-Owned Or New RV***

The decision to buy a new or a pre-owned unit has many variables. Again, for each purchase you must do your homework. Our Pace Arrow was two years old when we bought her after a three-year search and knew what we wanted. She was in pretty good shape with just a few flaws – she'd travelled considerable miles and her former owner had added a number of electrical toys. Many of his modifications, although important to him, were useless to us and, consequently, never used. Most were in the same condition when we sold the coach as when we bought it.

Another RVing friend purchased an almost-new Class A several years ago. Although the coach was heavily modified with extras and every bell-and-whistle, he purchased the fully-loaded motorhome at a fair price. However, he spent a considerable amount of money changing the modifications made by the former owners plus, for safety's sake, he removed one propane tank he felt was too low to the road.

Buyers of pre-owned RVs must be aware that there's almost always some after-sale modification required. On the other hand, you may save thousands of dollars because of the depreciation rate deducted from the original cost of used units.

When purchasing used, kicking a few tires helps. Check under the unit for faulty exhaust and other problems as well. Explore every crevice before you buy. It's possible that some previous modification may be hanging too close to the ground or not working properly. Another point to consider is the availability of parts for an older RV.

If you have friends who are knowledgeable about RVs, ask for their advice as well. After you read every piece of literature you can get your hands on, pay an expert to give the RV a conscientious once-over. Remember, most sellers only share good things about your prospective RV.

Even honest salesmen may miss some nasty buried problems. A fair price may not be the lowest but it is an amount that both the seller and buyer are happy with. When buying from a dealer, the follow-up service could justify paying a slightly higher price than through a private sale.

Be sure to check the date on the 6 or 12-volt house batteries[5], engine batteries and the date the tires were manufactured

> **When buying new (or trading up), always order the extra options you desire from the dealer before you sign for your purchase. This way they can become part of the overall cost of your RV. Dealers stock many luxuries and accessories in bulk for resale to customers at competitive or even low wholesale costs.**

First time buyers may benefit slightly from buying an almost-new pre-owned coach because dealers and manufacturers rectify – or repair most bugs or problems during the first year of use. Since the overall purchase price is lower, you're able to enjoy the RVing life while discovering what's important to you in a home-on-wheels.

If you're planning on buying a used model, be sure to educate yourself. Shop around at various dealers, scan newspaper advertisements, the Internet (if possible) and camping magazines to determine a fair selling price for the unit you have in mind. Know what you want before you begin shopping; don't depend solely on the words of sales personnel[6].

Remember, if a controversy surfaces at a later date, the only words of importance are those in writing. With a private sale, when you drive away, performance responsibility is all yours. On the other hand, when buying from a dealer, a one to three month follow-up service warranty is standard.

When you buy a new unit it comes with the latest accessories and, sometimes, the dealer will even exchange one accessory for another within the price of the coach.

> **If you add extra amenities aftermarket, the price will be higher (dealer's retail price of the appliances plus tax).**

---

5 *Les Doll, an award winning certified RV Technician and webhost of* www.rverscorner.com *features simple instructions to understand 6 and 12-volt batteries.*
6 *If you are shopping for a pre-owned RV be sure to purchase a copy of Les Doll's e-book,* Dummy's Guide to Buying a Pre-loved RV. *There is a direct link on the home page of* www.rvliving.net.

For instance, our new side aisle motorhome in Kastle #2 came equipped with two 13,500 BTU air conditioners. John and I asked the dealer to remove the bedroom air conditioner and install two Fan-Tastic vents, complete with rain sensors. We wanted one vent in the kitchen and the other in the bedroom. These climate-control accessories are much more efficient for the floorplan of our coach than the rear air conditioner could ever be.

Everyone has his or her dislikes and I, personally, will never use a gas oven. Simple enough, the dealership staff removed the stove and replaced it with a four-burner stovetop. Beneath the burners they built a large cupboard to store my pots and pans.

All discussion of these changes occurred prior to closure; they were agreed on before we signed for our unit; all accessories and modifications were included in the overall price.

Note: After the deal was signed I requested a micro/convection oven – the price then jumped to the retail cost.

Since everything at purchase is recorded on our invoice, when we cross borders, there is never a doubt as to what is original and what was an add-on purchase from south of the border. During any inspection, custom officers know exactly what we own and what we may have purchased outside of Canada that has duty and taxes owing.

The year following our purchase either the manufacturer or the dealer repaired any problems (we only had a few). This even included repainting the bottom portion of our coach because the original paint was less than perfect. Our warranty on many items was three years.

One big disadvantage to buying new is that, the day you drive your RV out of the dealership, your coach will depreciate several thousands of dollars. Once again, addressing the question of "Should I buy used or new?" is a dilemma with no correct answer. Either is a good choice but, only after checking all details and examining each option. If the purchase seems right for you, go for it.

Our first motorhome was two years old, which we bought in 1985. When we sold her eight years later, the loss difference between our purchase price and trade-in value worked out to $3000.00 per year.
We then bought Kastle #2 (NEW), and during trade-in six years later our loss was $60,000 (average motorhome depreciation on new units runs $10-$12,000.00 per year).
Kastle #3 was a four-year-old high-end diesel pusher; her resale amount drops approximately $6-$8,000.00 per year.

Moving up with Kastle #2.

No matter if you decide on new or pre-owned, before deciding on the unit you'd like, make a personal wish list from previous suggestions. Depending on your planned use, storage areas may or may not be a big part of your decision.

The capability of your tow vehicle to pull the trailer of your choice is another major factor to consider. If you plan on buying a motorized RV, will you tow a car behind? Is it possible to tow your present car? If it isn't then you may have to buy another car. That large fifth wheel may be a beauty but make sure that it's practical for your plans – this may not be the type of RV you need if you want to spend your time at a special secluded spot at the lake.

Although some compromise may be necessary, don't purchase an RV because it's a bargain. If it doesn't suit your needs or the floorplan and décor is not to your liking, you won't enjoy your getaways. Remember, no single RV fits every wish list. Set yourself a purchase budget and stick to it, however, buy the most RV you can for your money. Although it is possible (on some models) to add an aftermarket slide-out, this is a very costly route to go if you decide you want more space.

Service Follow-Up

Whether your RV is new or pre-owned, to ensure you receive hassle-free follow-up maintenance use the following as a guide.

1. Make an appointment by phone and explain each item you want looked at.

2. Have a list for service staff – specific problems stated in writing are more accurate than verbal. Make a list of the VIN, model number and the odometer reading.

3. As a rule, don't ask for extras the day your unit is in for servicing. Service personnel work by appointment and there probably won't be available time to schedule items not already allotted on work orders.

Remember that during the spring and summer, dealers are extremely busy. If you stay with your RV during repairs, the service is frequently faster than if you leave your unit for pick-up later. The staff will try to complete the work of visible customers first – just to get you on your way. However, expect to spend your time in the waiting room because many shops will not allow owners to stay in the work area due to insurance regulations.

Buying In A Country Other Than Your Own

*Dry camping at the friendly casino in Laughlin, Nevada
is a favourite with RVers.*

Free trade agreement between Canada and the U.S. opened the door to importing many vehicles from a country other than your own. Only after converting currency will the price differ. But you must consider all options – not all vehicles are available for import to another country. Most RVs are manufactured in the U.S.A. but those entering Canada require the odometer to read in kilometres plus daytime running lights are standard options. All vehicles must be approved by CSA (Canadian Standard Association with a Z240 seal of approval) to conform to Canadian laws for all plumbing, electrical, gas and propane fittings.

Several makes of American RVs (usually those with RVIA approval seals) come close or already comply with the above regulations and are sold with the price modification built-in. Others are easily adapted; however, some models cannot meet compliance laws at any price. Before Canadians finalize any RV purchases south of the border they should call the Registrar of Imported Vehicles[7] to ascertain that a specific RV can be imported to Canada.

---

7 *Contact the* Registrar of Imported Vehicles *at www.riv.ca: 1-888-848-8240 for information about* Importing A Vehicle Into Canada.

If it is acceptable, expect to pay a few hundred dollars in fees at the border for the completion of the paperwork plus GST (Federal Tax). After a short period for updating items such as the headlights or odometer or minor wiring, etc. you will have a follow-up appointment to register and licence your vehicle; the PST (Provincial Sales Tax) is paid at that time.

One lesson my sister Nancy and her hubby Bud learned the hard way was that when they imported a different vehicle two years in a row, they were charged tax on the full purchase price of both vehicles; not the difference on the trade-in price as is the case in Canada.

If importing a Canadian vehicle into the U.S.A. (or into any country other than your own) the situation is similar. You have to call the Customs and Import department of your country to discover if your vehicle is acceptable for import.[8] Ask what fees will be accessed including sales tax (is it on the entire vehicle?) and specific regulations. If the exchange rate is favourable for U.S.A. residents buying in Canada, it could save the purchaser big money. But remember the prices of most RVs in Canada are converted from the retail cost of the unit as it sits in the U.S.

Note: RV and auto dealers are usually well-versed in this import procedure. Some dealers have alliances in neighbouring countries, so for a fee, ask if it is possible for a one dealer to export your chosen RV to a dealership in your country of residence for the purchase completion. Ask. All they can say is "No".

RV shoppers will find deals everywhere in the U.S.A. and Canada. At first look, prices may appear extremely inviting but you must consider all hidden costs carefully before you buy. You should not have to pay the sales tax on your purchase if you do not live in the province, state or country where the sale took place. You pay this tax when you register and licence (or tag) your vehicle. However, extra costs such as import duties, federal taxes, U.S./Canadian exchange rates and the costs to modify the RV before it's acceptable for import can rapidly change the overall price. Financing will probably not be possible either because lenders rarely grant loans for non-residents, especially when the collateral can be driven to another country. Obtaining a personalized credit rating for customers from another country is not always easy either.

---

8 *Several websites covering* Cross Border information *are listed on the* RV WebLink page *of www.rvliving.net.*

Peggi McDonald

> **If buying 'extras' in a country other than your own, the extras become part of your allowed custom declaration. Additional duties and taxes may apply if you are over your entitlement.**

Even if you save a few dollars, buying in another country may not be problem-free with reference to service. After purchase, it does help to be conveniently accessible to your RV dealer for follow-up maintenance during a new vehicle break-in phase. The above concerns apply to all RVs, tow cars and tow vehicles – plus hitches and tow bars, if they exceed the amount you can bring home for personal use. Check out dealerships in your own country first – it may surprise you what you will find.

Remember, a fair price is one that satisfies both the buyer and seller. Paying a rock bottom amount may save you a little cash but cost you plenty in unsatisfactory service.

Note: We have met RVers who phone around the country looking for the lowest price. This may and may not work in your favour. The unit may not have all the bells and whistles on it that is standard equipment on higher price models. Adding these extras at regular retail prices can add extensively to the cost of your unit.

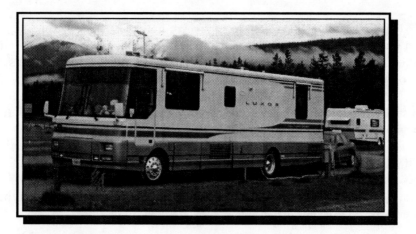

We hit the 'big time' with Kastle #3 – our first diesel pusher.

'Bigitis' Is A Common RV Ailment

Buying your first RV is always a difficult decision: "How long should it be?"; "How 'posh' should it be?"; "Do I need one, two or three slides?"; "Should it be new or pre-owned?" Oh the questions seem to go on and on. One thing for certain even when you find your perfect dream machine it seems that another a 'little nicer' or 'bigger' or 'fancier' 'or this', 'or that', or 'something else' has just surfaced on your dealer's lot or during your visit to the last RV show. Don't despair; this feeling is normal and, as a result, the average trade-up time is four-six years. Although John and I are finally driving what we feel is our perfect home – a diesel pusher that we emphatically say will be our last purchase – it is not always easy to stay with those convictions. Most RVers suffer from a constant ailment referred to as 'Bigitis'.

However, be aware it's not necessary to 'have-it-all' on your first RV, or on each follow-up unit either. Recently, while reminiscing about the fun and experiences of our early travels, we discovered some of our most enjoyable times were during our early days with our older and smaller first RV. We could go to almost anyplace we wanted to.

Our advice is to find a unit that suits your budget and fits your needs as they are now. There are two ways to buy a unit – one for the lowest price even if it doesn't have some main options such as a generator or an awning, etc. You can add these later or you can find one that fits your budget and ask the dealer to add extras and modification from your wish list and then negotiate on the final price. Either way works well but only you can decide the route you wish to follow.

RVING MADE EASY

*Bread stored in the oven extends space and
oven mitts cushion any noise from the burners.*

Extending Your Living Space

You did it! You bought your new RV and visions of exciting adventures crowd your thoughts. Although your unit might be big enough for your plans, now that you've brought it home, it looks so small compared to your house that it's difficult to imagine how you'll ever find enough space for all your 'must have' comforts.

Don't worry; there are endless ways to conveniently carry special extras in easily accessible places. This chapter explains **how to pack plus travel tips, outdoor hints, cleaning ideas, towing and driving techniques and simple maintenance tips** to make your travelling life fun and easy.

The first step to actually getting on the road to enjoy your new life is packing your RV. One cardinal rule for RVers is to never overload the unit. That, however, doesn't mean you can't make space for necessities and keeping these three simple guidelines in mind will help you to adjust.

1. Make your RV a comfortable home so you won't miss your other home.
2. Utilize every nook and cranny that you can find to extend space.
3. Don't pack things so deep you must dig for them. Buried items are rarely used. Eliminating non-necessities saves space for important 'can't live without' extras and also prevents overstuffed RV cupboards from an occasional explosion.

Over the years I discovered that many items serve more than one purpose. Here is my list of **'double duty detail'**; you can make your own up as you go along.

➢ If closet space is limited, add a <u>removable clothes bar</u> on brackets to the shower so it can double as a closet. For wet clothes that can't be dried in a machine, place tension-spring bars across a doorway or hallway as makeshift clothes dryer.

➢ Tuck folded blankets, jackets and sleeping bags neatly <u>inside of pillowcases</u>. The items are not only out of the way and easily accessible – the 'throw pillows' add a decorative touch to your furniture.

➢ <u>Tinted windows</u> contribute to privacy as well as reducing heat caused by the sun's glare. (Note: most window repair companies sell and install aftermarket window tinting.)

➢ <u>Café-style curtains</u> on RV windows add warmth to the décor as well as enhancing daytime privacy.

Café-style curtains add a homey touch as well as privacy.

➤ To avoid scratching refrigerator shelves, I dress every glass and metal container in my fridge with <u>non-skid booties</u>. These booties are a circle of plastic non-slip mesh held in place with an elastic band. I discovered they also do double duty – nothing moves when I forget to arrange the fridge for travel.

Note: Do not line the entire fridge shelf with anything because the refrigerator relies on circulating air to cool properly.

➤ <u>Bread and baked goods stay fresh</u> longer when placed in a plastic tub (to catch crumbs) and stored inside your air-tight microwave or oven.

➤ <u>Electric frying pans</u> double as excellent baking or roasting ovens plus they're convenient to use outside (or inside, if you prefer) for cooking food with an odour, such as fish.

➤ A <u>metric conversion calculator</u> is a must for Canadians travelling south of the border and for Americans exploring Canada. These calculators are inexpensive and can be used either as a conversion tool or as a regular calculator. (Note: These are easier to find in Canada than they are in the U.S.)

➤ <u>Pringle potato chips</u> travel well without turning into crumbs and the container is easy to store in minimal space. The containers also make excellent mailing tubes.

➤ Dawn dish soap (or any other mild dish soap) can be used as a substitute for a gentle shampoo. It also breaks up oil and dirt on John's ball caps and shirt collars so they wash cleaner.

➤ Shampoo (or dish soap) poured on a sponge and spread over the pebbly floor of the shower effortlessly releases dirt. A quick rinse with the shower cleans the floor.

➤ The empty squirt bottles from dish soaps become easy-to-use spill-free containers for adding distilled water to batteries. A meat baster works equally well.

> **Although John and I print business cards on our computer, some RVers pass out self-stick address labels to friends they meet along the way. The labels conveniently stick into the receiver's address book. This also works well at trade shows where there are many forms to fill out for draw prizes.**

Everything In Its Place

➤ My all-time favourite tip is a way to create extra drawer space. Attach an ordinary pocket-style shoe bag to the inside of a cupboard door. For stability, add elastic strips side-to-side across the pockets and fasten with screws to the door. These portable pocket 'drawers' work well in the kitchen to store long or large utensils; in the bedroom for underwear; in the bathroom for shampoo bottles plus toiletries and in a storage compartment for easy-to-find screw drivers and other tools.

➤ When non-slip vinyl mesh, originally designed for use on boats, is placed beneath kitchen appliances they won't move when the unit is in motion. If you line cupboards with this miracle fabric, dishes or pots and pans also stay exactly where you put them.

A collage of some of the many tips offered in this section.

➢ Over the years I discovered the mesh works even better if I place a <u>six-inch square</u> beneath each pile of dishes or pots rather than the entire shelf. This way when I pick up the last dish the entire shelf is not rearranged. However, this mesh will destroy the finish of some items such as the bottom of acrylic glasses.

➢ <u>Rubber stove and sink mats</u> work much the same way but cutting to size is more difficult.

➢ After our recent renovations I discovered that <u>lining the shelf</u> of our dish cupboards with <u>scrap carpet</u> added one more cushion of protection.

➢ <u>Hide a key</u> outside your coach for emergency entry. If you misplace your keys as much as I do, it's more convenient to use a spare key than it is to break in.

➢ Sometimes a motorhome will have <u>an overhead bunk</u>. If this isn't needed as a bed, remove the mattress; the resulting space is great to store shoes, dress clothes, bedding and more. If you pack any weight in this bed, you may need to add support straps to keep the bunk in place while driving.

➢ The <u>freezer in our refrigerator</u> in our second motorhome was one big compartment. To help organize this area, I purchased a simple one-level plastic-coated shelf. Everything stacked easier and remained within easy reach.

➢ A small <u>battery-operated fridge fan</u> circulates air and provides effective cooling.

➢ To <u>firm up the couch</u> in our first two units we added a 1/2-inch board between the couch and top cushions.

➢ <u>Eliminating magazine clutter</u> and storing large books like the atlas is always a challenge. If you don't have a corner for a bookrack, store them out of sight under the dinette or couch cushions (above the board mentioned previously).

➢ If your available <u>working area for sewing or crafts</u> is limited, try this easy modification – cut the two back legs of a folding table short enough to rest on the couch. The amount removed should allow the top to be level when the two front legs stand on the floor. Now you have a worktable that doesn't tie up the dinette.

➢ Trying to <u>restrain throw rugs from 'walking'</u> can be very frustrating. One way that works is to attach a strip of heavy-duty Velcro (needle side) to the underside of the throw rug. Fasten the opposing piece to your RV carpet. Products such as non-slip mesh for carpets and washable polyester felt also help to keep the rugs in place.

➢ <u>Rubber backed rugs</u> leave a stain on acrylic and hard surface floors.

➢ <u>Baby wipes</u> make great quick clean-ups and the square plastic containers are the perfect to store recipe cards, elastics, small tools, etc. List contents on the outside with a magic marker.

➢ <u>Pre-packaged cleaning cloths</u> treated with a wide variety of formulas from microwave cleaners to glass cleaners to wet and dry dusters are perfect for the RV lifestyle because they travel easily without spilling.

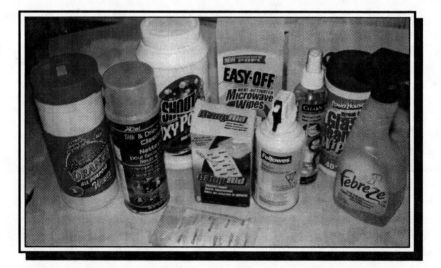

Products like this simplify life on the move because most do not spill.

➤ Glass liquor bottles remain safe and secure when stored in the bottom half of cardboard milk cartons. I wedge plastic containers between the cartons and everything is ready for your next happy hour.

➤ Empty sectioned liquor and wine boxes make versatile storage for shoes or craft supplies. In Kastle #2, I used these sectioned boxes to add a sense of order to my basement storage compartments.

➤ Café-curtain rods attached to the base of the bed or just above the floor level of walls create another perfect place to store shoes.

   o Our friends cut strips of pockets from a hanging shoe bag and stapled them to the bed support to keep their shoes out of sight.

   o Commercial-style shoe racks are also available with wide hooks to hang on the bed frame.

➤ Ultra-detergent boxes are convenient containers for audiotapes and toys or a good catch-all for a variety of small items. You can disguise the outside of the boxes by applying self-stick plastic such as MacTac.

➤ Jewellery is very difficult to store, however, neck chains and earrings hang neatly on wall hooks or an 'S'-hook on a piece of plastic craft mesh attached behind a closet door.

   o One friend added a corkboard to her bathroom wall and hangs her chains, etc., on push-pins.

   o Another uses a round, flat splatter screen to store her earrings. The handle already has a hole for hanging and all earrings are easily seen.

   o I have used the partitioned compartments of a fishing tackle box to separate my jewellery pieces.

Jewellery storage idea.

o   To store my earrings now, I keep each pair of earrings (and their backings) in a single small zip closure plastic bag available from Wal*Mart store craft area. I pin colours together and store all 50 pairs of them in a box with a flip lid. To make the box look pretty so it can sit on the counter I covered the box in decorative MacTac. For the first time in a long time I now wear the earrings of my choice, not whatever pair I find two of – each with backs attached as well.

➤   Adding adjustable shelves to your RV's short and narrow shirt closets considerably increases the storage capacity. To eliminate creases and minimize the amount of space needed, lay your clothes flat before rolling. They are easy to find if they are stored in a clear plastic bucket or if you stack the rolled clothes with the ends visible.

➤   An RVing friend places her folded clothes on the shelf, separating them with a sheet of cardboard between each item. They do not become rearranged when she removes them.

➤   She also does this with bedding and towels. Another friend uses empty beer boxes to hold towels and face cloths neatly in place.

➤   With the wide variety of plastic containers and tubs on the market, there's certain to be one available for each task. For instance, items such as socks or underwear stay put when stowed in plastic tubs on a closet shelf.

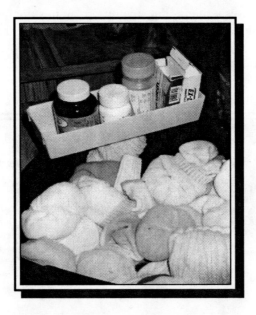

Buckets of all sizes make packing easier.

➢ Laundry baskets or the shopping buckets from places like Costco or Sam's are great organizers for use under the bed of some units.
➢ Small cutlery trays on the medicine cabinet shelves keep small prescription bottles securely in place. Fill the gap between the tray and cabinet wall with flat bottles or boxes from cold medicines. The advantage of using these trays is that nothing lands in the toilet when the door is opened after a rough ride.
➢ One friend wedges two-inch-high strips of Plexiglas in front of her medicine cabinet shelves. For tall bottles, she places a spring-loaded bar across the shelf. Other RVers attach strips of elastic across these shelves to avoid an avalanche that ends up in the toilet when they open the door at destination.
➢ I always found it a challenge to remember where we had put interesting articles on special places to visit. Now we keep these stories in a file folder in an upper cabinet. Make sure that you regularly eliminate old information because a large collection of pamphlets, maps and magazines all add excess weight.
➢ Car-type litterbags are perfect holders for maps and other travel information; so are the plastic sheet protectors used to protect files.
➢ Large plastic sports bottles filled with your favourite drink are wonderful to have when travelling. However, they don't fit into most RV drink holders. One friend inserted a dual size piece of PVC pipe – one end is three inches with four inches on the other end – into the existing holder; her sports bottle now fits. The small end fits the holders and the large end supports the bottles in an upright position.
➢ For objects that need trimming, MacTac or car striping is always a good choice. I fabricated a bathroom shelf from Plexiglas and mounted it on brass brackets. A window repair facility sold and cut the piece of Plexiglas (8" x 24") for me. After cutting, they heated the front edge of the shelf and curled it up to create a lip so that items would stay put during vehicle motion. I then added trimming to the edge with gold and black car striping, giving a professional touch to my creative modification.

Keeping Your Kitchen (Galley) Organized

The kitchen in your house or the galley in your RV is probably the most used room in your home. Over the years I've adopted many ideas to help simplify life and lessen the time needed to keep our unit clean and tidy.
➢ We keep our large cutting knives in a kitchen drawer in long narrow cutlery trays.

➤ Putting washed <u>plastic dishes and containers in the freezer</u> overnight removes most unpleasant food odours and freshens the dishes for future use.

➤ <u>Plastic clothespins</u> make quick and easy re-sealers for bags such as chips or cereal.

➤ <u>To keep potatoes from sprouting</u>, store them with apples.

➤ <u>To increase juice in oranges</u>, lemons, limes or grapefruit, either puncture the skin and place in the microwave for one minute or submerge in hot water for 15 minutes.

➤ <u>To soften brown sugar</u>, place sugar with apple slices in an air-tight container for several days.

➤ <u>To clean a burned pan</u>, add water and cream of tartar, boil for several minutes and wash clean. In an emergency, sand or pinecones also make good pot scrubbers.

➤ Dishes and pots and pans rattle and sometimes break when driving. Eating off of disposable dishes or purchasing an unbreakable supply isn't necessary if you simply place <u>circles of plastic bubbles</u> (available from stationery stores or packing supply stores) between each item. Paper plates or a layer of plastic mesh work equally as well. FYI – our hand-painted dishes cushioned with plastic bubble circles have travelled unbroken in our RV for nearly two decades.

Plastic bubbles cushion dishes – bungees keep cups secure.

➤ <u>Rectangular basket(s)</u> (under-the-shelf-type or wicker style, etc.) that sit on a cupboard shelf keep glasses and small stuff secure if plastic items are placed between breakable items.

➤ John and I use our silver wine goblets because they travel very well and keep drinks so cold. They always make a big hit when we use them sitting at the bonfire or the picnic table. These days there are pretty acrylic glasses available. However, the breakable variety will stay put at the back or side of a cupboard if you stretch thin bungee cords across the stems and hook the ends of the cords into eyehooks.

➤ Glasses placed in rubber or Styrofoam drink coolers travel well as do colourful acrylic patio glasses. Ribbed portions of worn out socks also make super travelling booties for glasses.

➤ Trying to keep pesky bug populations in control, especially ants is always a problem. You can either buy commercial traps or try some of these home remedies. So far they've worked for me.

  o Put an Ex-Lax square in a lid with a few drops of water near the entrance points.

  o Wrap cloths saturated with bug spray around hoses and cords.

  o Coat all outside hoses and electrical cords with a silicone-based lubricant – bugs hate the oily feeling.

  o Sprinkle ant powder or household cleanser around tires, jacks, hoses and cords.

  o Use a solution of approximately 1-teaspoon Borax acid powder with 1/4-cup sugar (any kind) and 2 cups hot water. Place in foil 'cups' to sit on the counter.

➤ Mice seem to hate the smell of Downy fabric softener sheets, so place these near every entrance point. Stuff 'brass wool' (similar to steel wool) in any holes where wires and hoses come in.

➤ Scatter bay leaves throughout cupboards and around openings to deter roaches from making your RV their home. As an added precaution, I remove groceries (even cereal) from cardboard cartons. The cartons may be home to a colony of roach eggs.

➤ RV kitchens are compact and where to put the garbage is always a Problem…

  o If placed in a cupboard, it uses precious space.

  o One RVer attached a container to the corner of her counter with small bungee cords and eye hooks.

  o We prefer to store our garbage out of sight. In Kastle #2, John copied an idea from our first coach. He cut a hole at the back of a deep cupboard with the opening the same size as the wastebasket rim so it would sink flush with the counter top. Then he added a wood frame to the hole (you can also cover the raw edge with a MacTac type of covering). Adding a colour co-ordinated strip of decorative elastic lace to the top of the basket (over the plastic bag) helps to streamline it. Re-sizing a cutting board tops it off. One advantage to this modification is that lifting the container allows easy access to items stored at the back of the cupboard.

Finding Unused Places To Store Things

Unless you design and build your own 'Dream Machine', most RVs have many areas of wasted space. With a little effort it's easy to transform these out-of-the-way places into creative storage spots DO NOT OVERLOAD – IF IT GOES UNUSED FOR A YEAR, REMOVE IT. Try to make as many areas as possible do double duty. The following should help to peak your imagination. Each RV is different, while checking yours out you may find more spaces.

Inside
- Frequently the space inside the cupboards is high. This means there is a lot of wasted space above the first level of contents. By adding an extra adjustable shelf all space can be utilized.
- You can also use this extra space to store small items in a rectangular cake pan above the lower contents either on a shelf or on top of dishes. The pan should stay put and travel well while doubling your space.
- Square or rectangle lidded plastic tubs stack well, again doubling or even tripling tier space.
- Some RVers puncture cello-type bags (chips, etc.) with a pinhole to remove unwanted air.
- If you browse home design stores you should find a selection of under-the-counter shelves and appliances. Holders for Kleenex, paper plates, napkins, coffee pots and more are designed to fill this unused space.
- Wall-mounted racks and holders provide magazines and maps with a special place while eliminating clutter.
- A wide variety of holders that attach to the wall are available for remote controls, alarm clocks, drinks and much more are available from dollar and discount stores, discount furniture places and thrift shops.
- Look for spaces under the dash or on the passenger side of your tow vehicle or motorhome that can house plastic file holders for maps or campground directories.
- To add working space inside, several friends built a shallow cabinet with casters on it. They wedge it beside the table during transit and move it to the blank wall when the slide is extended.
- Another friend covered her blank slide wall with space enhancing long narrow mirrors. What an impressive sight!

- Other RVers have built a <u>two-drawer cabinet over the engine cover</u> on their motorhome.
- We <u>removed the built-in TV in our last motorhome</u> and covered the space with a door from the factory. Our large floor model unit sat on the engine cover while parked and between the chairs while mobile.

Our dealer added a bank of cupboards over the couch.
This addition was negotiated in the purchase price.

- On our Luxor MH the dealer added <u>an extra bank of cupboards</u> over the couch. It was wasted decorative space with no purpose. Friends added cupboards within their slide area.
- Don't hesitate to ask a dealer to complete these options at the time of purchase – <u>before you negotiate on the overall price</u>. Keep an eye on the weight these changes may add.
- There is also <u>space under most couches</u> that can be transformed into drawer access.
- Look for <u>any small space</u> that could be utilized to transform into a storage area. Don't forget the space at the top and back of closets.
- On Kastle #2 we discovered two long 8" high spaces <u>under our night tables</u>. This became our shoe storage.
- There is about <u>6" of space designed to cover hoses and wires below drawers</u> in most RVs. The considerable space in and around these installations is great for necessities such as cookie sheets. Remove the panel for front approach or lift out the drawer for full access.
- <u>Narrow yet large items</u> like sewing machines can usually fit snug beside the dinette wall.

♦ A narrow cabinet could be built to fit along the same wall and used for items such as trays, photos and games.

***Take an ordinary $5.00 table from Wal*Mart and
cut off the legs so it sits secure on your motorhome's steering wheel.
Add a pretty cloth and you have an inexpensive, practical and decorative addition.***

♦ The open decorative areas with small railings in many coaches can easily be framed to provide yet another cupboard. Manufacturers will sell a matching cabinet door(s).
♦ To extend working space in a kitchen lay the sink cover over an open drawer during food preparations.
♦ Some RVers do the same thing with a special tray cut to fit over a drawer to make a night table in the bedroom.
♦ Many RVers have found very creative ways to adapt working space for their computers – on dashboards, converting dinettes, removing chairs or incorporating the small wall-mounted tables with filing cabinets.

Outside
♦ Keep tools accessible from the passenger side for emergency use – one idea is to store them in a small plastic bucket.
♦ Large lidded tubs stack well in the basement storage areas.

Lidded buckets keep everything in place.

♦ If <u>outside space is available above the tubs</u> it is a good spot for 'pool noodles', chairs, or unusual sized items.

♦ <u>Hanging PVC pipes</u> inside or outside of the RV frame can extend storage. Depending on the circumference, these can be used for fishing poles, cleaning brushes, extra sewer hoses and folding ladders. I recently saw a Class C with two mounted on the roof.

♦ <u>Slide-out trays</u> in the base of the pods ensure everything is accessible. However these are quite costly.

♦ We found two hollow areas <u>under each step</u> on our last motorhome. By adding a piano hinge to the back of the top step, two great storage areas opened up for our duck boots and outside shoes.

♦ If your unit has a <u>peg-board or a panel in an outside storage pod</u>, remove it to see what is behind. Sometime the panel is there to protect installation of hoses and wires but there is lots of useable space as well.

My Favourite Household Tips

Making up a <u>bed converted from an RV couch</u> can be a real stretching experience. I placed a fitted sheet over the back of the sofa first before opening the bed flat.

Wall space in an RV is always limited. Those without a viewing place for a <u>photo collage</u> could always arrange their favourite photos behind a cupboard door or on the front of the fridge. Cover the collage or photo with a sheet of acetate available from craft stores or a piece of Plexiglas and your family and special friends are always close at hand.

To <u>stop paper towels or toilet paper from unravelling</u> during travel, squash or flatten the rolls before putting them on the dispenser. Some RVers add bungees to secure the rolls.

<u>Plastic grocery bags</u> are extremely handy but difficult to store.

♦ One space-saver option is a handmade plastic garbage bag holder that hangs inside a cupboard or beside the kitchen window (a sleeve about 14 inches x 18 inches with elastic at top and bottom). One bag holder hanging on each side of the window along with small flounce adds a decorative touch.

♦ Another option is to keep the bags in a shoe box-style plastic container with a lid and stand the container on its end. (These containers can also be used for photos and craft supplies.)

♦ An empty paper towel roll is one more space-saving container that holds two-dozen or more plastic garbage bags – stuff them in the roll.

In the past, our <u>electric appliance cords stayed in place</u> when stored in empty toilet paper rolls. The rolls can easily be decorated to disguise their original purpose. More recently I discovered that wrapping elastic ponytail holders (with bobbles on the ends) around cords and wires contained them more efficiently. This works for computer cables as well as for appliance cords. Like the bungee cord hints, these holders have a million uses.

<u>Stretch cords (or bungees)</u> restrain numerous items from moving when driving. We probably have two dozen in use in our motorhome and another half-dozen available, especially the 12-inch thin ones and the models that have a bobble on one end of an elastic circle. You can make your own bobble-style mini bungee by looping an extra-large elastic around a small piece of dowelling in a half-hitch knot.

I found pretty <u>hanging brass hooks</u> that only leave one to two small holes in the wall if removed but they look so good you can leave them in place when you trade units. Look for these in hardware and regular department stores like Wal*Mart, etc.

Taking items off shelves and walls before changing destinations is a pain. However, if you place a small amount of caulking putty (called strip seal or fingertip caulking – available from hardware stores) on the bottom of objects, <u>nothing moves or falls from display position</u> between destinations. When applied to the corners of picture frames or other wall hangings, it prevents them from swinging side-to-side. This putty holds more securely than sticky products specially designed for this purpose.

<u>Goo Gone</u> removes sticky residue left on surfaces from tape or putty; WD-40 or cooking oil also works well. Rub it in and let it set awhile before wiping off. Repeat if necessary. This is effective on every hard finished surface I've tried. However, on fabric or carpet, the oil residue may require a specialized follow-up cleaning.

Attaching <u>Velcro</u> with glue holds items in place but it is extremely difficult to remove. Our first motorhome was two years old when we bought it and there was black Velcro everywhere. It was ten years old when we sold it and the Velcro was still there. On Kastle #3 we removed a picture from the manufacturer and the finish of the wallboard came off with the Velcro. I covered the damaged areas with a field of 'press on craft-style' butterflies, which added a decorative touch.

There are several ways to <u>remove decals</u> from exterior surfaces. Most will soften sufficiently for easy removal with a hair dryer (or a heat gun designed for this purpose). Be careful that it doesn't become too hot. Follow with a coat of denatured alcohol and a good polishing compound and fibreglass wax. WD-40, along with a commercial adhesive remover may also work. If these aren't effective, ask a professional. Other ways may damage your finish; it may require refurbishing. These days we add most decals and stick-on items to the windows rather than the coach skin.

<u>To combat dampness and condensation</u>:

1. Open containers of 'Damp-Rid' (a crystal-type dehumidifier/desiccant sold in U.S. grocery stores or RV dealers; 'No-Damp' is a similar product sold at RV dealers in Canada). These products remove excess humidity in an RV. Dri-Z-Air is another option and it comes in a fancy container.
2. Kitty litter has much of the same effect. Simply place the containers of crystals in choice locations and the moisture problem vanishes.
3. Desiccants also come in pouches to control moisture and humidity in closets. We add one to our tow car to remove the odour from wet rugs that are stowed while moving from place-to-place. These

pouches also eliminate a mouldy odour resulting from a water leak in a hard-to-reach area.

If your unit is not equipped with a <u>washer/dryer,</u> keeping ahead of the wash while moving around can become a constant aggravation, especially if the park's laundry facilities are limited. For easy hand-washing, try placing a bucket of soapy water in your shower and add your undies before you depart. The agitation created during driving washes the clothes; they're ready to rinse and dry when you reach your destination.

Travelling with your <u>water pump turned off</u> is a wise move. RVing friends in Mexico wished that they had – a bumpy road jiggled their motorhome shower tap open when the pump was on. Road noise obscured any sound of running water and, when they arrived at their campsite, an attaché case of very important papers – stored in the shower for travelling – was floating.

Unattended <u>water leaks</u> cause numerous problems including wood rot. A drip in one place may be the result of a leak from an opposite corner of your RV. During our early years, one of us left the bathroom tap running for 11 hours, with the sink plug in place. The mess was too extensive to clean with towels and at 11:00 p.m. renting an extractor was out of the question. It was necessary to become creative so, by scrapping the oven broiler pan across the floor, I was able to literally push the water out of the door. Several exhausting hours later, and after a session with the hair dryer plus the heat from the iron, our floor was, once again, dry.

As I mentioned earlier we <u>added support to our couch</u> by inserting a board below the cushions. RVers have numerous ideas of how to improve RV furniture; one RVing friend used oversized elastics to join groups of springs together on her sofa. This helped the springs to work as a unit for greater support.

To <u>avoid dented and mangled TV antennas,</u> don't drive away from your campsite with your antenna extended. Simple reminders help eliminate this embarrassing and very expensive mistake.

1. Take a large spring-loaded hair clip and place it on your TV antenna handle. When the antenna is up, move the clip to your motorhome's steering wheel, sun visor or a 'can't miss' final checkpoint near the doorway of your trailer. If it's there when you're ready to leave – check your antenna.
2. In a motorhome, place a dummy key on a key ring in the ignition when the antenna is extended and hang the dummy key ring on the antenna handle when it's in travelling position.
3. When your antenna is up, hang the RV keys on the antenna handle.
4. Some trailerists tie a scarf to a final checkpoint position.

5.   Hang a long 'can't miss' decoration to the handle when the antenna is up.

Cats like to scratch so put some carpet around a dinette table leg and introduce kitty to its new scratching post. Suspend a toy on a string and your cat will think the RV is paradise.

To simplify the life of the co-pilot and navigator, purchase an atlas that indicates highway exit numbers. Directions in travel guides and campground directories usually list sites by the closest highway exit number. In provinces or states where exit numbers coincide with kilometre/mile markers, this type of atlas makes it easy to compute distance. 🐾

Outdoor Hints And Set-Up Tips

Just like the RV's interior, there are many little tips you can follow to maintain the exterior and prevent costly repair jobs later on.

Poor caulking around the running lights on the top of the unit can result in water leaking through the front and back windows. When correcting this problem, remove the lens cover plus the old caulking of the running lights. Clean the area well then re-seal the running light unit with a bead of silicone. Put the lens cover back on.

For those who aren't mechanically inclined, when removing a battery for winter storage, place a small piece of coloured tape to each wire and terminal combination before disconnecting. Use different coloured tape for each combination and, to re-install, match up the coloured tape pieces. When we recently had our 6-volt house batteries replaced, the techs made a diagram of our set-up before removing the old batteries.

On sunny days when you would like to keep the main door open but it's too chilly for comfort, 'winterize' your screen door the easy way. Cut a piece of Plexiglas to cover the screen and attach with brackets that allow easy removal. With the new 'storm' window you can enjoy the sunny day without being cold.

Bike kickstands frequently sink into the soft ground. To keep your bike upright, attach a golf ball to the end of the stand.

One RVing friend carries a rake in his storage area to retrieve those hard-to-reach items buried in tight spaces between compartments. John and I find that the awning stick works equally well (another double duty principle).

> **Sometimes boards are required to lift one side or the other of your RV before using levelling jacks. If your unit has dual tires ALWAYS place the same number of boards under BOTH the inside and outside tire.**

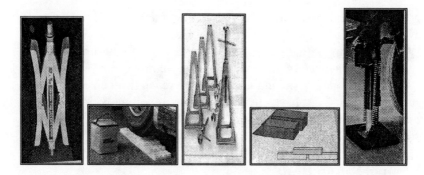

Levelling assistance props.

Automatic levelling jacks also add to the ease of campsite set up. However, be sure the ones you purchase are heavy enough for your unit. Our first coach came with an electronic levelling system that would stabilize but not lift our motorhome. When using any form of levelling system, don't forget to place a pad or board between the jacks and ground; make it a habit to put chocks behind the wheels to avoid rolling off jacks.

Our neighbour, after arriving late one rainy night at his campsite, pushed a button to automatically extend his levellers. The next morning he couldn't move without tow truck assistance as his jacks had sunk deep into the soft ground.

> **When you raise your awning, always drop one end several inches lower than the other. Rainwater is extremely heavy and if it doesn't drain the weight will tear your awning and/or bend the hardware. If you forget to lower one side, the water will puddle in the middle. Simply take a broom and push the water out before attempting to lower the awning side arms.**

Cleaning your awning is not difficult if you apply a coating of gentle soapy solution to the top and bottom of the fabric. Roll the awning up and wait for five minutes, extend it again and rinse with a hose. If it doesn't come clean, repeat. Using strong cleaners can damage the water retardant ability of the fabric. There are many solutions available designed to clean awnings from RV stores.

We always roll our awning at bedtime and, if we are going away for the day. Winds come up very fast when you least expect it. We also hate 3 a.m.

awning calls – when it starts to rattle and you lay there hoping the noise will go away. It seems the longer you wait the worse it gets.

Post the CB channel that you monitor on the rear of your unit. We frequently tune to channel 14 and, occasionally we monitor #19 – both are posted. Vehicles travelling behind know how to reach us in an emergency and frequently call to simply say hello. If you're travelling with friends, choose channels other than #13 (Good Sam); #14 (FMCA) and, #19 (the trucker's channel).

Campground Set-up Hints

We often see RVers use green garden hoses to connect their RV to park water supplies. This is a dangerous practice because these hoses are not insulated and the heat generated from the sun creates a perfect atmosphere for bacteria growth. RVers beware – always use the specially designed drinking water hoses to bring water into your RV. It's not only tastier; it's a lot healthier.

Attaching a water hose to the RV city water connection can be a difficult task unless you use a quick disconnect designed for home garden hoses. Place one end permanently on your coach with the opposing end on your water hose and connection is a snap. These handy adapters are also a convenient way to join two hoses together.

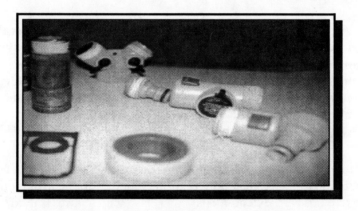

Regulator, 'Y' connection, quick disconnects,
washers, and plumbers tape.

In some parks, water pressure surges to an excess of 100 psi. A water regulator, placed at the tap end of the hose (park connection), reduces the water pressure to a recommended rate of 45 psi. In one campground, our neighbour's hose split lengthwise creating a beautiful water display. He had his regulator improperly installed at the coach end of the hose. Although it protected his plumbing lines in this position, if the regulator had been placed at the tap end as the manufacturer suggests, the water hose would still be intact.

We know an RVer who <u>attaches his regulator to the hose with chain</u> or gun-tape so he wouldn't forget it.

Periodically these <u>regulators need a soak in CLR</u> – if not the water to your unit will slow to a dribble. 'Been there, done that'.

If your fresh water tank fill port has no air release hole, adapters used for <u>filling fresh water tank</u> are sold in RV stores. It is also easy to make an inexpensive tank filler by attaching a piece of rubber surgical hose (from the pharmacy) to the male end of a quick disconnect adapter. Connect the adapter to your water hose and place it in the tank.

A good source of fresh water is most important while moving to various destinations. Keeping your <u>fresh water tank pure is easy if purged</u> after storage and at periodic intervals. To purge, add 4-6 ounces of chlorine bleach to 3/4 tank of water and let the water run through your taps until you can smell chlorine. Turn off the taps and, either let the mixture sit in the tank for several hours or take a short drive (to cause agitation), then drain. Refill tank and again drain by letting water run through taps until all chlorine odour disappears. Refill tank with fresh water and use as required.

Regular treatment is half a teaspoon to each 10 gallons of water. <u>Commercial liquid water purifiers</u> available from RV stores are much easier to use but they do cost a little more than household bleach. Remember that <u>every gallon of water or holding tank waste weighs approximately 10 pounds</u>. Choose carefully how much extra weight is actually a necessity.

'In-line' water filters can be a blessing during your travels. Although park water may test healthy, many campground systems have an objectionable taste or smell. Using either a one-unit style or the canister-type with removable filters helps to improve taste, quality and odour. However, many RVers still choose to use bottled water for drinking and cooking. Refill stations are located everywhere. In the northern U.S.A. and Canada these kiosks most likely will not be outside due to the weather; look for them in grocery stores and drug stores.

Several new RVs include outside showers as standard equipment. If your unit isn't so equipped, you can make your own <u>outside tap</u>. Place a 'Y' connection at the city outlet receptacle on your coach or on the park tap. Add a short piece of hose to one side of the 'Y' and, presto, you have an outside tap.

> If you plan to enjoy air-conditioned comfort, never connect
> with an orange or yellow 14-gauge, 15-amp extension cord to
> connect an RV to electricity. The wiring is not heavy enough
> to carry the electrical load. A fire did result in our
> neighbour's unit in Arizona.

All seasoned RVers carry <u>at least one extra water hose,</u> a 25-foot heavy duty, 10-gauge, <u>30-amp electric cord</u> as well as a variety of electrical dog-bone style adapters and plug-in adapters that connect 15 amps to 30 amps and vice-versa. In many of the new parks we found hookup choices consist of either 15-amp or 50-amp service. It's a good idea to include a 50-amp to 30-amp and a 30-amp to 50-amp adapter as part of your collection.

Not all campgrounds are properly wired. Some electric boxes have <u>reversed polarity,</u> others have an <u>open ground</u> and both are dangerous situations if you connect your RV to this source of power. Before connecting your unit to shore power turn the breaker off, test the wiring with a small plug-in tester/monitor then turn the breaker back on. If the monitor reads okay, turn the breaker off, remove monitor and plug in your unit. Turn the breaker on.

> Warning - NEVER tie your dog to the metal portion of your
> RV! If there is a power surge or an open ground the dog will
> complete the circuit.

Yes –   No –

Connect your unit with a three-prong plug.

A <u>surge protector</u> temporarily attached to the park outlet or an inline power line monitor (PLM) permanently installed in an RV's electrical system, will save appliances from damage caused by electrical surges exceeding 130 volts or a drop below 102 volts (brown-out conditions). PLMs simply turn off all power in micro-seconds (to avoid damage) for up to four minutes to provide time for the problem to rectify itself. This protects the delicate workings of appliances like your air conditioner.

When using our generator in a campsite, we routinely keep the <u>generator door open</u>. During our early days while at a large rally, our generator faltered, emitting a loud bang followed by a puff of smoke. We had left our genny on to run the air conditioner for our dogs; however, we were away from our coach attending seminars. Anxious neighbours couldn't shut it off because we had locked the compartment. Fortunately, no major problem resulted and, both the dogs and the genny survived.

Dripping water from an air conditioner can make a real mess of the side of an RV. One friend drilled a small hole in the pan below his air conditioner and ran a piece of clear plastic tubing, sealed with silicone, to the ground. A container at the bottom of the tubing is easy to empty and his coach remains clean.

Easy Cleaning

Wash the inside ceilings of your RV with a long-handled sponge and a no-rinse heavy-duty cleaner. If you have a fabric ceiling use the vacuum. If there are spots on this type of covering, most can be covered with white shoe polish.

Cleaning the high front of a basement-style motorhome or a fifth wheel can also be a real challenge. This same long-handle sponge with the metal part removed makes the task easier. Apply cleaner with the mop portion and cover with a towel to polish the area to a high shine.

A baking soda and water solution removes tar from vehicles plus it's a superior general household cleaner. Dipping jewellery into a mixture of baking soda and water makes it sparkle. John also uses a toothbrush and a thick paste of baking soda mixed with water to clean his battery terminals He rinses it off with clear water.

If the fibreglass on your RV has a white, chalky appearance, don't waste money on re-painting until you try the easy-to-use cleaners designed to remove oxidization from fibreglass boats. Many are on the market and for years we applied Meguiar's brand of Heavy Duty Oxidation Removers with a soft cloth, let it dry to a haze and wiped it off to reveal a lustrous shine. A coat of one-step RV/boat cleaner and wax sealed the finish. The dullness disappeared and both glistened like new. A wide selection of oxidization colour restorers and specialty waxes are available in marinas and RV supply stores.

However nothing John did would bring the finish of our Luxor up the way he wanted. Recently Murray, an RV friend, and a detailing expert, spent two and a half days using high-powered polishers along with Meguiar's commercial products on our coach. Our prize possession – front to back – looks as if it just came off the line.

Our shimmering, shining coach.

Most RVers will find one of the new <u>ultra UV-protection cleaner/wax</u> products is all that is needed to keep a 'like new' finish. Look for one that applies with minimum effort and wipes off to a shine.

<u>Spray-on tire shining products</u> make your tires look like new. These products also offer UV-protection – but only use brands without petroleum in the ingredients; petroleum is very damaging to rubber.

<u>Controlling black streaks</u> is always a hassle; the above-mentioned products and a range of others also eliminate these. But another favourite is Lysol Tub and Tile Cleaner (the foam type); it not only effortlessly removes persistent black marks, but also leaves a smooth finish, especially on a fibreglass skin.

One way to protect the skin of your coach, and proudly <u>display decals and stickers</u> from places you've visited, is to attach a cut-to-fit piece of Plexiglas to your ladder. Have an auto glass company punch holes into the edge of your display board, thread through heavy-duty ties and you're all set to go. When you sell your coach, simply remove your 'on-the-road' mementoes and attach them to the next one.

My hints could go on and on. As you travel the highways, you'll meet other RVers who love to share their special living tips as well and, eventually, your list will triple mine.

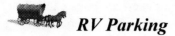 ## *RV Parking*

Parking an RV would be easier if dealers offered lessons to new RVers. Since this doesn't happen very often, newcomers to this lifestyle must learn handling techniques from their mistakes.

Most of us find this amusing because we, too, were all new RVers at one time and watching inexperienced RVers is a very interesting form of campground entertainment. Some perform a most creative and humorous act from the time they pull up to their site until they actually settle in. However, it can be somewhat embarrassing to hear the frustration of rising voices. And, when both the driver and co-pilot practise manoeuvring their unit until they are comfortable – including backing into a site – the rising tempers, knocked over picnic tables and crunched hookups would be a thing of the past.

Departing from a park can also cause problems. We once drove over a fire pit when we pulled out of our site. At the end of one RV rally, while everyone was saying goodbye, our friends drove over a huge cement cistern. Others left with electric cord attached. It helps if the co-pilot is outside watching where and what you are doing when you pull out.

Some RVers actually fear reaching their destination because their chosen park may not include pull-through sites and it may be necessary to back into a camping spot. Until both occupants understand a few basic driving hints, routine parking of their unit will always be a challenge plus a source of many spousal arguments. In reality, once you learn, backing a large recreational vehicle into a campsite is actually a simple procedure.

One tip all RVers should follow when backing up a **motorhome** into position is to place your hand at the bottom of the steering wheel and turn the wheel opposite to where you want the rear of your unit to move.

But, when backing up a **trailer** into a spot, place your hand at the bottom of the wheel and turn the wheel the same direction you want the rear of the trailer to move. Remembering the above will help immensely when backing up or parking an RV.

> **When using the 'buddy-system' to park your RV, make sure your co-pilot stands well back of the RV and always remain visible in the side mirrors.**

Several RVing friends prefer to talk each other into a spot. They use a walkie-talkie in conjunction with their CB. No one even becomes excited as the co-pilot guides their unit into place, usually on the first try. These compact transmitters are available from RV stores, Wal*Mart, home style hardware stores or RadioShack. These amazing devices are also very valuable any time you are in a busy place when you both prefer to go to different directions. John and I carry ours to communicate in grocery stores, malls and flea markets, etc. No longer do we waste time searching for each other.

Some RVers are more comfortable backing up with an expensive back-up camera system. Viewing a TV on the dash provides a complete picture of what's behind their coach.

One more group (usually novice) continue to think it helps to stand at the back of the RV and shout commands. I'm sorry, but no driver can hear or understand voice signals over the noise of an engine. Obviously, some RVers don't understand this point because frantic expletives occasionally echo over the campground. There are also a few who feel especially fit and strong because they attempt to stop an RV by pushing or leaning on the back of it as they scream 'Stop!'

John and I prefer to use hand signals. We find it easy to back up our motorhome and these same principles apply to trailers or fifth wheels.

"Move the rear of the coach to the left".

Both of us can direct our RV into a tight parking space without frustrating problems. When using hand signals to park a motorhome, the only major point to remember is the co-pilot must always be in full view of the driver's side mirror (if the co-pilot can see the mirror, the driver can see him or her). Trailerists may find it easier to use the passenger mirror. RVers have no specific signs to learn, nor is there a right or wrong way to guide someone into a site. As long as both the driver and co-pilot understand what the other is saying with their hands, the signals are effective.

At times, fellow RVers want to help, especially the men who feel that women aren't as knowledgeable as males in this area. If someone tries to help us, we simply thank them very much and continue using our own signals. No driver can receive direction from two sources. 'John only has eyes for me'. We (both of us share the driving) know exactly how to explain moves to the other with hand signals. Outside help only confuses the issue. With a little practise you, too, can settle into your spot with expertise and relax for the evening.

> **Devise signals for 'come straight back', 'turn right', 'turn left', 'temporary stop', 'full stop' and 'go forward'. If you cannot see the driver's side mirror the driver cannot see you.**

If you choose to use hand signals, you can develop your own variation. Our signals tell the driver where to put the rear of the unit. Your main goal is to communicate in simple gestures without yelling or screaming. Be patient!

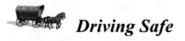 ## *Driving Safe*

I can't stress enough that good driving practices improve only after you feel confident handling your vehicle. Whether it's your first car or your first RV, it's wise for both pilot and co-pilot to become comfortable and proficient behind the wheel. Even if one person does most of the driving, a co-pilot never knows when he/she may have to take over in an emergency.

Large shopping centre parking lots – after hours, of course – can double as spacious training grounds for parking and backing into tight places. Until you feel confident, travel on quiet secondary roads to gain experience driving or towing that high, extra long and fully loaded RV.

Back To School

If you feel some professional instruction may help, contact a truck-driving school and sign-up for their basic course. If it's a bit costly, remember so is your RV. Even a local defensive driving course to update old habits could be a benefit. Taking control of your RV, instead of it controlling you, is the most important consideration. Practice makes perfect in many things but, especially in driving.

It's one thing to be confident on nice, sunny days but it's impossible to predict what the weather conditions will be after you set out on the road. During one of many seminars we attended, we picked up these tips on driving in adverse weather conditions.

Rain

When it first starts to rain, the roads become slick because of the water mixing with oils on road's surface. This is especially apparent during a light rain or heavy morning dew. Be careful, because until the road dries or the traffic increases, many roads can become as slippery as a skating rink. When driving in these conditions keep extra stopping distance between you and the vehicle in front. Reduce your speed so that you're not constantly using your brakes (braking too hard and too suddenly can cause you to slide). In heavy rain, when the water builds up on the roads, your vehicle will lose traction and hydroplane (ride on top of water), which makes your brakes virtually ineffective. If you must pull off the road, slow down before you move onto the shoulder. This is extremely important because the gravel shoulders are also very slippery when wet. When stopped, use your four-way emergency flashers to alert other drivers that you have stopped.

In recent years, many drivers seem to be using their four-way flashers when driving in conditions with poor visibility. If you do turn your flashers on and continue driving, you run the risk that those behind you may think that you've stopped and will pull into a lane of oncoming traffic to move around you. The safest move is to pull off the highway and turn your flashers on.

Fog

Contrary to what you may think, high beam headlights **reduce** visibility in fog conditions. Because the fog acts like a reflector, the bright lights of the high beams bounce back and impede your vision. Always use low beams when driving in the fog.

If the fog is thick and you can't see, pull off the road to the extreme right shoulder and put on your emergency flashers (see more info under the Rain section). Never turn your headlights on or sit in the dark when pulled off on the shoulder. Vehicles approaching from behind will think that you're either still mobile and on the road or, won't be able to see you at all and, in all probability, will plough right into you.

The safest stopping place is at a gas station or rest area parking lot. Eventually the fog lifts (especially true for morning fog) but, in low-lying areas, it remains dense for a longer period of time. Remember, if you can't see anyone else, they can't see you.

High Winds

If your vehicle is being buffeted or pushed around by high winds, reduce speed and keep both hands on the steering wheel. Keep the wheels in a forward direction and don't oversteer to compensate for the swerve caused by semi-trucks passing or when your RV is struck by wind gusts.

Again, practice makes perfect, especially when learning to cope with the increased height and weight of your RV. In the beginning, use secondary roads as much as possible. The lower traffic volume at reduced speed builds confidence and improves handling techniques.

Winter Driving

Even if the weather is mild when you start out, an unpredictable front can change a pleasant drive to one fraught with worry. Any driver living in or visiting a snow area should carry an emergency survival kit.

Always have a working flashlight, flares and triangles on board. Flares and triangles are especially important as they illuminate your vehicle during emergency stops and alert other drivers to a potential problem. In some states it is law that you have these on board but, since you never know when you will need them, no one should travel without them. Flares work well at dawn, dusk or in weather conditions when visibility is low. You can buy flares at RV automotive and department stores. Although the standard types are lit with a match for one-time use, battery operated flares are reusable.

Fluorescent triangles are the second most important accessory carried in your vehicle. These warning devices fold for packing and easily unfold for use. Because of the reflective surface that glows in the dark or shines brightly in the sunlight, triangles are a definite plus to have on board. In an emergency situation, put your flares or triangles about 300 feet in front and/or behind your vehicle.

> **Keep your windshield washer tank full and your wipers in good working order. You never know when you'll need them.**

In some parts of North America (in mountainous regions) tire chains are mandatory to travel through passes at high elevations on snow-packed roads.

Sand or rock salt (or kitty litter) helps traction. If you get stuck, sprinkle some in front of the drive wheels. Pieces of old carpet may also help provide traction. For extra traction, use good all-season radial tires.

Heavy work gloves make the job easier when handling icy chains and jacks. Ice scrapers, de-icing fluid and paper towels should be kept on hand to clean windows. In a freak snowstorm, a shovel may be a life-saver if you have to dig out. Always carry 12 to 15 feet of heavy gauge jumper cables.

Last, but not least, if travelling in the winter, carry a personal survival kit. Include boots, warm clothes (for layering), plenty of water and emergency high-energy rations. Make sure that you have candles and holders (for heat and light), waterproof matches and paper bags. The bags can be placed on your feet, hands and on your head (with eye-holes cut out). Do not use plastic bags. Plastic will suffocate you, while paper allows you to breathe and provides insulation from the cold. Since most of our body heat is lost through the head, keep your head covered. Include a fully-stocked first-aid kit in your vehicle. Make sure you check and replace supplies as needed on a regular basis.

Snow And Ice

The first rule when driving in blowing snow is to never travel with your high beam headlights on. (Read the Fog section for details.) When driving in cold-weather conditions, you must always expect to run into ice. Because they are so difficult to see ice patches, especially black ice, are extremely hazardous. Slow down and never slam on your brakes. If your brakes lock in position, you will lose control of your steering and go into an uncontrollable skid. In light snow and on thin ice, heavy vehicles have the stopping advantage; however, when the ice is thick and the snow is packed, your heavy vehicle will slide farther than a smaller car.

In these conditions, reduce speed and increase the distance between you and the vehicle in front. Just like driving a car, be prepared and don't take foolish chances, especially when travelling on snow covered or wet roads. Remember, most bridges, ramps and overpasses become icy before the road does. Slow down.

When conditions are poor and visibility is drastically reduced, wait until the weather improves. If you're on the road, pull into a rest area and move into your home-on-wheels, turn the genny on if you have one to power the furnace and relax. No appointment or timetable to be somewhere is worth the risk of an accident and your life. One winter two of our friends were on their way to Florida in their fifth wheel when a bad storm hit, so they checked into a hotel with a pool and hot tub and waited it out in comfort. You have to do what you have to do.

Peggi McDonald

Mountain Driving

*Magnificent Red Rock Canyon near Zion National Park, Utah
is carved through the heart of a mountain.*

In a large or heavy RV always gear down when climbing mountains to save wear-and-tear on your transmission. When descending a steep and lengthy slope, especially where it indicates that trucks should use 'low gear', gear down. Let your engine do the braking and only use your brakes to control your speed when you have no choice and for very short bursts. The rule of thumb is to descend a hill in one gear lower than you used to climb it.

John and I learned this lesson – also the hard way. Travelling through Oregon our first year, we had put new brake pads on the motorhome when we came out of Mexico. On our route north, we climbed a four-mile steep grade before descending for seven miles.

Unfortunately, neither of us was aware of engine braking. Since we had new brakes, we descended using the brakes to control our speed. We were passing a truck at the five-mile descent mark when the overpowering smell of burning brakes hit us. Of course, we thought it was the truck. Thankfully, for us, we decided to stop at a rest area around the next bend and discovered that it was our RV with hot brakes. Once again, the good Lord and our guardian angel protected us from a major disaster while teaching us a valuable lesson.

For anyone driving in the mountainous regions of the U.S.A., there is an excellent book called the *Mountain Directory – East and West Editions* written by Richard Miller for truck, RV, and motorhome drivers. This book is a great help to RVers when assessing grades and wondering what's around the next bend. Having the *Mountain Directory* on board takes the guesswork out of mountain driving and provides such peace-of-mind to the journey.[9]

Drive Alert

Most experienced RVers drive short distances every day, with frequent stops. The stops (especially if you do some sightseeing) can make getting there part of your travel adventure. A large percentage of accidents are caused by driver fatigue. The following hints may help you keep alert (and alive) when driving.

Change drivers frequently if your driving day is long. Only sit behind the wheel if you're well-rested.

If nighttime driving is uncomfortable, arrange your schedule so that all driving is done during daylight hours.

Several years ago we discovered Blue Lights (or jokingly what we call 'over 65 lights'). These low beams do not bother other drivers but they do provide a wider light path. Since I began wearing glasses all the time, headlights reflect and cause a glare to the point where my vision is less than perfect. As a result both John and I only drive after dark when it's unavoidable and, even then, for just a very short distance.

Eating helps you to stay awake but adds unnecessary calories. Try chewing gum (like your life depends on it) and you'll accomplish the same effect without adding extra pounds.

Don't take any medication (either prescription or over-the-counter) without carefully reading the label. Some drugs may cause drowsiness and put you to sleep. Be very careful when mixing medications, mixing could cause adverse reactions and decrease driving ability.

A little coffee keeps you awake but, too much coffee can act in reverse and cause you to nod off. And, save the partying for after your arrival – drinking alcohol or suffering from a hangover doesn't mix with sitting behind the steering wheel of a moving vehicle.

Recognize the signs of drowsiness, such as yawning and heavy eyelids. Stop the vehicle and change drivers. If this isn't possible, stop the vehicle (in a safe place – a truck stop or restaurant), and take a nap or, at least, take a walk-around break as soon as possible. Frequent stops sometimes help drivers cope with drowsiness.

---

9 *For info on* Mountain Directory East and West, *log onto* www.mountaindirectory.com *(1-800-594-5999). For more references see the* RV Books *section on the* RV WebLinks *page of* www.rvliving.net.

Keep the inside of your vehicle cool with a breeze on your face. It's easier to stay alert in cool temperatures and your passengers can always cover up if they get cold. Turn the radio on to an interesting talk show or strike up a conversation with your travel companion. You can also talk to yourself when there's no one else around. Who knows, that may prove to be the most informative conversation of your life and you know that the response will be what you want to hear. Ignore the strange looks from others in passing vehicles, talking will keep you awake and that is your top priority.

Tire Safety

A few weeks before trading in Kastle #1, we narrowly escaped a complete wipe out because of poor tires on another vehicle. A lady driving an older model car was passing us in the left lane on an interstate and a van that was tailgating her forced her into our lane. As she began pulling over in front of us, her right rear tire blew. It pushed her towards the inside shoulder, directly into the path of the van. No one was badly hurt because both vehicles were moving at the same speed and both drivers retained control of their vehicles. Had the left rear tire blown, she would have collided with us resulting in a much different ending.

Tires are one of the most important parts on your RV and your tow vehicle. Learning all you can about tires may mean the difference between an enjoyable vacation and one overflowing with problems. Most RV tires have a life of four to five years. Even if the tread seems perfect, when the sidewalls show signs of cracking it's time for a change. They are expensive but do not take chances with unsafe rubber.

If your unit has dual tires, spend the money on a quality set of valve extenders. When checking air pressure, it's extremely difficult to reach the tire valves on the inside tires of a dual system. With a valve extender, one end fits on to the valve and the hose is clamped on to the wheel hub allowing easy access when needed to read or increase tire air pressure.

It's difficult to put air into RV tires at a service station. With our gas units we carried a three-quarter horsepower air compressor on board so we could inflate our tires in the campground. Our diesel pusher has an adapter that connects to the compressor of the air brakes. Using this on board system makes it easy to keep the tires on Kastle #3 at the proper inflation.

BrakingTips

Motorhome owners with air brakes need special licensing in many states and provinces. The qualification can be a simple written test or a one-three day course. Frequently you have to re-qualify when you renew your licence.

All brakes should be tested periodically, especially after driving through water. In wet weather, to avoid locking your brakes, apply pressure (brake, release, brake, release, etc.) until your vehicle can be safely stopped. With an automatic transmission, you can get your vehicle back under control and avoid going into a skid on slippery roads if you shift to neutral or, with a standard tranny, depress the clutch. This disconnects the drive wheel so it won't compete with the brakes. When the wheels grip the road again and traction returns, release the clutch or shift to drive and maintain a safe speed.

Don't brake and turn at the same time. When turning, momentarily remove your foot from the brake.

Anti-locking brakes are now part of many vehicles. Anti-locking brakes automatically go through a repeated brake/release action as soon as the brake is depressed so, there is no need for the driver to pump the brake. There is a weird feel to the brake pedal and a different kind of noise with anti-lock brakes. Don't panic – keep your foot on the brake.

According to a driving pamphlet titled *Good Driving Practices* that I picked up from the Ontario Ministry of Transportation and Communications, there are three main types of braking on good road conditions. Contact the Department of Transport for pamphlets containing other hints for drivers.

1. Threshold braking: This is when you press as hard as possible on the brakes without locking up or skidding the wheels. Release pressure if wheels lock and re-apply – don't pump the brakes. Use the heel/toe method – keep the heel of your foot on the floor and use your toes to apply firm, steady pressure on the brake pedal just short of lockup.
2. Steering around an obstacle: This is another way to avoid an accident. Use the threshold braking method and then steer to the left or right. If you must enter another lane, check to make sure it's clear.
3. Four-Wheel-Lock Braking: This is when a quick stop is mandatory. Hit the brake as hard as you can and hold it to lock the brakes. This is the fastest way to stop but, with locked brakes, the car continues in a forward direction and you have no steering capabilities.

Other points mentioned in this pamphlet are rules that I knew at one time but have forgotten over the years. One tip that a whole slew of other drivers have also forgotten is to keep a safe stopping distance from the vehicle in front of you. Some roads have measured chevrons painted on the surface to indicate the safe distance. If there aren't any chevrons, mark your distance by counting off three-second intervals. Take note of a checkpoint (hydro/electric pole, etc.) on the side of the road; when the car in front comes to that point, count off 'one-thousand and one, one-thousand and two'. (Increase this distance even more when travelling in an RV.) Drivers following at a safe distance will not have reached the same check-point before the count is finished.

Adjust your driver's seat to a comfortable position. The seat should be close enough so that your left foot sits flat.

Before starting the ignition, adjust all rear-view and side mirrors (clean if necessary) so that the mirrors are positioned for optimum viewing suited to the height of the current driver.

Watch for blind spots and frequently check all mirrors for traffic conditions both behind you and to your sides.

Be extremely cautious of children and animals in suburban neighbourhoods – they have a habit of darting out on to the road without looking.

Watch for open car doors in your path or for other vehicles pulling out without warning. Be wary of bicycles, mopeds and motorcycles. Give road maintenance workers a 'brake' as well.

Always signal, you may know where you're going but others don't unless you signal your intention. This is especially true when you repeatedly travel the same route. Signal; don't assume that the other driver is as familiar with the road as you.

Keep a driver's handbook with emergency road rules handy in your glove compartment. Take it out every once in a while to familiarize yourself with emergency guidelines.

If possible, keep a cell phone with you whether you are in your RV or your car. A second choice is a CB but everyone – including not-so-nice people, will hear everything you broadcast. Being able to call for help in any situation offers additional peace-of-mind.

***Learning to handle your unit in all driving situations allows you to join friends
for good times such as at this Explorer RV Club rally in Sicamous, BC.***

Driving skills depend on good reflexes, wise judgement and treating
other motorists, as you would like to be treated. At this time, RVers don't
need a special licence to control very heavy vehicles and driving preparation
or extra road training is almost non-existent. This shows signs of changing
in the not too distant future. Give yourself an edge by doing your own extra
training – a little practise and preparation is all it takes to increase driving
skills and improve your on-the-road travel.

Peggi McDonald

Maintenance Service on the Road
(See also How To Buy A Pre-owned Or New RV*)*

Most of the time RVs perform exactly as you expect them to, however, on occasion problems do surface. Of course, this frequently happens when you are away from home and in unfamiliar territory. When your tow or towed vehicle and/or your home-on-wheels requires some TLC, the following tips may help you find a quality repair facility.

Ask a local RVer or campground staff where they have repairs done. Early on in our adventure we stopped for gas in the small town of Van Horn, Texas. We were leaking coolant and the attendant sent us down the road to a repair shop. There, helpful mechanics replaced a rad hose clamp and pressure-tested the radiator for a mere $5.00 (1991 prices but extremely low even for then).

Call your emergency road service (ERS)[10] personnel for a recommendation. Once, when we had minor valve problem on our tag axle compressor on a late Friday afternoon, I phoned various shops for service. After continually hearing, "No, we can't look at it until Monday," I called our ERS. The agent stayed on the line until we found a facility to look at our problem. The shop agreed to repair it – if we didn't need new parts. We were on our way in 15 minutes.

Many vehicle manufacturers provide a toll-free 'hot-line' help line. Look for yours in the operating manual. Before you leave your home country, make sure that the toll-free number works from the area in which you are travelling. Ask for the regular phone number and if they have an international toll-free number.

If your engine needs looking at, take your unit to a Chev, GMC, Ford, Cummins, CAT or specific dealer, your tires to a speciality shop such as Goodyear, Firestone or Michelin. Many times it is more economical to have an oil change done at a service centre that specializes in quick turn-around service. If your RV needs repairs, call an in-park service company or take it to an RV dealer. If you are camped near your RV dealer, contact them for assistance.

---

10 *Keep your* ERS *contact numbers close at hand. You never know when you will need it. This applies to a contact number for your RV dealer as well. Being aware that someone is close at hand to talk to in an emergency makes for peace-of-mind travels.*

Camping World[11] is a discount chain of RV stores located throughout the U.S. and their service is second to none when it comes to RV repairs. All installations carry a lifetime warranty, if one store does the repair, a second store will honour the service contract if you run into any problems. They also provide limited service to many products they sell even if you did not buy them there.

When you have found a qualified facility, be considerate. Make an appointment, if possible. Travellers simply dropping by can pose a difficult problem for mechanics that already have a full workload.

Give the service manager a written list of required maintenance or repairs. Include your vehicle identification number (VIN) and your mileage. When your request is in writing everyone understands what maintenance you are requesting and the service manager can schedule sufficient time for proper repair. Ask for an estimate – it may come in handy if charges differ from what you expected. Enquire if they have a checklist of all components they will look at so you know your RV will receive a good once over.

We have always stayed in our unit at the garage during service, occasionally for an extended period of several days and more. In all cases, plan to stay with your vehicle or RV at the facility. The service you receive will be faster and, possibly, of higher quality when you are visible. Staff simply want to complete your work and get you on your way.

If you must leave your vehicle for extended periods (major engine jobs), pre-arrange a set time every day to discuss problems with your mechanic. An RVing friend of ours blew the engine on his towed car. Because he had important commitments 160-km away, he left his car at the garage for a week with promises of completion on his return. Guess what? When he called a week later, the mechanic had run into problems and the car wasn't ready. Our friend had to modify his travel plans. A daily phone call to the service manager may have eliminated this delay or at least prepared him for his altered plans.

Ask to see the parts that the mechanic plans to install and for the return of all parts removed from your unit – at the very least ask for a detailed explanation of the cause of the problem. Another hard lesson learned – once we left a garage with mismatched spark plugs. When another mechanic discovered the mistake, we informed the dealer who made the error. Thankfully, he refunded our full parts and labour costs. On a different occasion (same situation) only five of the eight plugs replaced were new (two brands were in our coach) and at another maintenance tune-up, a plastic fuel filter was used instead of a metal one (needed for larger and

---

11 Camping World has a chain of stores throughout the U.S.A., www.campingworld.com 1-800-626-5944 for info.

hotter engines). This is just one more reason to check all parts before (and old ones after) installation.

Our emergency repairs have been quite minimal over the years, mainly because we strongly believe in preventive maintenance. As a rule, we stay well under our maintenance budget for both our motorhome and car.

All RVs, towed and tow vehicles need periodic service. Most RVers set up a maintenance schedule to remind themselves of when and how often their vehicles require maintenance.

Regular car-style maintenance is required for spark plugs and cables, air filter, battery charge system, distributor cap and rotor, fuel filters, belts and hoses, PVC valve.

Diesels require periodic oil and filter change, fuel filters plus a class B service (lubrication, a visual check and inspection).

Note: When we bought our diesel motorhome, John switched to synthetic transmission fluid (synthetic engine oil is also available). The switch resulted in fewer fluid changes. If you're considering a diesel engine, researching the benefits of synthetic oil/fluid might be worth your while.

When you are setting up your maintenance schedule calendar, remember to have your brakes and fuel lines, shocks and suspension system checked. Inspect your tires for wear, etc., and have your coolant system flushed.

Attend to wheel alignments and repacking of bearings as needed.

It helps if you purchase a mechanic's helper book. Shop around, you may find one specific for your unit or, collect handouts at mechanical seminars. Sometimes these manuals help mechanics at repair facilities to understand the problem.

FMCA's (Family Motor Coach Association) convention in Brunswick, Maine during 2000 – over 7000 motorhomes were registered.

Being part of a national convention at one of the larger RV clubs is a perfect way to learn more about RV maintenance. At the conventions, experts from the leading engine and chassis manufacturers hold seminars to teach you how their chassis and engines work. Other seminars cover diesel engines and a host of additional mechanical topics. The information gathered here is worth much more than the price of the convention.

> **Don't forget to change your oil and fuel filters. This is especially important for diesel engines.**

Some RVers feel more comfortable when they carry easy-to-store spare parts in their RV. Even though many of us can't fix even minor problems, there's usually an RVing neighbour or friend who can do the repair if you have the required part.

Regular RV maintenance should include inspection (and replacement if needed) of non-mechanical items, such as water heaters and furnaces.

Most appliances are extremely reliable accessories; however, all propane appliances should receive an annual preventive safety check by an authorized dealer licensed to perform propane repairs.

The carpeting and furniture in your RV is used more than they would be in a house. If the furniture requires repairs or modification, attend to it immediately. The dusty environment that RVers live in at many destinations doesn't help and demands extra-special care in cleaning and maintenance.

We have dogs, however, I don't like living with sheets or blankets covering my furniture. So in Kastle #2 I made decorative seat covers for the couch, captain's chairs plus the pilot and co-pilot seats. The covers take the beating, blend in with our décor and are easy to remove for washing away day-to-day dirt and dog hair.

Excess wear on carpets is the other main concern in an older RV. Over the years we've tried correcting this several ways. In Kruisin' Kastle #1 we removed the carpet and replaced it with a sub-floor of mahogany covered with a heavy-duty vinyl. I simply loved it. For an added touch and warmth, I placed throw rugs throughout the coach.

Cleaning with a broom and dustpan was a dream. A quick wash and wax restored the shine. It was amazing to see how much dirt and dust was tracked into the coach every day.

In Kastle #2, we placed area rugs on top of the carpet for added protection. These rugs not only protect the carpet, they are easy to take outside for thorough cleaning. Eventually in that coach, too, the carpet was replaced with easy-to-clean vinyl flooring dotted with throw rugs.

Our present coach is a high-end diesel-pusher that we bought when she was four years old. We love our Luxor by Winnebago but it doesn't have a slide. To increase the space of our living area we renovated by removing the couch and big barrel chair and again the carpet (carpets in RVs look good when they are new but they quickly show wear and are extremely difficult to keep clean). This time we hired a professional installer to add vinyl planking that looks like hardwood over a 3/8-inch sub-floor. We replaced the original furniture with two wine coloured loungers on a circular base along with a couple of end tables. Covers for the valences and a circular table to hide the steering wheel completed her new décor. [12]

Getting To Know Your Appliances

When we began our extended travels, I could never remember which RV appliances functioned on electric, propane or, occasionally, from the engine battery. These simply exceeded my realm of comprehension.

Mastering the art of living with a 30-amp service carried its own long list of frustrations. I quickly learned that if I operated the fridge on propane, I had extra power to use an air conditioner, the microwave, coffee pot and the toaster. If I turned some appliance off for a short time, I could even add the TV and my curling iron to the list – without blowing the park breaker.

> **If you are in a park where you must pay for power you will save money by operating your fridge on propane.**

I eventually learned to 'trust' these appliances until, one time, two days after arriving in Mexico, I was overwhelmed by the smell of ammonia. There wasn't a repair facility within miles.

Searching through all available RV maintenance manuals, we discovered everything about the fridge operation, except how to correct, drain or cope with ammonia leaks.

In these manuals we found no repair suggestions, nor did we find out what would happen if we just left it. Apprehensive and unsure of what health related problems may arise, we slept for three nights with the main door of the coach open. We did find out later that this wasn't necessary. As long as we kept the fridge door closed, the aroma of the ammonia coolant solution remained trapped inside the well-insulated fridge.

---

12 For complete details and photos of our renovations log onto www.rvliving.net for the story – The Space Of A Slide From The Inside *(non-computer owners can go to the library to view how we did this).*

Our refrigerator was an absorption-style model and the only repair technician within a 50-kilometre radius was overbooked with several months of work ahead of us. Even though he couldn't come to our rescue, he assured us that the strong odour was not life-threatening and took time to explain how to remove the plug and drain the ammonia cylinder.

The only long-term remedy for leaking coolant is to replace the fridge or the condenser/coolant and, since we couldn't buy a fridge in Mexico and it wasn't feasible to drive 1,000 kilometres to return to the U.S., we had no choice but to deal with our problem until late March.

To keep our fridge cold, we turned it into an <u>old fashioned icebox</u>. I put triple-bagged ice in the crispers and placed a large covered cake pan filled with ice in the freezer compartment plus a triple bag in the ice-cube container. They each needed replacing every two days. I added newspapers to the top shelf as further insulation. Both the refrigerator and freezer of RV fridges are so very well-insulated, the temperature remained a constant 40 degrees Fahrenheit, as long as we only opened the door when necessary.

No make-do solution is ever perfect but, on the other hand, it's better than ruining a perfectly good vacation. At least with having a non-running ice-packed fridge we didn't have to worry about exact levelling the coach at the various campsites we visited. My sister travelled with us that winter and she loved ice cubes in her glass of water. She was in seventh heaven.

***Well-maintained RVs lead to unique getaways
such as a swim at Radium Hot Springs in British Columbia.***

Fridges and other RV appliances do malfunction and, as a rule, help is generally nearby. RVers whose adventures take them to interesting out-of-the-way places may also take them away from convenient repair shops. A breakdown doesn't necessarily signal an end to your travels but it may tax your imagination to learn how to cope when an appliance doesn't work as expected.

Delays associated with unscheduled maintenance and repairs can be upsetting. Nevertheless, these are only minor irritations RVers must put up with in exchange for the freedom to explore. Most RVers feel that working and maintaining a home is much more stressful than a few minor maintenance irritations usually encountered in your home-on-wheels.

Understanding Your Sanitation System

Les Doll, an award winning certified RV Technician and host of
www.rverscorner.com provided tech support editing to this subject.

Travelling along the highways with bathroom facilities close at hand is
one of the many benefits of exploring by RV. But, like all things, this
convenience is quickly taken for granted until the toilet does not work.
During our first years we made just about every mistake possible and
encountering preventable problems with our marine-style toilet was no
exception. Hopefully, with a few tips that we've accumulated from personal
experience, you'll avoid many of our costly mistakes.

Emptying holding tanks is easy – you simply pull a lever and the
contents drain through a hose to the campsite receptacle or into the dump
station. Be a considerate camper and always leave a sewer area the way
you'd like to find it. If you are a new RVer, get instructions from the dealer
on how your system works. If this isn't offered, ask for it.

> **When draining your tanks, always dump the black (toilet)
> tank first, followed by the grey (kitchen/shower) water. This
> leaves your hose fresh and clean and ready for storage and
> your next hookup.**

Remember, all RVers, even those driving the elaborate condos-on-
wheels must empty their holding tanks. Some RVers don rubber boots,
coveralls and gloves to dump but, if your hose is in good shape and long
enough to reach the receptacle, emptying your tanks is really a clean, simple
and trouble-free task.

RVers constantly learn lessons from their life on the road. My most
embarrassing holding tank learning experience was on our first weekend
out. We checked into a park without sewer hookups on a Friday night and
both of us had long relaxing showers Saturday morning. No one had
explained how to use the **water saver on the shower** nozzle handle– we
simply let the water run till the hot water ran out. Our grey tank overfilled in
a hurry.

As new RVers, we did receive a thorough instruction from our dealer,
however, our memory of each detail faded as soon as we reached our
campsite. Since this was fresh shower water, I decided to drain a little on the

ground until we could visit the dump station – good plan, except I pulled the wrong lever. Yes, I closed the valve in a hurry and spent the next ten minutes trying to clean up residue left from our black water tank. Thank heavens we were only in the RV for about 12 hours and this tank was almost empty. As co-pilot I decided then and there to become familiar with this procedure along with all the others, even though I don't have the 'pleasure' of performing this task very often.

RVers who follow and understand a few basic rules of operation will find RV marine-style sanitary systems give years of satisfactory service.

Problem: Many toilets have a scissor-like trap (more expensive commodes have a ball style trap and are less prone to this problem) in the toilet bowl neck that closes when a pedal or lever releases it. Occasionally, when there's insufficient water in the bowl before flushing, paper frequently becomes caught in its path and gets packed under the seal. Sometimes granules of non-dissolved toilet chemicals also get stuck around this rim and force the trap open a few millimetres. If the water won't stay in the bowl you have a problem. When the trap no longer closes completely, tank gases can enter the RV and the seal begins to dry out.

Solution: Instruct all occupants, visitors included, that the paper must 'float' before flushing. Removing the packed residue under the trap is sometimes possible by working a home-made right-angle tool around the seal. Try to construct your adapter without sharp edges to avoid damaging the rubber seal. In severe cases, RV mechanics must completely remove the toilet to fix this problem.

Using a heavy spray nozzle (connected to a water hose from the outside) to flush the toilet neck along the partially opened scissor valve is another trick that sometimes dislodges any residue collected around the seal. This may only work if you have a window nearby.

Spraying with silicone helps keep the seal pliable. However, if RVers leave this irritating problem uncorrected, replacing the dried seal can become a major repair job.

Purchasing a new seal by itself is not always possible either. Frequently, the new seal is part of an expensive kit that includes the gears. On one occasion we found that it was more economical to replace our entire toilet at a sale price than to purchase the package of replacement parts. John and I also learned this lesson the expensive way – we replaced two toilets and one set of gears during our first six years. It was one of our more costly learning curves. So remember – if your scissor valve does not close properly and water drains from the bowl, attend to the problem immediately. It will save you big bucks in the long run!

Special RV toilet paper breaks up easily in RV holding tanks but it is more costly than budget priced household brands. Many brands of biodegradable one-ply tissue works equally as well in the marine toilet system. While in the U.S.A. we stock up on Scott tissue one-ply toilet paper with 1,000 sheets per roll (this is equivalent to just about three rolls of regular size rolls; storing one roll takes less space than three). It is now available in Canada at stores like Costco, etc. The paper is biodegradable, economical and packages of four (a month supply) are easy to store.

> **To test if your favourite toilet paper is biodegradable put a few sheets in a container of your mixed chemicals. If it breaks up in a few minutes it is OK to add to your tank.**

Some manufacturers include a tissue digester in their chemical product line for those RVers who have tissue build-up inside their black water tank.

To effectively deodorize and break up waste add a small amount of liquid **holding tank chemicals** to the tank. Solutions come in easy-to-use applications from liquids, powder or pills to deodorant, formaldehyde or enzyme-based products. (However try to avoid formaldehyde-based solutions because they destroy the good bacteria necessary to keep septic systems functioning properly.)

Tank chemicals are available in a full range of formulas to cover all situations.

Mix a small amount of chemical with one gallon of water to your empty black water tank. Add a touch more at the 1/2 level mark. Your tank always remains fresh this way and you stretch the amount of chemicals used. For more savings stock up on these costly products while they are on sale at RV supply stores.

Because most RVers dump before these reservoirs are completely full, we usually reduce the amount of chemical solution recommended by manufacturers for a 40-gallon tank. Always dump your black tank when it is between 1/2 to 3/4 full – add water if needed. The pressure from a volume of liquid in the tank makes for a cleaner flush.

Movement of the liquid aids in keeping the tank clean, especially the black water tank with its added chemicals. Periodically, when we expect to have sewer hookups at our next stop, I add a double dose of solution and lots of water before we change destinations. The agitation caused by driving ensures that our tank is squeaky clean when we reach our park. However, be aware that each gallon of water adds 10 pounds to your vehicle weight.

My washer/dryer is my most valued accessory.

Several years ago we **added a washer/dryer combo** to Kastle #3. We would hate to be without this great machine. However, due to the design of our coach plumbing the W/D drains into our black tank. This took some adjustment but there are pluses to this type of drainage because our black tank is constantly being rinsed. Two loads fill an empty tank so on the days when we must leave it open for a while we occasionally have a build up of solids. Guess what? The awning stick (wash and wipe it down when you are finished) works well to dislodge any temporary build-up. We then close the black and add a double dose of chemicals; our tanks once again operate as we expect them too.

Using **grey water tank disinfectant** freshens your drains and tanks but how much and how often you use grey water chemicals depends on the degree of food residue in your kitchen sink drains. John and I leave our grey valve open when we're camped with sewer hookups. If you keep yours closed until the tank is full before dumping it, you will probably use more chemicals than we do.

> **Wise RVers do not use home remedies in their holding tanks. These solutions may control odours, but they could damage sensitive components, seals and valves. Most home brews do not kill the bacteria that can grow in your tanks. RV plumbing is constructed differently than that in a house.**

Some RVers prefer to occasionally **flush their black water tank**. They dump the contents, rinse the tank with a hose or specialized rinsing wand or a back-flush attachment, close valves, add solutions and water to the 3/4 level. If possible, they take a short drive and drain their tank again. Close valves and add small amounts of solutions and the tank will be fresh and ready for use. Although it is NOT necessary to thoroughly rinse your tank every time you dump, flushing and treating your tank is extremely important if your RV will be sitting idle for an extended period of time.

There is considerable controversy about the pros and cons of **grey water draining on the ground**. When water from the sink and shower does not sit in the tank, it has no odour to it. However, if it drains directly into the ground, environmentalists say that the earth becomes contaminated. We spent many summers in one park that catered to a number of seasonal residents. (Seasonal is when the RV is parked on a site for an extended – sometimes years – period of time. These units take the place of a cottage.) Those park owners recommended RVers dig a hole and drain the grey water into the ground. This may be OK but no matter where you are, never, never, never do this with your black water.

Camping directories, tourist offices, welcome centres, Chamber of Commerce offices and even the Internet, should be able to direct you to a proper dumping facility when needed in an emergency.

The **gauge indicators** inside most RVs are frequently inaccurate. This doesn't necessarily mean paper or residue has stuck to the measure device – believe it or not – some recorders are so sensitive that even brand new they never provide correct readings. For instance, the indicator on Kastle #1 was only accurate when the tank reached 1/4 full. On Kastle #2, even after servicing, our gauges continued to be less than satisfactory.

On our present coach we don't even check the gauges since it's easy to see how full the black tank is with a flashlight through the toilet neck. The grey tanks overflow into the shower and we can see the level in our fresh water tank. To us it really isn't a big problem when gauges read incorrectly; however your coach designs may be different than ours and you will have to find solutions that work for you.

> **It's OK to leave your grey water valve open when you're hooked up to sewer. If you keep it closed and the tank overflows, stale water will back up in your shower basin. It will smell like something died and everything you store in your shower will be saturated with the same foul odour.**

There are many things that will help you keep your sanitation system working the way it is supposed to work.

➢ The first is to always use **biodegradable products** in your black tank.

➢ Placing used toilet tissue in a separate container rather than the toilet is an unhygienic practice and isn't necessary with the wide variety of holding tank solutions on the market. The paper completely dissolves when deposited in the proper commercial tank chemicals. If one product isn't satisfactory, try another – the choice is extensive.

➢ Even though facial tissue is colourful and softer than toilet paper, do NOT flush it. When wet, facial tissue clumps into a sodden ball and shouldn't even be used in your home toilet let alone your marine toilet.

➢ During a Thetford Sanitation seminar, the staff explained pointers on maintaining your sanitation system.

  o They stressed the importance of **NEVER using any petroleum products (Vaseline, WD-40, etc.)** on sewage valves. Using these products over time will swell the valves and dry them out. Instead of correcting the problem of a sticky valve, petroleum products add to the difficulty.

  o Thetford toilet manufacturers recommend using a silicone-based spray to loosen a sticky valve.

  o A drain valve lubricant can also be added periodically to the tanks to condition the tanks from the inside.

When camped in a park with sewer hookups always keep
your black (toilet) water valve closed. If it's left open, the
liquids drain away and the solids collect on the tank bottom
and clog your system. This too, is a messy task to clean up if
you do it yourself and costly if an RV repair tech corrects
your problem. We also learned this lesson the hard way!

General Tips

1. If trying to **connect the sewer hose to a standard adapter** seems
   impossible, fill a container with hot, soapy water then place the end of
   your sewer hose in the water. While it is soaking, lubricate the bottom
   of a wine bottle with liquid soap and coat the hose attachments with
   liquid soap, as well. When the sewer hose is warm, stretch it over the
   bottle, remove the bottle and connect the hose to the fixtures. On the
   good side of things many of the new-style adapters have easy and quick
   connectors for sewer hoses.

One type of sewer adapter and a donut.

2. A wide variety of handy **sewer attachments** on the market provide an
   excellent air-tight seal when your hose is connected to the park
   receptacle. In many campgrounds, especially in the south, it is still
   mandatory to add a rubber donut between the hose and the PVC pipe to
   achieve an air-tight seal. These donuts are available from any RV store
   and from the campgrounds enforcing this rule. Since these rubber
   donuts are inexpensive, it is wise to carry one on board. Buying an
   adapter just to comply with park regulations can be very frustrating.

3. When **camped with sewer hookups**, it's easy to frequently dump and,
   during these times, our entire system works more efficiently if we use
   an excess amount of water with each toilet flush. But, when we're only
   using holding tanks and must conserve liquids, we find using our toilet
   spray hose in conjunction with a round-styled toilet brush efficiently

cleans the bowl and neck without excess water. However, always keep a small amount of water in the bowl so the seal does not dry out.

4. Though most RVs have showers on board, some people prefer to use park or campground facilities. Before heading off to the shower, check to see if you need coins to activate the water – this is more common in rural areas. Carrying coins and shampoo bottles from your RV to the shower can be awkward so creative RVers find numerous ways to transport these supplies.

    o   One lady we met refills trial-size bottles for each member of her family and, if these mini-containers are left behind, there's no waste.

    o   Another finds that the removable cutlery basket from her dishwasher is a convenient tote to carry shampoos and bath gel to park showers. In time you will find your own ways to accomplish tasks like this.

There are so many different ways to do things when RVing that there is no right or wrong way. Talk to others you meet on the road – it's surprising how many ingenious solutions RVers come up with to make life easier.

The bathroom might be the smallest room in your RV but it can ensure that your travel is more comfortable, especially when you don't have to worry about the cleanliness of public washrooms. Take care of facilities in this room and it will return years of satisfactory service.

Winter Storage – Spring Ready

Winterizing an RV or taking it out of storage and getting it ready to hit the road is a big job. You may want to hire a professional to do everything but the cleaning. However, the following tips will guide the do-it-yourselfer through each step.

A pretty winter day in an Ontario campground.

It is possible to <u>live in an RV over the winter</u> but it is not without problems. There is a complete 'how-to' story complete with photos on our website[13]. In general, if you decide to live in your RV for an extended stay in the north, the following guidelines should help. Expect to add RV antifreeze through your pump and fresh water tank. You can still use city water if you wrap your water hose with a heat strip covered with foam cylinders. Plan to dump only when your tanks are near full, be sure to stow your sewer hose when finished or it will freeze if it's left out.

---

13 Go to <u>www.rvliving.net</u> under the Advice and How-to *section to read a story about the winter we spent at a RV park in the snow. If you are not on the Internet, visit the computers at the public library – take a grandkid with you for help if you need to.*

We rented a large auxiliary propane tank that was re-filled by a propane supplier every three weeks. We also placed four trouble lights with 40 or 100-watt bulbs (enclosed in their protective cages), in crucial areas to increase heat where the furnace didn't quite reach. In some cases this is the only way to avoid frozen water lines in these areas.

> CAUTION: I checked with the local fire department and they stressed that if you are following this procedure be certain that the lights are not close to any combustible materials. Do not leave them turned on 24/7 and check on the surrounding areas frequently – look for area that show signs of excess heat.

Most days were great and comfortable but over the winter, a portion of five to six days, our water lines froze even with all our preparations. Many people seal their windows with plastic and surround their units with skirting plus most of us added press on strips of insulating foam tape to our doorframe. That winter was a fun experience, especially walking among the clean, white undisturbed snow on a picture-perfect evening. However, we don't look forward to repeating the experience in the near future.

John and I prefer to go south each fall and return in the spring, therefore, the 'how-to' of winterizing our unit was not familiar to us. So we asked many seasoned RVers what they do to ready their RV for the winter and the following is a synopsis of their procedures.

Putting Your RV In Hibernation

> Les Doll, an award winning certified RV Technician and host of www.rverscorner.com provided extensive tech support editing to this subject.

It was a very pretty, but very long winter.

<u>All lines must be free of water to avoid freezing</u>. One option is to clear lines by blowing compressed air through the system. Though some people swear by this method, it's not foolproof. Unfortunately, some water residue may remain that can freeze and cause future problems. The recommended choice is to add RV antifreeze to the system. It's suggested that RVers bypass the fresh and hot water tanks (drained of course) when adding non-toxic RV antifreeze.

> **You can purchase an easy to install bypass kit from your RV dealer. To save money on the cost of RV antifreeze, you can also install a second valve. This valve fits between the fresh water tank and the water pump. There is a short piece of hose that is placed directly in the antifreeze bottle and when the pump is turned on, it pulls the antifreeze through the water lines, bypassing the fresh water tank, when you open the taps. See your dealer for details.**

<u>The first step is to clean, flush and drain all tanks</u>. Add RV antifreeze to the water lines – be sure to bypass the tanks.

Locate the water pump, disconnect the inlet fitting...

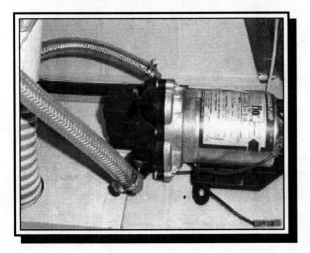

and install the winterizing hose...

then insert the other end of the hose into the antifreeze jug.

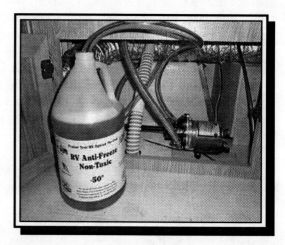

Note: If you add antifreeze to your fresh water tank it may be difficult to remove in the spring due to the location of the drain – on many RVs it is located on the side of the tank near the bottom. If this is the case, several gallons will remain in the tank if the valve is left open. When flushing, it mixes with the water and takes a long time to totally remove the antifreeze.

Starting with the tap the farthest from the pump, turn each one on (don't forget the shower) until you see antifreeze flowing out of the faucet. Turn faucets off and flush the toilet, then pour a small amount of antifreeze down the toilet and through the drains to the grey tank

Note: If you are going to use your RV in below freezing weather over the winter and your tank valves are not in a heated compartment, always add 1/2-cup of RV antifreeze to both grey and black tanks after dumping so it will collect next to the valve areas.

A word of caution – NEVER add windshield wiper antifreeze to ANY part of the water system. It is poisonous to both you and to the earth.

Another point to remember if you're winter camping and you don't have your water hoses wrapped in heat strips, do not connect to campground hookups. Either carry water on board in containers or if your fresh water tank is heated, fill the tank, disconnect the water hose and store it away. This also applies to your sewer hose; wait until your grey and/or black water tanks are nearly full, then connect your hose, dump and stow the hose away again. Hoses that are not heated will freeze and split open.

Clean, check and charge your battery. Top up your batteries with distilled water, but do not overfill. If you don't plan on using your motorhome over the winter months, remove the battery and store it somewhere where it will stay cool, but not below freezing. (If your battery gets too warm, it will discharge.) Remember to make a diagram of the battery connections before you remove them.

> **Top-up the charge at least every two months. Deep cycle batteries self-discharge when in storage**.

Note: Recently technicians from a battery store at a FMCA RV convention changed our four golf cart-style house batteries. I was impressed to see that these techs who change batteries for a living, made a drawing of how our batteries were connected before they removed them.

Thoroughly clean the inside and outside of your unit. After cleaning, turn the fridge off, prop open the door(s) to eliminate odours and stop mildew from growing. Leave several open boxes of baking soda inside the fridge and freezer. Cover all external vents and openings where pipes and cords enter the unit with tinfoil. Stuff 'brass' wool (similar to steel wool but it won't rust) into crevices to stop pests from making a nest. Don't forget to protect the air conditioner with a cover.

Mice do not like the smell of Downy sheets so spread them around at the back of your cupboards where the floor joins the walls and near openings where wires come into your unit. Filling these holes with brass wool (available from grocery stores for cleaning pots) provides extra protection.

Placing several containers of 'Damp Rid or No Damp or Dri-Z-Air desiccant crystals throughout your unit helps to control moisture build-up. These are available from RV dealers and some grocery stores. (See *Kitchen Tips* for more details.)

Close all drapes and blinds to prevent the sun's rays from deteriorating and fading fabric. It is also a good idea to crack open a vent or window for ventilation. Reduce air pressure on the tires and jack up the RV, if possible, to extend tire life.

> **If you install covers over your roof vents, you can leave the vents open to allow air to circulate. This keeps rain, snow and pests out, plus it eliminates the stale closed-up smell of an unoccupied RV.**

<u>Keep your gas/fuel/propane tanks full to prevent condensation</u>. Turn off your propane at the tank and make sure that the place where you are storing your RV is level. Extend or add jacks to stabilize your unit – it helps to relieve stress on the frame.

Spring Into Action

The incredible International Peace Gardens – complete with an on-site campground – on the border of Manitoba and North Dakota is something every RVer should see.

At the first hint of spring northern RVers, especially those who weathered our blustery winter, are anxious to get on the road. It's really difficult to hold back the desire to load the RV and take off for parts unknown.

However, while we may have been active over the winter our RVs have been hibernating, some under a blanket of snow. Although these units are made to withstand all sorts of weather, they do need a bit of TLC to bring them back to tip-top shape. RVs, after all, are investments and a little bit of elbow grease and preventive maintenance each spring could save you hundreds of dollars in costly on-the-road repairs.

Now that winter is over, it's time for spring-cleaning, RV style. Most of the following you can do yourself but, for any difficult parts don't hesitate to ask a dealer for help. To nip potential problems in the bud, wise RVers set up a simple maintenance and clean-up schedule. First of all, open all the windows and let in some of that fresh spring breeze to get rid of that musty, closed-up smell. Do a visual check of connections, propane, water hoses, pipes and valves. Make sure that none are cracked or corroded.

Look behind the fridge and inspect the area for any signs of mice, birds, spider webs and any other blockages. Clean the area. If there are any signs of rust on the coils, lightly rub the surface with a dry steel or brass wool pad.

While your coach is airing out, check thoroughly for any sign of water seepage on the walls, floors and ceiling. A build-up of snow may have weakened the roof.

Water stains could show up on the walls or rust stains may be apparent on the roof frame. Check carefully – there is probably a leak and treat this as a major repair. If the leak is extensive it may be time to call in the professionals.

While you're on the roof, check again for signs of birds and remove all nests and other debris.

If your air conditioner is leaking, the gasket will have to be replaced. This is a 1" thick gasket that is compressed to 1/2". NEVER use caulking or sealant to control leaks around the A/C. This may be a repair for your dealer.

Take a walk around the outside of your RV. Check all handles and hardware to be certain each one works properly. Look in every nook and cranny for mice or birds and other pests (especially in your storage pods). Examine the skin of your RV for anything that is out of the ordinary.

Next look at all the electrical connections, check for cracks or breaks in the wires. If there's a chalky-looking substance on the connectors, it's just a residue left courtesy of winter and road salt. Brush it off with wire brush, steel wool or even sandpaper. Make sure that the road salt hasn't plugged any outside electrical sockets. This could cause corrosion leading to shortages. If the sockets are corroded, replace immediately. Check your battery – electrical shortages may be the result of low electrolyte levels. After cleaning the terminals and connectors, top up the electrolyte levels with distilled water.

> **If your batteries say 'maintenance free', the 'eye' will tell you the status. Batteries that require water should be topped up monthly with distilled water especially if you're in a hot climate – but do not overfill. Clean the cables and terminals regularly to keep them corrosion free. Use a meter to check voltage.**

For motorized RVs, check all the parts of your engine and fluid levels before starting. Verify that no furry little critters have taken up residence. While you're at it, check all lights (this also applies to towables). During one winter when we were stationary for several months in Mexico, birds built a nest around the A/C coil for the dash air.

Repack all bearings and connections on tow hitches of **fifth wheels and trailers**. Test the electrical connections of the brakes. Connect the brakes to an ammeter and a battery. If the ammeter doesn't register amperage, the magnet isn't getting any energy and will have to be replaced. (This test should be done at least once, maybe twice a year and, if you don't want to do it yourself, take it to a professional.)

A definite must is to ensure that your tires are in tip-top shape. Inflate your tires and check for leaks, sidewall cracks or uneven wear. If you log many miles with your RV some manufacturers suggest rotating the tires annually. Follow the recommendations of your chassis manufacturer. The next step is to wash and spray tires with a non-petroleum protective cleaner.

Now it's time to flush out the plumbing. Remember when your RV was stored for the winter and you poured antifreeze into the tanks and lines to prevent freezing? Well, it's time to purge that solution.

Partially fill your fresh water tank (it was drained last fall), and open both bypass valves, all your faucets and flush the toilet. When the water stops bubbling, the antifreeze is gone.

To purge the fresh water tank, fill it about three-quarters full with warm water and add four to six ounces of chlorine bleach. Drive your RV around the block a couple of times to agitate the water and give the water tanks an extra cleaning boost. When back home (or at the campground), drain the tanks. Refill with fresh water and let it run through the faucets until clear and chlorine free. Refill the tank with fresh water and a very weak solution of chlorine bleach (1/2 teaspoon per 10 gallons of water) to purify it. RV dealers sell commercial solutions for fresh water tanks; these are more convenient and have a pleasanter taste than the bleach.

If water is pooling around plumbing lines and fixtures or you find damp spots by your water pump, there is a leak. It may be a loose clamp that just needs tightening or it could be a damaged hose or pipe that needs replacing. If water stops flowing from the hot water tap take a look at the check valve for your hot water tank.

With all the flushing and draining, your black and grey water tanks are also being cleaned. Don't forget to check the holding tanks for leaks. The best indicator of a problem is an unpleasant 'backed-up sewer' smell. Even if you can't detect any odours, get down on your hands and knees and feel around the toilet for water.

Add an extra dose of toilet chemical, let sit for a while and gently scrub the pipe with a round toilet brush. When everything 'moves' as expected, clean and disinfect the bathroom – add grey and black water solutions to the appropriate tanks.

Check all propane lines and valves with a soap bubble test. Mix liquid dish soap with a bit of water. Take a soft toothbrush and brush the soapy mixture all over the hoses, line, valves and gas regulator. If bubbles appear you've found your leak. Turn the propane off immediately and leave it off until the problem is corrected. NEVER make propane repairs yourself. All connections, the burner flue and fridge coils should only be inspected and repaired by a service mechanic with S-4 propane certification.

Cleaning Inside

Continue with a thorough spring-cleaning. Sweep away any cobwebs and dead bugs. Sprinkle your carpets (and upholstery) with the appropriate freshener and let it sit before vacuuming away. While you are waiting for the carpet freshener to take hold, remove dust and use a no-rinse cleaner on the inside of cupboards and closets. Clean the counters, fixtures and appliances. Don't forget to check for creepy crawlies, mice and birds (in every area). One tip to keep mice away it to place fresh Downy fabric-softener sheets under the cupboards and near any crevices that they may can come in. (No guarantee that this works but we have not had mice since we have been following this tip.) Sprinkle bay leaves (apparently roach-type bugs do not like bay leaves either) to your food cupboard shelves.

Then give the carpet a thorough vacuum. Apply lemon or orange oil to all your wood cabinetry; it adds a special gleam and helps preserve the wood.

Check all door handles and hinges for stiffness or looseness and lubricate or tighten accordingly.

Shine up the surface of your appliances, your sink, taps and counter-top with a vinegar and water solution. Used fabric-softener sheets add sparkle to appliances, sinks and faucets. These sheets do an excellent job of cleaning the TV, VCR, stereos and computers.

Before tackling the windows take down the curtains and check the window seals for leaks. Wash the curtains and wipe the blinds with special anti-static dusting sheets. Use a no-rinse cleaner for tough spots. For the final touch, clean the windows.

Next, wash the interior and exterior of the fridge, turn it on if the propane soap test checked out OK (it was turned off and the door left open for winter storage). To avoid overworking the fridge cooling system let it run on medium-low for a day or two before loading it up with supplies.

Hint: Try to have most of your food cold or frozen before transferring it to your RV fridge.

Cleaning Outside
Finally, <u>wash the exterior of your RV</u> – if you have the opportunity. Begin at the <u>roof</u> using a mild soap and water solution or products designed to clean roofs. Look for a one with UV protection and make sure it is petroleum-free. Follow with a wax or sealant protection. The chalky residue is caused by oxidation that should be removed during the cleaning and wax process.

Follow with a complete <u>wash and polish</u> with products designed for the type of finish on your RV. Again look for those that offer UV protection.

Because many parks have a 'no wash' policy, at those times John uses (I only clean or polish the coach occasionally) one of the many types of no-rinse cleaners on the market. <u>We fill a spray bottle with a mixture of the cleaner and water</u> (manufacturer's recommendations) and spray it on. Simply wipe it off with a soft cloth.

If your RV is really dirty, add <u>no-rinse cleaner</u> to a bucket of water and, using a brush or a large sponge, clean the unit and dry it off with a soft cloth. No rinsing is required.

While you're doing all that exterior washing, <u>unroll your awning and examine carefully for tears, worn spots or mildew stains</u>. Never use abrasive and strong commercial cleaners on your awning because they can remove the water repellent qualities of the treated fabric (for more awning care, see *Set-up Tips*).

Before re-rolling or <u>patching the awning,</u> make sure it is completely dry. You can buy patching kits for awnings and, if you do see a tear or worn spot, patch immediately following the manufacturer's recommendations. Paraffin wax will plug small holes such as those that result of sparks from a fire.

When the awning is extended, <u>a square corner of your screen door</u> can catch and tear the fabric. However, there are inexpensive protectors – either a wheel-type or plastic awning saver – that fit over the square corner of the door.

<u>Wash and dry every part of the awning hardware</u> with a brush plus mild soap and water solution. Lubricate with silicon-based spray and tighten all loose bolts and screws, then finish with a polish.

If you see <u>chips in your windshield</u> or windows, take your unit to a window repair specialist. The techniques used to renew chipped glass will help you avoid the cost of a new windshield. Even if your deductible is a couple hundred dollars, your insurance generally pays for stone chip repairs.

95

Peggi McDonald

Before long you will <u>develop your own routine</u> of getting your RV ready for the road. Use these hints as a guideline and adapt them to your system. But remember, preventive maintenance is the first step to enjoying your on-the-road summer fun. And, once these necessary chores are done, you won't have to repeat them again, until the fall. But that's another story. Enjoy your summer.

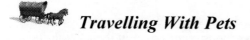 ***Travelling With Pets***

These fulltiming pets range in age from 2 to 16.
Six months after this picture was taken,
our 'old girl', Susie Q, passed away.

Not all RVers have children and grandchildren but quite a few of RVers have pets. John and I always travel with our dachshunds in our motorhome and, without exception, these four-legged angels love the RV lifestyle. We have yet to encounter problems with our pets on board while exploring anywhere in North America from Canada to the U.S.A. to Mexico.

There have, however, been times when our plans to stop at some state parks or the occasional private campground changed because of a 'no pet' policy. John and I simply avoid these places. Our pets are fulltimers, too, so when our pets are not welcome we do not feel welcome either. North America is so vast that it's impossible to see it all and we concentrate on areas where our dogs are as welcome as we. Travelling with large dogs, and/or more than two pets, (cats or dogs) may open the door to more problems.

When our pets see us getting ready to change destinations, they immediately assume their driving positions – curled up in their favourite spots. Their kennel is new in Kastle #3 and sits next to my computer station. It is their 'house' when we are away from the motorhome but while we are driving between destinations they nestle on the dash or on a special bed that we have made for them beside my chair. Our dogs love travelling and they know another location with new smells, pet walks, sights and sounds is waiting for them to explore.

Our dogs are small but many RVers travel with large four-legged friends. Crossing any border is no problem if your pets receive their required annual shots, especially rabies. Always carry the International Statement of Health provided by your local veterinarian for each pet on board with you. These regulations apply to dogs and cats – for other types of pets such as birds or fish, ask your veterinarian about border crossing regulations and restrictions.[14]

> **Most rabies shots are for a three-year period but many vets request an annual vaccination. During our most recent visit I asked our vet about this and she took the label off the vial and added it to their rabies certificate with a note explaining they were protected for three-years.**

Wise travellers also have a copy of their pet's history with them. This is particularly important if your pet has health problems or requires special medication. Make sure that all pet medications have descriptive labelling and, if possible, carry a copy of their prescriptions with you. In an emergency, it may help an unfamiliar vet diagnose your pet's problem plus, if you are delayed in returning to home, it's easier for the vet to refill a prescription if he/she knows what medication your pet is taking. The written prescription is also proof (if ever needed) to custom agents that you have legally acquired the medication and why it is necessary.

> **Rabies vaccinations are only required once every three years to come into Canada. If the certificate is not dated it will be considered as a 12-month vaccine to enter the U.S.A.**

---

14 *More info about* Travel to Canada *and* Travel to the USA *is listed on our website at www.rvliving.net. (Those not online can use computers at the library – take a grandkid to help if this is a new experience.)*

RVers who travel with pets do encounter one re-occurring and frustrating problem – controlling fleas and ticks. Each area of a warm climate has its own breed of annoying tick and flea population. Some places are much worse than others but, with the regular use of an effective flea spray and pet shampoo, it is possible to keep the infestation under control. A combo flea, tick and heartworm pill is also available. It is costly but very convenient. Administered monthly, this pill is reported to work extremely well controlling these dreaded problems.

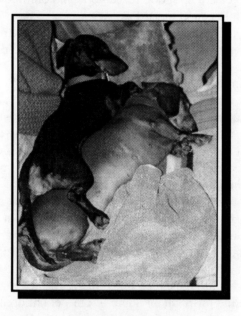

Our present 'kids'.

If you're in an area where your flea control seems ineffective, visit a local vet to see what they would recommend for conditions of the area you are in. Both pets and their beds require regular flea control maintenance. Don't forget to flea proof your RV as well. John and I spend a considerable amount of time travelling in warm climates and, as much as we love it, mosquitoes love it just as much. As a result, we keep our dogs on heartworm medication for the whole year. We discovered several years ago that some brands of heartworm pills sold in each country contain different ingredients plus in the early 90s we couldn't even buy heartworm pills in Mexico. To simplify things, our dogs are on a monthly pill and we now purchase the whole amount during their annual check-up each summer.

Sometimes, at new destinations, it's difficult to find a particular brand of food or supplies that your pet particularly enjoys. Most RVers carry a back-up supply of all essentials in their RV but excess pet food weighs heavily. As a result our dogs are now on a home-cooked diet recommended by our breeder – consisting of ground meat, veggies and potatoes. They also take a selection of vitamins and minerals. Their diet suits them perfectly; they are both healthy and we no longer waste valuable touring time trying to find a particular brand of dog food. This works well for us because unnecessary changes are not good for anyone and our babies are (spoiled) valued family members and treated as such.

Unfortunately, pets do become lost or venture away from campsites. At times they can't remember where 'mom' and 'dad' parked their travelling home. RVers with animals should consider registering with a lost pet service or have your vet implant an identification chip.

Our two each wear a special tag with their name and an 800-phone number of a friend on them. Some RV clubs also offer lost pet service as well. Veterinarians, too, offer a service that connects missing pets and their owners. As a 'lost pet' member, your pet wears an identification tag bearing a membership number plus a toll-free number to call. If your pet does get lost, simply call the number to record your location. With luck, the person who finds your four-legged friend will also telephone the number to report finding your pet. If all goes well, you and your 'baby' can soon become travel partners again.

Our dachshunds are senior members that we adopt from a show kennel. When they first came into our care they were already into their retirement years (ages 5 - 7) and, like us, they had already formed many (some bad) habits. While outside for fresh air some of our pet children preferred a collapsible playpen rather than being tied to a leash. Because they are small, fellow campers always want to stop, say hello and pet them. Our 'children', although tiny, quickly change into very protective and ferocious guard dogs. To protect ourselves (and others) we displayed a sign with the words **'guard dogs on duty'**. This lets visitors know to keep their distance and that the playpen is off limits.

The dogs we have now only go outside to potty or for a walk. They prefer to be inside most of the time. These two are getting very old and when one goes to doggie heaven another will come into our house as soon as possible.

Pets are loyal friends but they do need conscientious owners to take care of them. Remember that pets can't clean up after themselves plus noisy animals irritate and frighten others. Most campgrounds welcome pets but, if pet owners hope to keep it that way, cleaning up after your pets and respecting fellow RVers is mandatory. One prominently displayed sign we saw in a campground in Nova Scotia said it all,

> ### *"Got a Dog? Got a Shovel? Get the Picture?"*

One Arizona Park we were in had an 80-site pet section. It was wonderful camping beside RVers who understood dogs or cats. Everyone accepted an occasional barking dog and other pet owners were usually ready to help out if problems occurred when you're temporarily away from your RV.

Another challenge when travelling with pets is trying to keep the temperature of your RV comfortable during the times when you have to leave them alone in your coach. If you leave your RV early in the morning it may be too cold to turn your air conditioner on or to open windows. Unfortunately, cool mornings frequently turn into extremely hot afternoons – especially in a closed-up RV. We discovered a solution to this dilemma – when we upgraded to Kastle #2 we had three Fan-Tastic vents installed. With these thermostat-controlled vents the interior of our unit always remains comfortable, both for us, and our pets. In that RV when we went out, we closed the blinds and set the vents so the air would come in. Our vents were equipped with rain sensors and automatically closed when the weather turned less than perfect.

Kastle #3 came with a 2500-watt inverter that powers all our electric appliances except the A/C and our overhead vents. Now when we go out we still have two Fan-Tastic fans but we also have two regular table fans which stay running powered by the inverter/batteries if the park power goes out. Again, by closing all blinds we no longer worry about our pets. In this coach we also have space for a large travelling kennel for our babies so it is easy to keep them in one spot with the fans directed towards them when we go out.

> **Occasionally some campgrounds have a 'no pet' policy. RVers travelling with cats or dogs are not welcome in these parks. Check campground directories or ask at welcome centres/tourist bureaus if the stopping spot you are considering accepts pets.**

Travelling with a pet adds to the RV experience. Pets offer companionship plus provide a sense of security for RVers, although, I must admit, they occasionally do tie us down. When something comes up that excludes our dogs we board them with an animal clinic. Since our dogs are older, we prefer to leave them at a facility where a doctor is close at hand – just in case. Animal hospital boarding rates are similar to rates at kennels and it's comforting for us to know medical help is available for our 'old girls'.

Unfortunately, pets don't live as long as people. Since ours are seniors when they begin travelling with us, we must face the prospect of a pet becoming ill or even dying in distant places. This is a situation no one likes to think about but, if faced with this decision, we look for an animal clinic that will not only quickly send our pet to 'doggie heaven' but provide burial or cremation services as well.

> **It's apparent that non-considerate pet owners have effectively worn out their welcome (yours too) in some areas so always be a responsible pet owner. If you are welcomed back – you have done your part to smooth the way for pet-owners everywhere.**

Several years ago one of our dogs became sick with pneumonia. The vet couldn't work miracles and she died. There was so much love, concern and caring in that clinic and the staff not only offered us a spot in their special cemetery behind the clinic, they also sent us a unique pet sympathy card several days later. It was a welcome and comforting touch especially since we missed our old girl very much.

Yes, travelling with pets does carry some responsibilities and restrictions. All things considered though, we would never even consider travelling without four-legged 'children' on board.

More Money For Your Trade-in
(by updating your unit)

No matter how much you love your present RV there comes a time in every RVer's life when trading-in your present unit for a larger (or smaller) RV is necessary. We all suffer from 'Bigitis' – the need to have a larger, glitzier unit. Once you've made the decision to trade-up, getting the most value for your old unit is your top priority. Although most sellers don't go to the trouble to update or modernize an older RV, John and I did just that when we traded Kastle #1 and we found the redecorating experience a rewarding challenge.

When we traded our 1983 Pace Arrow in May of 1993, she glistened. Our Kruisin' Kastle #1, a renovated showpiece celebrating her 10th birthday, had served us well. Her last year was one of her finest but we had to make a big decision – do we run her for countless more miles and lose trade-in value or do we go for the brass ring?

We dreamed of the pleasure associated with driving a new 38-footer; we could feel it, we could even see it. Especially when a twin to our new 'dream machine' backed into an adjoining campsite five months earlier. John and I gazed in awe, envious of that beautiful motorhome and wondered if owning an RV so elegant could ever become a possibility.

We had to face facts and take care of what we had. Even though we knew it was time to replace our 32-foot Class A, we wanted her new owners to enjoy our Kruisin' Kastle as much as we did. John and I spent many hours over the winter adding the final touches of her face-lift.

To bring her interior décor into the 90s, when she was seven-years old we recovered the furniture in a soft green upholstery fabric. The upholsterer added the same covering to existing fabric wall panels plus creating two extra sofa throw pillows for an added comfy touch.

Using a mint and emerald green colour scheme, the kitchen, bath and bedroom received an elegant uplift with new wallpaper (including inside of the cupboards and the air conditioner covers). New bedspreads, mini-blinds, curtains and valences completed her interior décor. We used pale blue fabric to update the existing front windshield drapery and, and lace café-style curtains provided a finishing touch to the living room. A year later we replaced her worn carpet from front to back with an easy-to-clean, quality vinyl floor that resembled huge patio blocks. With the addition of emerald green carpet runners she was showing her finest hour. Each of these inexpensive modifications enhanced the value and appearance of our 10-year-old coach.

Kastle #1 shows off her new mint green décor.

Finishing the wood cabinets with a generous dose of lemon oil finalized and accented her new image. All things considered, the inside of our reliable older RV was ready to move into another decade.

Next step was the outside. Replacing old caulking on the roof and around several windows ensured she was leak free. Heavy-duty boat cleaner removed every trace of oxidization from her fiberglass skin. We completed her make-over with a coat of protective boat wax, plus a once-over of chrome polish and tire shine. Our Kruisin' Kastle #1 was ready to show off her sparkling image at the dealer's lot. We were certain that her attractive appearance would quickly attract new owners. Several years later we received a letter from her new owners; they instantly fell in love with her and bought her with no changes two days after she arrived at our dealer. I recently talked to that owner of our Pace Arrow and they are still enjoying and driving this 20 year-old coach.

We learned a lot from this experience and, although it was time-consuming to modify an old RV, it really wasn't too difficult. RVers with even the minimum of wallpapering knowledge can use the same principles that are used in a house in an RV. The only difference is that in the confined space of an RV there's more cutting around corners. Vinyl-to-vinyl adhesive, designed to secure border surfaces, works exceptionally well as a medium for sticking wallpaper on to covered RV wallboards.

*It is easy to add a face-lift to your RV by wallpapering
over the vinyl walls. There is no need to strip the original paper.*

It wasn't possible to take our unit with us when we began trade-up discussions, so we took along recent exterior and interior photos to our first negotiation meeting with the dealer as well as a list of all modifications, additions and important maintenance repairs for the previous three years.

For instance, this was an 83-gas model but we upgraded our tires with 'F'-rated Michelins, our three-way eight-cubic-foot Dometic refrigerator was new the previous year and so were the radiator, alternator, batteries and much more. Each item increased the trade-in value of our motorhome and, when presenting our resale unit this way, the dealer knew exactly what we had and could offer us a realistic trade-in value.

Although you may not want to completely redecorate, before you take your unit in for an appraisal, at least clean both the interior and exterior of your RV. If you are still using your unit, tidy and organize the cupboards and closets. Make sure that the bathroom and all appliances are spotless. Rearrange your counter top so that it doesn't look cluttered (it makes it appear smaller) and, while you're at it, move any old magazine or newspaper collections out of sight.

Rent a carpet cleaner to shampoo the rugs and upholstery. Wash (or dust) the walls, floors, ceiling, blinds and curtains. Vacuum the ceiling if it has carpet covering or wipe it down with a no-rinse cleaner. Use window cleaner on the windows, mirrors, glass doors and faucets.

Next, complete minor repairs. Remember, the better your unit looks, the more trade-in value it will command. If you are trading a motorized RV have the engine tuned and replace spark plugs, etc., if needed. A few dollars spent before an appraisal could translate into hundreds of dollars extra from the dealer.

If you are downsizing to change retirement plans into another direction there are several RV dealers that specialize in consignment sales. Ask about the service they provide and their percentage fee for selling your unit. 🐛

ON THE ROAD

RV travel opens the door to outstanding destinations like
this popular campsite at Playa Amor, in Aticama, Nayarit, Mexico
(between San Blas and Santa Cruz).

 *Weather Watch*

Although travelling in your RV is a great way to spend a vacation, there are some points you should take note of before you set out. When John and I began our life on wheels we were looking for perpetual summer sunshine. The previous four years we'd been holidaying in Florida each November and March and it was always beautiful and warm. With retirement approaching, we could see no reason why we wouldn't enjoy the warm sunshine all year-round.

Most areas in Canada and the U.S. have several outstanding seasons, unfortunately, they also have snow, cold, rain or extreme heat and none, not even the sunny south, has a perfect year-round climate every year.

We did, however, find as close to perfect as possible when we discovered the perpetual warmth south of Guadalajara, Mexico. At a place called Lake Chapala, we enjoyed heavenly temperatures hovering around the 21 to 28 Celsius mark (75 to 90 Fahrenheit) for seven winters. Unfortunately, to enjoy this weather, we had to drive an extra 1,000-kilometres south of the U.S. border. With the purchase of our larger units we no longer fit into the laid-back places we learned to love, so more recently we roam and explore different areas of the U.S. southern states.

RVers searching for memorable travels must be flexible and ready for anything. That means packing a substantial number of clothes for any type of climate. Along with your bathing suits, shorts and sandals include a few items for cool weather, such as jackets and sweaters. Although it's possible to follow the sun, sometimes the weather doesn't co-operate and, even in the sunbelt temperatures can fall. You will also need the appropriate clothing for the northern spring and fall temperatures.

Driving north in the spring is such a beautiful and uplifting experience. Wild flowers adorn the highway and everything slowly is waking up from its winter sleep. Autumn is our other favourite season for travel, especially in areas to the north where trees dress in brilliant colour – the whole area transforms into a vibrant, fiery collage of intense hues.

When John and I travel, we plan to drive for one short day (approximately six hours) and then stop for three to four days to explore our surroundings. Besides staying rested *en route* and taking in the sights along the way, we enjoy the added advantage of seasons that last for weeks as we slowly move from one location to another. Travelling this way is relaxing and the journey is every bit as pleasant as the stay at our winter-stopping spot. To increase our enjoyment we try to use secondary roads when it's possible. Not only is the scenery more interesting than on the fast-paced major highway and interstate systems, the traffic is lighter and driving is more relaxed.

RVers should be wary when travelling during the spring season. This is the prime season in the mid and southern U.S.A. for tornados, violent thunderstorms, flooding (especially flash flooding) and even the occasional and unexpected snowstorm. Such weather disturbances occur more frequently during the summer up north. In Canada, bad weather conditions and storms are reported by towns and cities (only occasionally by counties), however in the U.S., counties report this information.

> **If a tornado is imminent, get out of your vehicle and look for a low-lying area such as a ditch. During a tornado, cars, trucks, semis and RVs plus every other object in its path are tossed around like twigs in a brisk breeze. Observe the warnings and be thankful if they are overstated.**

Our education never stops and this includes learning about unfamiliar weather patterns. Early in our travels one spring afternoon in Iowa we were watching TV and the continual reporting of a tornado watch listed by counties was on the corner of the screen. This was a new experience for us, especially when the park manager knocked on our door to warn us of the impending 'watch'. When we asked what that meant, he advised us to evacuate our motorhome and come to the park's reinforced clubhouse/restaurant. RVers and their children and assorted pets all gathered in our temporary refuge. Only then did we learn that a watch preceded a warning when reporting weather conditions. If a warning is on the screen, take cover immediately. Our evacuation experience wasn't a false alarm – a tornado touched down 1/4 of a mile away.

The tornado incident showed us that we needed a more complete understanding of strange weather patterns as well as knowing what action to take. To keep on top of the complete storm picture, RVers are wise to have a weather radio on board and/or to stay tuned to local radio and TV stations for constant local weather-watch updates.

Before this incident, as the primary navigator, I completely ignored county markings on road maps. I really never cared what county I was in, as I had no plan to pay their taxes or apply to vote. Believe me, after this frightening experience, both John and I became much more conscientious of travel during adverse weather conditions.

One additional reason for being aware of county markings is that radio announcers not only report what county is under warning, they also report where the weather is coming from and where it is headed. Knowing the path of a weather pattern helps you to make an educated decision about whether or not to keep on driving.

These same DJs suggest helpful tips and precautions travellers should take during specific weather situations, including flash floods or even earthquakes. The radio (and truckers on CB channel 19) also report accidents or delays on the highway, broken down by county markings. Suddenly we realized that these insignificant map markings are very important to our immediate travel plans.

As RVers, we have the privilege to experience the joys of all four seasons, plus we have the option to shorten our stays in the not so pleasant locations.

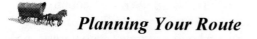 *Planning Your Route*

***Plan your route to include unique outstanding
destinations such as Peggy's Cove, NS.***

Much like one unit won't be perfect for every RVer, there is also more than one correct way to plan your trip. Travellers find almost as many ways to plan a vacation getaway as there are RVers on the road. Some like the freedom to stop when they feel the urge, others want each detail checked, double-checked and verified weeks in advance – although most RVers find a common ground between these two extremes.

RVers who don't feel comfortable planning a vacation may prefer to use the trip routing service offered by many of the large RV clubs plus CAA (Canadian Automobile Association) or AAA (American Automobile Association). There are also a number of computer programs available to help travellers with route planning – many can be used off-line. You can also find information on trip routing preparations at bookstores and public libraries for information on trip preparation. [15]

---

15 *Several websites listed on the* RV WebLink *page of www.rvliving.net also offer free trip routing and distance listings in miles and km. We use www.freetrip.com as our primary source but many others are available. Some RV clubs also offer* trip routing services *to the members.*

Seasoned RVers are aware that, during holiday weekends, campgrounds in Canada and the U.S.A. are extremely busy. In southern sun country, the busy periods are from January to March, spaces in popular RV parks are quickly booked to capacity. Even RVers who like to travel with unrestricted freedom and without confining plans make reservations for busy times in high season.

Many RVers use a GPS software program on their computer to plan their journey but in our family, John does all the trip planning. If I want to visit a particular spot, I make my wishes known and he fits it into the schedule. These days when John plans our trip he plots a route between our two main destinations using the Internet to find the approximate distance. He then fine-tunes it using a descriptive atlas. During our early travels he used a Rand McNally Dist-O-Map (automatic mileage dialler) to estimate driving distances and then followed with detailed maps or the atlas.

Next, he looks for interesting stops along our route using the atlas plus various campground directories listing all of North America. He also takes notes of places that are promoted in the directories by each park and from travel articles in RV magazines.

As we like to limit our driving to a maximum of 400 to 700-km (250 to 430 miles) per day, John researches the location of the best stop-over places and how long it will take to do some sightseeing. Relaxing between driving days, contributes to a healthier and less stressful trip.

Once we reach our destination and after setting up camp, we fine-tune our research of the area by talking to the park staff and other RVers about must-see places. We also visit local tourist bureaus and welcome centres.

Our military training to follow a schedule is deeply ingrained into our make-up. If we arrive at an unreserved campground and we can't stay because the park is full or for some other reason, both of us become irritated and words, which shouldn't even be thought of, are spoken. The air inside our motorhome takes on a vibrant shade of blue as we try to decide where to go next. Neither of us works well in an impulse situation.

However, many RVers prefer to travel without reservations and stop at attractions on a whim when they see something interesting. In our case we settle into a campsite and unhook the car to explore the area. We also don't like to camp or stop in unprotected areas.

Because the rate of crime is high at some rest areas, many truck stops have redesigned their stations to accommodate and encourage RVers to stop for the night at these facilities. The Flying J in particular has become very RV friendly. Most stations even have an RV island with gas, fuel, propane, dump and fresh water available.

TravelCenters of America (TA) have also redesigned some of their facilities to be more RV friendly. Specialty services include overnight parking plus discounts on fuel/gas.

Ambest and '76 Truck Stops (among others) have also put out the welcome mat for RVers. Along with fuel (gas, diesel and propane) and mechanical service, most truck stops have restaurants, convenience stores, restrooms with showers and a safe place to park for the night. Many have dump stations as well. In the centres without special areas for RVs, we are welcome to park with the trucks. It doesn't cost anything to stay overnight in these areas and they do come in handy when you wish to take a break from driving or get off the road for the night. Some restaurants with large parking lots may also allow overnight parking but, before you stop for the night, always ask the owners or managers if it's allowed.

At times provincial and national parks, community campgrounds and conservation areas plus state and Bureau of Land Management parks in the U.S. may be more economical than private campgrounds. Look for listings from welcome centres, tourist bureaus and maybe North American campground directories. These are worth checking out to compare prices, especially if you're travelling on a budget. Ask if the site price includes the day-use fee or if that is extra. The additional fee (and some reservation costs) can considerably increase your camping costs.

While at the welcome centres, information booths or tourist bureau offices check to see what other out-of-the-way places are waiting for you to discover. Ask if there are any discount coupon books for the area you are visiting. With a minimum amount of planning, RV travel can be the most exciting time of your life.

Keep your timetable flexible! Frequently, our most interesting stops have been on the advice of other RVers. Make time to visit and investigate the places where you camp – your stopovers will take on a whole new meaning.

Discovering unique and colourful places add another dimension to your journey. We frequently find several ideas for places to visit from local newspapers at our stopovers. These side trips are not only fun, they're also educational.

Don't try to, nor expect to see everything the first visit. It's more interesting if you save some experiences for return trips. It's only natural for new RVers on holidays or beginning their retirement to try to see it all 'yesterday'.

It is no big deal if you get lost; look at it as an expansion of your adventure. Find a safe place to pull over, take a deep breath and examine the map and continue your adventures wherever they take you.

A good atlas is a necessity and it should list counties, highway and interstate exit numbers, major city maps and provinces and states in alphabetical order rather than in regional order. We find the atlas sold by Wal*Mart is one of the best plus it lists the locations of all the Wal*Mart stores.

By the way many Wal*Marts encourage RVers to stop overnight, but always ask first because in some areas local by-laws do not permit extended stopovers. Never set up camp in these parking lots and if you have to put your levellers down on the asphalt be sure to put boards beneath them. As an added safety precaution always park with your doors facing the people (and the cameras) rather than towards the spacious grassy area at the edge of the pavement.

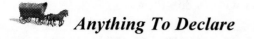 *Anything To Declare*

When crossing the border, follow the car lanes NOT the truck lanes.

Although we may consider our RV to be our home, when crossing a border, RVs come under the same rules as cars and your RV is no different than a suitcase at the border. That means that custom agents do not need a search warrant to enter and search an RV. If they unpack cupboards it is your responsibility to put things away. Just because you have nothing to declare, doesn't mean the next border crossing won't result in a complete inspection of your unit.[16]

When approaching the inspection station, be calm and take off your sunglasses so that the agent can look into your eyes. Always be polite and remember the Golden Rule – 'treat officials as you want to be treated; with respect'. Answer each question but don't get smart or attempt to be 'funny'. Also, don't provide more information than asked for – keep your response

---

16 On *www.rvliving.net* there are comprehensive pages explaining both;
　　Travelling to the U.S.A: *www.customs.gov* or *www.cbp.gov;*
　　1- 877-CUSTOMS, press 0 and
　　Travelling to Canada: *www.Canada.gc.ca* or *www.ccra.adrc.gc.ca*
　　1-800-CANADA.

short, to the point and pertinent to only the questions asked. If you are asked if you have cigarettes do not answer with, "I don't smoke!"

> **Some border crossings now have a separate RV lane. Agents will frequently come on board. At other border crossings, some RVs are directed through the truck lanes so x-ray machine can scan your unit. Times are changing and it is up to you to stay on top of the current rules and regulations.**

All RVers must have a permanent 'home' address that is your official residence for voting, census, licensing vehicle registration, etc. You are also only legally allowed to be in another country for up to six months without special visas that allow you to stay for extended periods. Therefore, RVers may be required to prove they have ties to their country of residence and the length of time they plan to visit another country. Presenting gas or toll-bridge receipts helps verify where you have travelled and for how long.

Besides relaying the location of your official home residence, stating that you have a reservation in a campground for the following year or that you have a phone line placed on vacation or even a business location in your home country may help prove you have a reason to return home. At this point we all have a choice of where we choose to sleep each night.

Although the agent inputs licence numbers into the computer as vehicles pull up to a custom's station, they are mainly looking for outstanding traffic tickets and warrants. Unless they have a reason to question your criminal history, most times the computer never goes to the second level.

When entering another country, there's a possibility that immigration agents will ask for proof of permanent residency and information regarding any property owned in your home country. They may ask you to produce a phone or utility bill. The agents are merely trying to determine if, as an RVer, you will be returning to home country after your getaway. They do not want you to be a burden on the host country. A seasonal site at a campground, business commitments, or a phone service on vacation, etc. may be enough to satisfy the officials.

> **Even if you spend most of the year in your RV, do not admit or brag about being a fulltimer or that your RV is your only home, especially to an immigration or customs officer. Every RVer needs an official residence even if you do not sleep at that address.**

Regulations and dollar amounts each country allows visitors to bring home changes periodically. Somehow it is always more enticing to buy things in a country other than your own, even if the item in question is not a bargain. To ensure that you know what is or isn't duty-free, either pick up a current copy of Canada's *'I Declare'* or the *'Know Before You Go'* booklet for U.S. travellers from any custom's office of your home country. The phone book lists locations. Personal exemptions do not usually include items and gifts sent separately but, it does include gifts carried in your luggage or RV. Ask officials for updates before you leave your home country.

Yes, it does take money to live but we purchase very few extras when we are in another country, mainly because we have so little space to stow stuff. When we cross the border we usually round off our purchases to the nearest Canadian dollar amount.

> **Carrying a passport or a certified copy of your birth certificate plus a photo ID such as a driver's licence is a must. Your landed immigrant papers will also verify the country you call home.**

To calculate the number of days you're away, count the day of return – the time (hour) isn't important – but don't include your day of departure.

Generally you cannot combine the exemptions of several travellers nor can you use part of your exemption on one visit and carry the balance over to the next time you're absent. Excess amounts will be assessed at a flat rate and the balance will be charged regular duties and applicable state, provincial or federal taxes.

Tobacco And Alcohol

Limited amounts of tobacco and alcohol are duty free – see booklets noted above for actual amounts. Travellers must reach the age requirements of the state, province or territory where they enter another country. For amounts greater than allowed, current duties plus applicable taxes will be added to the overall cost; however, there are limits to import amounts. Liquor remaining in open bottles may be counted in your overall total.

And, even though North America is part of 'free trade' and some duty charges have been reduced or eliminated, import duties still apply to a wide variety of purchases, alcohol included.

> **Legal age of the person purchasing tobacco and/or alcohol is determined on state, provincial or territorial laws where you ENTER a country.**

On one occasion, because I forgot to check the regulations before arriving at the border, we were carrying too much alcohol. We had wine and beer on board. I soon found out that it's not 'and', it was wine 'or' beer. When asked, I told them the truth but we had a choice of paying the hefty duties or pouring my four-litre bottle of wine down the drain. I chose the drain because the extras were too excessive.

Permanent Records Of Your 'Toys'

I'm always apprehensive as we drive up to a border crossing, even if we didn't buy any declarable items. But, when travellers are informed and know in advance what to expect, their crossing should be uneventful. Most custom officers allow a verbal declaration but, by law, they can demand a written declaration for all items. If asked, don't complain, just fill out the form.

Travellers using other forms of transportation such as an airplane or bus should always expect to give a written declaration at the custom's checkpoint.

Note: Canadians can fill out a Y-38 wallet card (Identification of Articles for Temporary Exportation) for valuable items with serial numbers, such as cameras, sporting goods, etc. before leaving home. These cards are available at the border or any custom's office. A bill of sale stating the price and country of purchase will also suffice for both Americans and Canadians.

If the items are mounted in an RV (TVs, VCRs, air conditioners, etc.), it may be necessary to present your unit for inspection. You may have to prove these personal items and RV accessories were purchased in your home country. Carrying the original receipt is the best way to prove your ownership.

When we purchased our RV we asked the dealer to record each appliance and all accessories included in our purchase on the bill of sale.

This way there was no question at the border as to what we bought in a country other than our own.

Jewellery

It's always better to leave expensive jewellery at home. However, when taking pieces across the border, bring along a photo, a written appraisal and a bill of sale (or, if previously imported, carry the custom's receipt). When jewellery that has been taken out of the country is altered in any way (new setting, replacement stone, etc.), it is subject to the same duties as if it was a newly purchased item. All modified 'new' jewellery should be declared in full, regardless if it was originally purchased in Canada.

Weapons

Canada has strict rules about importing weapons into Canada, but the U.S.A. also has rules against some firearms. If you plan to transport a firearm across the border, ask customs for rulings concerning '*Importing A Firearm or Weapon*'.[17]

Call 1-204-983-3500 for custom regulations entering Canada and 1-877-CUSTOMS for the U.S. (press O to speak to an operator). Ask for the phone number of the proper department to import firearms.

Rules change depending on hunting seasons and other factors so asking questions before arriving at the border eliminates surprises. Some times it takes several weeks or longer for paperwork to be processed. Importing explosives, fireworks, ammunition and similar items may need authorization as well as a permit.

If travelling to Canada, handguns and automatic weapons cannot be imported into Canada. Defence accessories such as pepper spray and mace are also classed as weapons and are prohibited – a fine could result if you do not declare these items.

---

17 More detailed info is listed in the Travel to Canada and Travel to the U.S.A. pages on www.rvliving.net. Those without a computer can ask a friend to gather the info for you. Phone numbers listed in next footnote.

Drugs

If you're carrying prescription drugs, leaving the meds in the original bottle or carrying photocopies of all prescriptions may also be advantageous if you are ever questioned. Carry verification if you need the use of syringes as well. It could prevent hassles and many questions from agents on both sides of the border – especially with the Canadian and American zero drug tolerance policies. This includes pet meds as well.

Food And Plants

Everyday groceries carried in a self-contained RV are usually not questioned because customs realize the food on board is for personal use. The import limits on meat, dairy products and fresh fruits and vegetables are very generous for the personal use of RVers. However, what is allowed occasionally changes depending on circumstances and present bug/disease infestation. Citrus is the one item that frequently cannot be transferred from one country to another or at times from one province or state to another (this might also apply to bananas). From time-to-time other items move into the prohibited category. RVing friends could not bring potatoes on the ferry from Newfoundland. During inspections these fruits and maybe others could be confiscated. As a result we limit fruits and veggies we have on board when crossing the border. These inspections can also occur when travelling from one southern state to the other especially when entering California. However, additional regulations may be enacted at any time, anywhere.

Some RVers also travel with freezers stocked with food but this is no longer wise. Both countries have just gone through a period where no meat (fresh frozen or by-products – even dog food) from animals with hooves can go south due to disease, and for the same reason no poultry or by-products can come north. Contact customs on each side of the border before you leave.[18] The type of food you can bring across the border depends on current diseases at the time. RVers are usually allowed enough food for personal use, but rules are more stringent for those travelling by car – see *Travellers Tip brochure* (available for U.S.A. and Canada) for detailed listings.

It becomes too complicated to transport plants across a border. Each one must be inspected and prepared for import by an agricultural agent prior to

---

18 *Canada Customs 1-204-983-3500.*
   US Customs and Homeland Security is 1-877-CUSTOMS. Dial 'O' for an agent.

your trip. Do yourself a favour and leave them at home. Contact the Agricultural department for further information[19].

> **One point many travellers may not realize is they cannot drive a vehicle licensed in another country across the border - even for a temporary period. This includes a rental car or borrowed vehicle for personal use.**

Obtaining Maintenance In A Host Country

Routine vehicle maintenance acquired in a country other than your own can be subject to duty charges if it is over your declaration amount. And, although "I didn't know!" may well be true, it is not an acceptable excuse. Ignorance and words won't eliminate the cost of duties and/or taxes assessed at the border. Revenue Canada and agents for the U.S. Customs service accept MasterCard, Visa, cash, traveller's cheques and certified cheques for payment of assessed charges.

> **Under the law, no modification to your vehicle or RV is exempt from tariffs. However, in most cases, emergency repairs necessary for the operation or safety of your vehicle are allowed tax-free.**

But, take note, a tire 'blow out' only requires one new tire to accomplish the emergency repair, not three! If you change or improve on the condition of, or transform your unit in any way and the alterations are extensive, you could be charged import duties on the entire value of your RV and/or vehicle. Just like upgrading pieces of jewellery, any modification is treated like a new purchase that you are importing.

If your revisions or repairs are minor (make sure you keep receipts and know the value of your unit), then duties and taxes may only be assessed on the modification or repair. If you have no other purchases, your personal exemption can be applied to the amount. If you buy accessories to install when you return to your home country, these too can be included as part of your personal exemption amounts and you will only have to pay duties and taxes if you are over your personal exemption.

Don't try to avoid duties and taxes by not declaring your conversions. We have heard first-hand stories from RVers who purchased items south of

---

19 More info can be found under Cross Border Information *on the* RV WebLink *page of www.rvliving.net,* the border and brought them back into Canada without declaring them. Later, when they sent in warranty and rebate forms to manufacturers, they received a call from federal custom agents and had to pay a severe fine plus duty and applicable taxes. Credit card purchases can be traced.

Customs agents are federal law-enforcement officers under Revenue Canada and Homeland Security in the U.S.A. They have a wide-range of constitutionally legal rights to recover lost revenue to each country.

Rules constantly change. Call each country to keep up to date on what is and is not allowed.

Times are changing and visiting RVers who are considering RV modifications or plan on updating major items, such as computers or used vehicles, should call customs offices in your home country for the latest information reference duties and taxes.[20] This also applies if you're planning to have extensive maintenance completed. Custom import rules are constantly changing, many to the benefit of the consumer. In North America, free trade has also opened many more doors that eliminate duty payments. But do your research and shop around before you buy out-of-country. Compare exchange rate and applicable duties, it may be cheaper to buy at home.

---

20 U.S.A Custom: *www.customs.gov* or *www.cbp.gov* 1-877-CUSTOMS – dial '0' for an agent or General Canada Info: *www.canada.gc.ca* 1-800-O-CANADA. Border/general customs info *www.ccra.gc.ca* 1-204-983-3500 – dial '0' for an agent. Revenue Canada/customs: (importing, taxes, duties, etc.) *www.ccra-adrc.gc.ca* 1-800-451-9999.

Don't take the chance when crossing the border. Become aware of all custom regulations. If in doubt, phone your local custom office. In a dispute, it is your responsibilities to prove that all duties and applicable taxes have been paid.

Never try to con custom agents – it's not worth the risk of having your RV or personal property confiscated. Make a point to understand applicable regulations to return home.

Keep all receipts for emergency repairs, maintenance and major purchases accessible for presentation to border officials. If these modifications require payment of duties and taxes, the official will direct you to the office to fill out forms and pay appropriate fees. This is also the procedure when a written declaration for duty-free purchases is requested.

Over the years both Canadian and American RV magazines were inundated with letters relating horror stories of border crossings from RVers. There are always two sides to every story so I won't go into who's right and who's wrong. In more than two decades, we have only had a very few less-than-perfect crossings and none were bad. If you do encounter problems or feel that an inspection agent treated you unfairly, address your problems to their superior officer. There is a chain of command from on-site staff to regional managers. Obtain badge numbers and name just in case you may need it. The complete details are listed in *I Declare* (Canadian) and *Know Before You Go* (U.S.A.) booklets. Another option is to contact your embassy to intercede.

Keep in mind that custom officers are legally entitled to examine your luggage (or car or RV). While at the border you have no rights. You may be responsible for opening, unpacking and re-packing your belongings. You could also be asked to leave your RV during a search. If you prefer to have more than one agent alone in your unit, you can request a second officer to be present. However, this could cause an extensive delay because you may have to wait until two officers are free at the same time.

Pick up your personal copies of *I Declare* (Canada) and *Know Before You Go* (U.S.A.) guides from any customs office or at the border.

Recently after one of my seminars an RVer asked if she could take some treasures out of her unit in a small attaché style case. I see no problem with this option but the officers will want to inspect it. Again because this is out of the ordinary it may be wise to ask officials before you reach the border.

Keeping In Touch By Voice Contact
(See Also Keeping In Touch By Post And Email)

Twenty or thirty years ago keeping in contact with those at home was no easy task. However, we now live in the computer age and it's more convenient and a less expensive endeavour to stay on top of things. Being aware of what's happening from across the continent is no more complicated than from across the street. Whether on a weekend getaway or on an extended trip, the following methods are only a very few of the ways RVers stay in touch.

Statistics show that Canadians and Americans love their phones and residents of these two countries primarily exist in day-to-day living simply because of extensive telephone use. Phoning from Canada and the U.S.A. to just about anywhere in the world is relatively simple and inexpensive.

Several years ago automated pay phones with slots to insert a card appeared in communities throughout North America (including Mexico); they accept Visa, MasterCard and American Express plus telephone company phone cards as well as coins. When using a card, a voice prompt tells you how to proceed before and after you slide your card through a special slot.

Message Service

The simplest way for RVers to stay in touch is to use a message service. Many camping clubs include voice mail in their benefit packages. Some message services are free for club members; others charge a small fee. Depending on the plan, subscribers may only be able to pick up messages, or leave and receive unlimited messages, or record a personal welcome message to keep friends and family aware of your whereabouts. Each plan differs and here, too, it may be wise to shop around.

Occasionally telephone companies plus a few private businesses offer inexpensive message services. Many of these limited services are accessible by a toll-free number from any phone in both Canada and the U.S. and, in some cases you even talk to a real person, not a machine. Check with the company of your home (or cell) phone or, look for advertisements in international RV magazines for services suited to your needs.

For years John and I used the voice mail service of FMCA (Family Motor Coach Association). Each evening we dialled a toll-free number to pick up messages. This way, we're only 24 hours away from important news and we saved long-distance calls for necessities. Phoning family just to say where we are and where we're going became unnecessary. At times, thanks to the message service, we coordinated rendezvous meetings with RVing friends who happen to be in the same area we were visiting.

Our toll-free message service number, along with our personal membership club ID# number was on our address card so others could leave a message for us too.

For the past few years we use the message service on our cell phone (a home phone that remains connected works too) to stay in contact. We can pick up these messages from any pay phone, or after hours when our cell rates are low. Whether you choose to use a limited service or one of the more advanced programs, using a message service ensures peace-of-mind travel. Thanks to a message service we are never out of touch.

Phone Company Calling Cards

The first step to eliminate frustrations associated with pay phones and the necessity of carrying a pocket full of change is to obtain a phone company calling card. These are free for the asking from your long distance service. If you're a fulltimer and don't have your own home phone, you can ask a friend or relative to share their phone number and card. This card doesn't have to be in your name, however, you must have access to their telephone code numbers and since they will receive a statement of your calls, you do need permission to use their card. A minor point of interest, calling card rates can be slightly higher than home phone costs but the card adds convenience.

During our early years we shared the phone number of a relative at our home base. Using her phone card and telephone number reduced costs and took the hassle out of long distance calling. Telephone statements listed the place where the call originated so, when the bill arrived, it was easy to determine our portion. Each month, my sister, (also our banking power of attorney – see chapter covering *Banking Power of Attorney* for more details) simply wrote a cheque on our account to pay our share of her calling card costs.

Several phone companies also offer a selection of low-cost calling cards to their residential customers. For some, it is not even a requirement to be connected to an in-service phone number, a great solution for fulltimers. Ask about services available from your phone carrier, you may be surprised at the savings.

Discount Or Pre-paid Calling Cards

Many RV clubs, especially in the U.S.A. also offer low-cost calling cards to make it easy for their members. Others are available on the Internet and over the counter in numerous convenience stores. Sometimes there are surcharges or hidden fees to use these cards – plus a low flat rate of pennies per-minute cost. They advertise only pennies a minute, but read the fine print; occasionally every call consumes a minimum number of units even if the call is short in length. For calls from one country to another, the connection fee can 'cost' 4 to 6 units or more to connect.

John and I have used a similar calling card by Win-tel[21] based in British Columbia. The per/minute cost is slightly higher but there are no hidden fees and costs are the same in U.S.A. or Canada 24/7. It also includes reduced long distance home phone rates. Our invoice is automatically paid by credit card but it can be accessed on the Internet or mailed to a particular address.

Toll-Free Access Number

If your calling card does not have a toll-free access number before **placing calls from pay phones in the U.S.A. to calls within the U.S., dial 1-800 CALL ATT** to take advantage of AT&T's lower rates. Completing a long distance call at a pay phone without an access code can become extremely costly. The company that installs the phone can charge what they like for long distance calls. American visitors to Canada can also use this access number when calling to the U.S.A. **To call Canada from the U.S.A. dial Canada Direct at 1-800-555-1111**. An operator may answer to assist you in completing your call.

At times U.S. pay phones require a few coins to dial both local and toll-free numbers. Pay phone charges in Canada are also low for local calls and toll-free calls are still no cost. Situations like this change without notice so it always pays to carry some change with you when you use a pay phone.

Fax Machines

Although these have been around for many years, John and I retired before fax (facsimile) machines became second nature for doing business. RVers unaware of what these marvellous machines can do are in for a pleasant surprise. We even have a 'no-cost fax number' on our computer –

---

21 Contact Win-tel at www.win-tel.ca, 1-888-266-1313.

our faxes come in as an email. Unfortunately we can only receive faxes through that number, not send them

Lawyers' offices, travel agents, stationery stores, postal facilities and many more outlets offer public fax service. We know of no faster way to send important papers across the miles and, in most cases, a signature sent by fax on a document is considered to be legal. The cost of $1 or $2 per page (for receiving or sending) is standard and includes long distance rates. Shop around, some businesses charge much more.

To send a fax, the fax number (it's like a phone number) of the receiving fax machine is dialled and the page(s) of information are placed in the originating machine. It sends a photocopy of each page to the destination fax. Faxes can be sent across the world or across the street in a few seconds per page. No additional copies are necessary as the fax machine returns your original papers.

Ham Radios

Several RVers we know have discovered the joys of staying in contact through their ham radios. They call friends and family from wherever they are and compared to long distance phone service, they talk longer and more frequently without paying for the call. Of course, they originally had to buy their equipment, study Morse Code extensively plus pay an annual fee for their licence. Before anyone can be licensed, operators must pass an exam.

In times of natural disasters sometimes the only form of contact is through ham radio operators. To expand their horizons, many RVers join a ham radio RV chapter of one of the many RV clubs. Sharing such common interests and fellowship can greatly enhance your RV travels.

Cellular Phones

The latest way to stay in touch is with a cellular phone. In the fall of 1993 I was having minor health problems and we decided that a cell phone would add peace-of-mind. Frequently campground pay phones are located quite a distance from the site locations. We felt if there was an emergency or, one of us had a heart attack, we wanted an accessible phone to call for help. Neither of us wanted to have to choose whether to give CPR or drive to a pay phone.

Our first phone was a 3-watt bag phone that plugged into the cigarette lighter. Since it continues to function in analogue areas (slow and very basic but it covers expansive service region) we still keep it in the car for emergencies. AAA and CAA (American or Canadian Automobile Association), 911, plus services across Canada and the U.S., are all free calls. Local after-hour usage is relatively inexpensive but analogue rates increase drastically if you move to a country (and maybe from a specific area) other than where your phone is registered. Roaming and long distance fees are not included in monthly charges. This phone is also much larger than the small compact digital phones many RVers carry, but they are extremely reliable plus with a steady rate of power. In an emergency situation there is a better chance you will connect in out of the way places using a bag phone than using one of the compact ultra tri-mode phones.

Hopefully the following information will explain and help you understand the benefits of a cell phone. It took us time to economically learn to use our phone, but we'd be extremely lost without it. While in Canada we stay the majority of the summer in one park as a seasonal renter so we add a landline. As a result, after-hour cell phone minutes are more valuable for us Canadians while we are south of the border. Bell Canada offers a similar program for users in Canada who make local calls or use toll-free numbers.

When we first obtained our cell phone it was difficult to keep costs in control, partly because usage is very different from your home phone. Although a cell works like a home phone, usage is much more expensive. The big difference between a regular house-style telephone and a cell phone is that the regular phone transmits sound along telephone wires and cell circuits travel along airwaves. Hills, valleys, trees and isolated areas can all interfere and interrupt these airwaves. Modern technology is slowly reducing these 'no use' areas but users still must pay for airtime, long distance and roaming fees (when away from where your phone is registered) unless you have a one-rate plan.

RVing friends purchased a cell phone to use with a $30.00 prepaid calling card (300 minutes at .10 per minute). Their plan only works in the U.S.A. and although they can make calls, receiving them is very costly. Each company offers different plans, so it pays to shop around.

Most of us agree that in an emergency cost doesn't matter, however it is important to plan your cell phone usage. Every call that you make or receive is subjected to fees. Although using a cell phone is very convenient, it is not cost efficient. Monthly usage charges are much higher than household phone rates. There are a host of rate plans available ranging from the emergency only plan, to pre-pay, to a full-service one-rate package with bonus free airtime. One-rate plans include airtime, long distance and roaming fees.

Several cell companies in the U.S.A. and Canada include valuable 'free' after-hour minutes to use in the country where the phone is purchased. These 'free' minutes do not travel across the U.S./Canada border, but technology is changing and, when purchasing a new phone anywhere, it generally includes an annual commitment paid for as a monthly fee – even after you return to your home country. If you change phone companies, most will insist you buy a different phone model because the software is locked in. Economical cell phone plans in Mexico are very limited. Most visitors use a prepaid calling card to communicate.

Depending on your cell phone company they may add an inexpensive rider to use your phone in a country other than your own. Our U.S.A. provider charges $10.00 extra per month to allow calls to Canada from the U.S.A. and, within Canada.

With my U.S. cell plan, I pay in U.S.$ – but my rate is comparable to Canadian cell plans. While I am in the U.S.A., I have unlimited evening and weekend minutes but as soon as I enter Canada I no longer have access to these 'after hour minutes'. Some phone plans purchased in Canada also offer local after hour minutes on out-going calls while in Canada but not on incoming calls. Digital phone service plans function in both countries but roaming service that connects in 'analogue-only' is not usually available.

Routine charges for each call include a per minute airtime cost even for a local call. Of course, long distance charges increase the cost of the call. One-rate plans on the other hand help make these costs more affordable, although they generally do cost more than a landline. Usage can be paid automatically by credit card. Decide what you want to use your cell phone for then shop around to negotiate the best plan and rate for your situation.

More About Cell Phones

If possible try to register your cell home phone number near where you spend the most amount of time because that area becomes your home cell location – local calls may be less expensive. Our original analogue cell 3-watt bag phone connected to a cigarette lighter – the phone number was listed in Brockville, Ontario, our home base at the time. That cell plan covered all of Ontario and Quebec. If we left that area we still used our phone, however, we then went into roaming. No matter if we were in the U.S. or New Brunswick, as soon as we moved away from Ontario or Quebec we left our cell coverage area and calls reverted to either local only or to a per minute fee for airtime, plus roaming and long distance. Digital packages are more economical.

Cell phones come in a variety of styles and sizes and many have a hands-free voice-activated option to allow you to talk while driving. In some areas it is illegal to use your cell while at the wheel. Phones that plug into a cigarette lighter have a longer range of coverage than battery operated ones. Originally we purchased a 12-volt extension cord that we connected to the 12-volt appliance adapter in our motorhome. It draws amps from our house batteries and works effectively to power our phone. While driving, we plugged into the cigarette lighter as needed. An optional phone battery is available but, for us and our limited usage, we didn't feel that it's necessary.

Later we purchased a 12-volt/120-volts converter called a 'brick' to power our phone (and any other 12 volt appliance). We plugged the phone into the jack and the brick into the wall. This was more effective than the extension cord. More and more people are using cell phones; their operation has become second nature. Because John and I knew very little about this modern form of communication, we made some costly mistakes. To help future owners avoid our pitfalls, I'm sharing some cost saving information you may overlook when you begin to use your phone.

The best way for mobile communication from across North America is to subscribe to a digital one-rate plan. With a specific area local cell phone plan, it is possible to receive calls from anywhere, but they will cost more. Other unknown and hidden charges that apply to local area usage plan include…

♦ If a person called us – frequently two long distance charges were incurred.

♦ They paid long distance to Brockville and so did we pay charges to Brockville.

♦ But if the caller dialled a special roam number before punching in our cell home number (at the dial tone prompt), the caller paid the long distance charge to the special number and the call became a local one for us.

♦ The same double charge also applies if we received what appeared to be a local call from our next-door neighbour. If the caller first dialled the local roam number before our cell number, it then became a local call for both of us. A list of roam numbers is available from the parent cell company.

♦ Unless your plan includes free airtime, charges may be added for each minute your phone is in use.

♦ When your statement arrives, check it carefully. Airwaves travel along the water easier than on land. When we were near water such as the St. Lawrence River our calls frequently connected to a cell network in New York and our statement showed expensive roaming charges that we never used. This problem affects users and boaters on both sides of the border – call your phone company to correct billing errors.

◆ Cell phones are not secure either because calls travel over airwaves. During one trek through northern communities TV reception was limited before we had satellite TV. John listened to analogue cell phone calls for entertainment while sitting at the picnic table on his $14.00 radio.

◆ Though rates continue to drop, using our cell phone is still one of our major monthly expenses.

◆ One-rate analogue cell packages are not available. Analogue service is the most costly if you are out of your local calling area.

There are many ways to stay in voice touch – 'One-rate' cell plans with after-hour free minutes are one very economical choice but the least expensive is with a voice mail message service and a discount telephone calling card. To reduce these costs even more, make calls selectively and choose low rate times such as evenings or Sundays. Keeping in touch can still be easy and very inexpensive. ➤

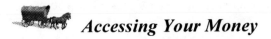 **Accessing Your Money**

Client/Debit Cards And ATMs

When we began RVing, to ensure we had enough money for travel expenses (and emergencies) for the entire trip it was necessary to stash an abundance of cash and travellers cheques in our RV. Modern technology has changed all that.

Using debit cards in both Canada and the U.S.A. has become second nature. Once you've registered your card with a Personal Identification Number (PIN) from your bank, it is so convenient to withdraw cash at ATMs (Automatic Teller Machines) everywhere. No interest is charged because you are using your own money; however, your bank will access a small fee if you use a machine other than one that is part of your bank system. At ATMs operated by your own bank you can also deposit cheques or pay bills. In Canada all ATMs are connected with 'Interac' – withdrawal fees at any Interac machine are minimal for Canadian cardholders. You will pay a transaction fee to your bank when using ATMs in a country other than your own. Generic ATMs located in convenient places frequently charge an additional small fee to withdraw cash.

Today, easy-to-use ATMs are located in grocery and convenience stores, gas stations, shopping malls and, of course, in almost every bank – some have drive-up access but for your safety be aware of your surroundings. ATMs are as popular in small towns and out-of-the-way places as they are in large metropolitan communities. It's no longer necessary to bring your life savings with you on your journey – you can leave it behind to earn interest. When you need money, go to an ATM, insert your card, punch in your PIN (personalized identification number) and pick up your cash. The convenience of getting money when you need it is worth the small fee. Although the bank limits the daily withdrawal amounts from the machines, it is normally sufficient to cover most expenses.

Note: Debit cards are only effective when money is available in your account. If you take 'cash-back' during purchase transactions you can avoid the above-mentioned ATM fees.

While in a country other than your own you may incur two fees – one at the ATM and one from the bank, however, we recently discovered a way around this. As we go through the 'cash' at Wal*Marts or large grocery stores in the U.S.A., we use our Canadian Bank of Montreal client card (affiliated with the Harris Bank) as a debit card for purchases and we request cash-back – we have not paid a cent in ATM fees for several years. This should work in reverse although not all cards function as a debit card in a country other than your own but it is worth a try – technology is changing. Tell the cashier you'd like to test your card. If it works you too can save ATM fees. (FYI – all international PINs should be only four digits.)

Note: Your bank client card (debit card) usually displays the logos of affiliated bank transfer systems (i.e. Interac, Cirrus, Plus, etc.). If the store where you are shopping uses the same banking system, your client (debit) card should work.

From the beginning our pension cheques have been direct-deposited each month. This makes it easy to ensure cash is available to meet our expenses. It is easier for us to budget if we take out our monthly amount and set aside suggested amounts in designated envelopes to cover various expenses. When I move about with a wallet full of money, I seem to always find something to spend it on. Nevertheless, by budgeting I don't feel deprived and we live extremely well if I limit how much I have on-hand. By the way, remember your PIN number but for security reasons never write it down. Anyone with your number and your card has full access to cash from your account.

> **John and I each carry ONE credit card at a time. Additional cards are kept in a safe place for emergencies. If we lose a wallet we are inconvenienced but not incapacitated.**

If you punch an incorrect number into an ATM three times, it will either destroy your card or refuse card transaction requests. Early in our travels this happened to us. I had both cards in my wallet and inadvertently punched John's number into the machine using my card. Unfortunately, that year we didn't understand why our cards no longer worked until we reached British Columbia six months later. It is not so critical these days but at that time we had to wait until we returned east of Winnipeg, Manitoba before our bank's computer could verify our accounts and issue new cards. These days most banks will re-issue new cards by courier service. On the other hand, if you ask a relative near your home address to become your 'banking power of attorney' ('P of A'), they could also intercede on your behalf.

> Note: To become a banking 'P of A', the relative or friend simply signs a paper stating that if they take any money out of your account after you died they would have to pay it back. As a banking 'P of A' they can write cheques and deposit cash plus intercede on your behalf if a problem with the bank surfaces when you are many miles away. Our bank will not provide a third client card for our 'P of A' (unless their name is on the account) so we give our contact one of our cards.

ATMs sometimes fail but don't despair; there are several ways to obtain money while travelling – besides using an ATM. With two forms of identification (one with your photo plus at least two credit cards), we found many bank managers will authorize you to cash a personal cheque during emergencies.

Paying bills and obtaining updated information by telephone is the easiest way of staying on top of your banking records while on the move. All banks offer this comprehensive service – some for a small fee. Subscribers can move money between accounts, pay bills, obtain statements, apply for loans and much more simply by phoning the 24-hour 1-800 number supplied by your bank. (See more reference to telephone banking in the *Budgeting For The Good Life* chapter.)

More recently many RVers use their computers to access their bank accounts on-line. The majority of campgrounds offer modems for campers to connect their laptops; some even provide instant telephone hookups at each site and WIFI (highspeed wireless Internet service where you connect from a short distance without wires) is popping up everywhere.[22] (For more info about online activities see *Staying In Touch Electronically* under *Mail Call And Cyberspace*).

---

22 Accessing the Internet changes rapidly so updated current information about RVing in Cyberspace *is posted on our website of www.rvliving.net.*

Credit Cards

Credit cards work almost everywhere but, sometimes, the merchant will add a three to eight percent surcharge when payment is by credit card, even if paying for a campsite or at small gas stations.

Cash advances on credit cards may also be convenient, however, interest begins the day you receive your money, not the day of your statement due date. RV friends in Mexico asked their son to deposit a $1000.00 or more into their credit card account the first of every month (the bank will also make a monthly payment at your request). They simply took cash withdrawals whenever they needed cash. Their account showed a credit balance before the withdrawal, so they avoided any interest charges on their cash advance.

Note: If you plan on using your credit card in an ATM machine for cash withdrawals, you do need a PIN. You can get a PIN by going into or calling your bank.

Some RV clubs and other organizations offer credit cards to their members. Although, obtaining credit cards in a country other than your own can be somewhat difficult. Credit history does not easily travel across the border. Companies (no matter in which country they are located) prefer not to extend credit to non-residents but it is not impossible. This, too, goes for clubs or financial institutions offering RV financing. Not too many want the risk of an out-of-country client who can easily take their 'collateral' across the border.

However, for years we have had a U.S.-only credit card. We phoned for the application and every time the clerk asked a question such as "How much do you make?", "How much do you owe?", etc. we would answer "X-amount in Canadian dollars." That card came in handy when we needed U.S.$ cheques (before we were able to open U.S.$ accounts in Canada), as well as if we wanted to buy something with a high U.S. dollar amount.

Traveller's Cheques

ATMs were not available when we first explored Mexico. To add to our cash flow we visited the local American Express office to cash a personal cheque in exchange for traveller's cheques or the local currency. The cheque could be written in Canadian or American funds depending on what exchange rate was most beneficial to us.

135

There is only one problem with using American Express services – it's easier to find an American Express office in foreign countries than it is in many areas of Canada or the U.S. When we accepted the currency of the country in cash, there was no fee, however, if we purchased traveller's cheques, we paid a low one-percent service charge.

Bank Accounts

Many RVers who spend extended time in a country other than their own open an account at a local bank. If you maintain an account balance in a local bank it is not necessary to wait for a cheque to clear your home bank before you receive your cash.

To receive courteous service and maximum bank benefits, it helps if you introduce yourself to a new bank with a letter of credit from your home bank – especially if you return to the same area and wish to open an account near your favourite destination.

As you can see, acquiring money away from home is not too difficult and the available choices of easy access are continuously growing. To protect yourself, leave your cash in your financial institution to earn interest and, although you can withdraw as often as you wish, don't withdraw more than you need to enjoy your travels.

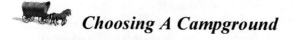

Choosing A Campground

Many campgrounds are located in picturesque surroundings
such as this one located at Radium Hot Springs, British Columbia.

Campgrounds aren't all equal and when you begin RVing, it's difficult to know what features will make your holiday enjoyable or create a disaster.

For John and me, the most important plus in any campground is a level site with good hookups, easy access into the park and sufficient space to manoeuvre our unit. If it's close to highway exits, that's an added bonus.

We also appreciate a well-maintained campground. When park staff trim and remove large tree overhangs, it shows that the owners are aware of the damage that low-hanging branches can do to RVs. Each year, manufacturers are making units taller, longer and wider and parks that provide ample turnaround space for large fifth wheels and motorhomes with car in tow are places we mark on our map as 'must return' stopping spots. No matter how pretty a place or how great the amenities; we don't repeat a visit to any place where it's difficult to set up camp.

A steady and correctly wired power source is also important. We can cope rather well with either 15-amp or 30-amp service. But, reverse polarity (when the line circuit and the neutral circuit are reversed), an open ground or power surge are dangerous and damaging to appliances.

Tasty, pure and odour-free water follows close behind a good power source as a significant factor for us. The inconvenience of connecting water filter units, especially on overnight stops, is also a bother. Although you should always keep your water tank at least one third-full when camping (for emergencies), it can become stale and so occasionally we drain and refill ours with fresh water. We add a few capfuls of commercial fresh water additive to keep our water tasty.

One other point when dealing with water and electric (hydro) hookups – we want handy connections. Although some parks have yet to learn what that means, no RVer should need 100 feet of electric cord and five feet of water hose, or vice versa, to attach an RV to hookups.

Many parks add weekly activities such as pancake breakfasts, hayrides, evening movies, crafts, tournaments, bingo and more that enhance your stay.

Over the years, we've found a few 'no-frills overnight camping' parks with easy on/off access to the highway. At these stopovers campers set-up within the security of a campground, complete with all necessary – but basic – amenities. Although sites at these campgrounds aren't overly spacious, most are usually full hookup pull-throughs. Showers, too, although hot, may be very basic as well.

Since these no-frills campgrounds are for overnight stops only, there's no need for more elaborate amenities. We love to see these no-frills parks advertised along the highway, especially when payment is usually under $10 a night and we're *en route* between destinations.

Other types of low-cost camping spots charge for only the service used by having a stepping-stone fee schedule. RVers wishing to park within a secure compound pay one low rate. Overnight prices increase depending on what power amperage you select or if you need sewer or plan to use electric heaters or air conditioners. Unfortunately, there aren't very many no-frills campgrounds available – appreciate it when you find one.

➤ *Highway Truck Stops*

Several campers prefer to stop for a nap in rest areas *en route* to their destination parks – please don't do it! In many areas of North America, especially in the isolated areas, this is becoming a dangerous practice. A safer alternative is to pull into one of the large truck stop chain stations I discussed in the *On The Road* chapter under *Planning Your Route* section. Each truck stop is open 24 hours, 365 days a year and, although these are not as plush as five-star campgrounds, they're definitely more secure than highway rest areas.

➤ **Good Sam Parks**

Many full service private campgrounds in North America are also members of the Good Sam Park system. Each year, staff members visit and rate each park to determine the quality of washrooms, park amenities and surrounding scenery. A high minimum standard is necessary to qualify as a member park. These parks are listed in the 4-inch thick *Trailer Life* and *Woodall's* campground directories. Every RVer should have one of these books on board. They are available from bookstores and RV dealers.

The smiling Good Samaritan Angel logo identifies each Good Sam Park where members of the club receive a 10 percent discount on all daily rates paid in cash.

➤ **FMCA (Family Motor Coach Association), Escapees And Other Clubs**

Several RV clubs have attained a collection of campgrounds throughout the U.S.A.: with a few more in Canada that offer 10 percent off the daily rate to club members. This savings is not large but it frequently offsets the tax. Cash payment is usually required. See chapter under *RV Clubs* for contact info.

➤ **Military RV, Camping And Rec Areas**

This comprehensive publication from Military Living features campground information for active military personnel and retirees around the world. Some parks are open to non-military personnel as well.[23]

➤ **KOA (Kampgrounds Of America)**

You'll find these campgrounds everywhere, usually convenient to popular tourist hotspots, with easy access from interstates and major highways. Although every park offers different features, each provides clean rest rooms, hot showers, laundry facilities, convenience stores, children's playground, swimming pools and level sites with handy hookups. Many also offer bike paths, hot tubs, saunas, beach access, mini-golf, boat docks and more.

At KOA kamps, campers pay for only the services used. Rates begin with a basic fee – dump stations are free but electricity (hydro); sewer, cable TV, etc. are extra. Rates are based on two people and there is an additional fee for extra campers, including children, in your unit. KOA franchise owners offer a 10 percent fee for those carrying a KOA Value Kard. These

---

23 *To contact Military Living call 1-703-237-0203 or log onto* www.militaryliving.com *or* www.usmilitaryrvcamping.com

are available from any KOA kampground or the Billings, Montana head office.

> ### *Premium RV Resorts*

There is a new choice of campgrounds on the market these days. They consist of large high-end resorts where RVers can purchase a site or rent one on a long-term lease. These five-star resorts offer every amenity to make your stay extra special – some even have hot tubs on site and a free morning paper is the norm. Cost to camp is also high. Although a few of these parks also have strict regulations as to who can stop (such as your unit has to be over a selected size and younger than ten years old). You can find these parks listed in the new *Big Rig Campground Directory* and in most comprehensive North American campground directories. Most are located in the sunny south.

> ### *Provincial/State Parks*

In Canada, we have many provincial parks scattered throughout the country. The same is true for state parks in the U.S.

Several parks are for day-use only but others have spacious sites nestled among tranquil scenery designed with those who want to get in touch with nature. All campers are welcome from backpacking tenters to those in RVs. If you have a large RV, check ahead, although most sites are wide some are short in length. Many of these parks have no hookups, but there's usually a water tap spaced throughout the campground and a dump station near by. Washrooms and/or showers are usually available. Contact Tourist Bureaus for location.

On the other hand, John and I have stayed at several breathtaking provincial and state parks with full hookups, some even had spaces for physically challenged RVers, nature centres, paved roadways and blacktop sites. One park loaned their customers pre-recorded cassettes explaining the habitat and lifestyle of animals native to the park

At one time, these parks were less expensive than private parks but they now charge a comparable and occasionally higher fee, at some you are required to purchase a day-use pass in addition to paying a daily camping cost.

Occasionally seniors who are camping between Monday and Friday can receive a discount – ask if there are any restrictions. In most places it's only applicable to residents of the province or state that you're visiting.

Also check about the 'no pets' rule. Several states do not allow animals in the campground.

Reservations are possible as well as recommended during holiday weekends, but they may come with a fee.

➤ *National/Federal Parks And Forests*

These parks frequently offer a wealth of adventure. In both Canada and the U.S., day-use or annual fees may be required. If there are campgrounds on site, many will include full hookups plus numerous amenities. Costs vary depending on activities; in some cases rates may be higher than provincial and public parks.

➤ *Bureau Of Land Management (BLM) Facilities*

Some RVers prefer to dry camp in the desert of the southwest and other secluded spots in Bureau of Land Management areas. The book *Adventures on America's Public Lands* highlights destinations in 20 states featuring activities from canyon climbing to mountain biking to hang gliding and more. Passes are available for stays of a few weeks to several months. Although inexpensive, in most cases, there are very few amenities and no hook-ups. In some areas water trucks and pump-out vehicles make regular visits.[24]

➤ *U.S. Army Corps Of Engineers Campgrounds*

Parks operated by the Corps are located on U.S. government-owned land throughout the U.S.A. Facilities range from low-cost, primitive locations to modern, full-service campgrounds. The Corps of Engineers is one of the nation's largest providers of outdoor recreation, operating more than 2,500 recreation areas. Many are located in the southwest desert.

All Corps campgrounds offer a 50% discount to U.S. citizens aged 62 and older. Many parks provide a variety of recreation facilities from camping to marinas and more. The book *Camping with the Corps of Engineers* outlines specific details of parks owned and operated by the U.S. Corps of Engineers.[24]

➤ *Municipal Campgrounds And Fairgrounds*

John and I were surprised to find that quite a few small communities maintain municipal campgrounds. Payment of the inexpensive camp fee is usually by the honour system. These are not listed in most camping books but you will find them if you follow signs as you drive through towns along your route.

---

24 *Look for your copy of these publications in bookstores plus they are listed under* Campground Directories *on the* RV WebLink *page of* www.rvliving.net.

Some sites have full hookups; others have 15-amp electric only. At the least a water tap will be nearby and most parks have a dump station. Many locations are within walking distance to downtown. Staying at these campgrounds is a superior and friendly way to explore small town North America.

➤ *Seasonal Camping*

Many RV snowbirds who head south for the winter settle into a campground for three to four months. Rates are lower the longer you stay and the parks activities are designed for seniors that are away from their friends and family. These parks offer such a busy calendar it is impossible to take part in all of it. Paying for electric (hydro) power is always the RVers responsibility on long-term stays.

In the summer some RVers travel to see all they can while other fulltimers flock north and settle into a campground near family and check in for the six-month season. This definitely lowers camping costs. Canadians who head south in the winter usually stay in Canada for the summer since in any calendar year visitors are only allowed to stay in a country other than their own less than six months. RVers from the U.S.A. tour the country but they can also take advantage of the Canadian six-month seasonal rate – sorry three to four month stopovers that are popular in the south are not common.

Most parks feature a few get-togethers and activities for families over the summer, but very few northern U.S.A. or Canadian resorts offer an abundance of activities for seniors such as RVers find in the south. The park we were in while I was writing this is located in southern Ontario. Our season rate is a mere $1300.00 Cdn for the six months. That equals $216.00 Cdn. per month; there are a number of similar parks like this. Considering the daily rate is $29.00, staying the season translates as a good savings, (of course a one month rate is a bit higher but it is always less money than a daily or weekly rate). Refer to the campground directories from each province or state for the area you wish to stay, find a park and give them a call.

General Info

The previous information provides an overview of the various types of campgrounds available. Look through your North American campground directories mentioned above or check with Tourist Bureaus, Welcome Centres and Provincial Tourist offices. Load your RV, find an interesting camping hideaway and get set for the time of your life.

Two main requirements that John and I look for in a good campsite are a level site and good source of power.

Reading A Campground Directory

Several large international campground directories available from bookstores make it easy to locate RV parks and resorts throughout North America.

If you're using a campground directory there are some things to know about interpreting the descriptions. Remember, although I recommend that you travel with reservations, make sure that you understand the campground's cancellation policy. A number of campgrounds charge a fee if you cancel your reservation – no matter the reason.

Terms Used In Campground Directories

- Back-in – this means that tow vehicles must be detached before backing into a space.
- Beach – sandy shore that borders a lake or a river or ocean. Swimming is popular.
- Boondocking – another word for dry camping (no hookups).
- Cable – a cable TV hookup is available.
- Dollar sign ($) – means that the hookup or amenity flagged with this symbol costs extra and is not part of the camping fee.
- Dry camping – boondocking, no hookups.

- <u>Dump station</u> – a place to dump your holding tanks.
- <u>Electric (Hydro),</u> 15, 20, 30 or 50 amps – informs you that electric hookups are available and what amperage is used at the site.
- <u>Groceries</u> – basic supplies are available.
- <u>Ice</u> – you can buy ice on-site.
- <u>Instant site phones</u> – phones lines are available at each site. You must have a phone available to connect inside.
- <u>Laundry</u> – there's at least one machine on-site.
- <u>Modem</u> – adapter is available within the park to connect a laptop.
- <u>No hookups</u> – no water or electric (hydro) or sewer hook-ups, although water and dump may be close at hand.
- <u>Pets</u> – you can bring your four-legged friends. Note: Most pets are only allowed if you clean up after them and they are on a leash. Some parks stipulate 'small pets only'.
- <u>Playground</u> – usually indicates that families are welcome.
- <u>Pool</u> – a swimming pool.
- <u>Private phone</u> – park owners will share their phone.
- <u>Public phone</u> – pay phone in park.
- <u>Pull-through/pull-thru</u> – these sites allow RVers to set-up without unhitching vehicles.
- <u>Pump-out</u> – a honey-wagon visits your RV site and pumps out your holding tanks.
- <u>Seasonal</u> – campers stay put for an extended season, sometimes years without moving their unit.
- <u>Security</u> – the park provides some kind of patrol and/or security gate.
- <u>Self-registration</u> – drop money and registration forms into a box, find a site and connect to available facilities and enjoy your stay.
- <u>Sewers</u> – sewage hookups at the site.
- <u>Showers</u> – shower facilities are on-site – if there is a ($) next to showers, this means that it will cost you approximately one to four quarters to run the shower water.
- <u>Swimming</u> – but no pool listed means that swimming is in a river, lake, pond or even a creek.
- <u>Telephone</u> – jacks are available for long-term residents.
- <u>TV</u> – jacks to connect cable are available.
- <u>Water</u> – water hookups at the site.
- <u>Water sports</u> – implies a lake or extra large river for boating, canoeing or water skiing.
- <u>Wooded area</u> – some sites are by shade trees (don't forget, trees can interfere with the use of TV satellite dishes and low-hanging branches can damage your RV).

Special Tip For Campers

Compliments of – rvliving.net RV Lifestyle Consultants – Peggi and John McDonald	In case of Emergency
In Case of Emergency We are _____ **Our RV is parked at –** Resort/Phone .... Dates..................................... **Pets on board** (type/name)_____ **During Any Emergency** Please call_____	*************** **We're Peggi and John McDonald** **Our motorhome is parked at** Resort Name.......................... Phone #................................. Dates.................................... We have two Dachshunds on board *'Maddie' and 'Katie'*
Reproduce as required – fill in a new one each time you change locations. Keep with your driver's licence.	*During Any Emergency, please call* *Peggi's sister Diane -519 xxx xxxx* _____ Sample only – This is the one we use.

When you're travelling, even though you carry personal identification, you may not be carrying the address of the campground where you're staying. In the event of an emergency, this information could be crucial.

As soon as John and I check into a campground, we fill out our own self-produced emergency information card that we each carry in our wallet with our driver's licences. In an emergency, rescue personnel know who we are, where we are staying, where our RV is parked and how many pets are on board.

The illustration above is a sample of the card we use. Modify the card to fit your individual circumstance. This security measure is only effective if you complete a new card for each person on board at each new stop. Keep the form with your driver's licence.

Membership Campgrounds

Coast to Coast, Resorts Parks International (RPI) and Thousand Trails (TT) are the three main membership park parent organizations. Several smaller groups recently entered the market but most form an affiliation with one of the larger three to provide more benefits for their members.

Coast to Coast

As the group idea caught on, the park system grew and **Coast to Coast,**[25] **(C2C)** is now the largest membership park organization. It began in 1972 with 13 affiliated parks. In 1973, their independent reciprocal network camping system was started. C2C now has more than 500 camping resorts in its system plus a large collection of Good Neighbor parks – private parks that extend one or more overnight stays to visiting C2C members at a rate of approximately $10.00 per night.

Note: Although I have placed Coast to Coast under membership parks, this organization is also know as an 'association campground network' because C2C has an affiliation with parks from various smaller groups of membership parks – some resorts in the parent system are individual private parks as well.

Some parks also include **Coast to Coast Resorts (CCR).** These resorts combine RV campsites with on-site RV rentals and cabins. International destinations, reduced hotel rates and travel services are a few other bonuses offered to C2C/CCR members.

C2C's latest edition is **Coast to Coast Deluxe**. This program includes longer stays, a reservation service and more benefits. Of course, there is an extra cost for membership – your home park sets the price of the deluxe upgrade.

John and I were avid members of Coast to Coast for 10 years. Members can stay at their home parks at 'no-cost' for two, occasionally three weeks; leave for a week and return for more 'free' camping. When visiting other parks members pay a low fee.

This form of camping may save some day-to-day camping costs but that is only after members pay a hefty home park buy-in price plus annual dues.

---

25 Coast to Coast Resorts: *www.coastresorts.com, 1-800-368-5721.*

In our case as our lifestyles, wants, needs and desires changed we spent less time in this type of campground. Although we enjoyed the savings of our early days, later years we gravitated to areas where member parks were not located. We felt the cost of our annual membership dues was a waste of our travel income. So it was time for us to sever these ties. Since we were not boxed in with a long-term contract we simply sent a letter stating we wanted to cancel our association and walked away. Being able to walk away is one reason for not buying in for a lengthy period.

In the beginning John and I thought we hit the jackpot. Our home membership camping resort had level sites, spacious patios and convenient hookups – including cable TV – excellent recreation facilities, clean showers and a fully-equipped laundry room. An extensive activity calendar of dances, bingo, craft classes, BBQs, pot-lucks, church services and, of course, friendly staff were the icing-on-the-cake on this stopover. It was located in the heart of a popular tourist area but since it was a distance away from our home base we could only visit it occasionally.

Although not all membership parks are five-star resorts, many of these campgrounds are nestled among beautiful scenery surrounded by mountains or lakes. Most are located within easy access to tourist areas. Whether snuggled in the woods or resting in a secluded valley on the edge of a city, each membership park has its own charm.

Thousand Trails (TT)

TT was the first membership RV park system and now there are close to a hundred preserves (campgrounds) in its system. They also offer rental accommodations for members travelling without an RV. TT has recently changed its policy[26] and, while overnight use is still free, annual dues vary by the amount of time spent in the park. There is one price for limited preserve use and a higher cost for the opportunity to use the resort year-round.

Resort Parks International (RPI)

RPI has close to 400 parks in its group. In addition, RPI also offers inexpensive vacations[27] at many quality condominiums throughout the world. The majority of these parks are affiliated with C2C as well as other membership park systems – you cannot buy into RPI on its own. Overnight

---

26 Thousand Trails: *www.1000trails.com* *1-800-388-7788.*
27 Resort Parks International: *www.resortparks.com* *1-800-635-8498.*

rates are extremely low. RPI also offers a low cost reservation service but you do have the choice of reserving or driving up for a site. Again visits are restricted to twice per year to the same park.

Rules Of The Game

It definitely pays to **shop around** and DO NOT buy in for the long term. These parks occasionally do phase out of the system. The membership park system works when RVers buy into a home park for site access plus paying a low cost membership into the parent park system. The one-time 'buy-in' cost for a home park ranges from a low $400 U.S. to a high of $8,000 U.S. You have to shop around; many are available for less than $2500.00 U.S. The more benefits, the higher the cost. The parent organization, the area of location, number of sister parks and the available facilities all determine park site price. Annual dues can be frozen at less than $100 U.S. to $400 U.S. and higher. Another fee between $50.00 U.S. and $65.00 U.S. is paid annually to the parent club.

Memberships may contain a three-time resale clause. Although, in principle, this option is a good idea, it's rare that anyone reselling his or her membership will ever recoup the value. In some parks, members can also buy a lower cost one-lifetime membership with no resale value. This purchase is only good for the lifetime of the member. (In most cases, it is not transferable to a spouse if the spouse is not listed as the member.) Occasionally resorts may offer a one or two year trial package as well.

On-site resort staff is employed mainly to sell memberships in each park; however, in many camping magazines; clearing house advertisements list reduced prices of resale home parks. This is a convenient place to begin searching for pre-owned club affiliation memberships.

The majority of membership campgrounds are in the U.S., however, Canada has its share of C2C and RPI resorts. A couple of parks have also signed on in Mexico.

There are two main factors to consider before buying into your home park. If a park is close to where you live, you can enjoy the home park facilities on weekends and holidays. But, if you don't want to stay in one area, make sure that you have enough time to travel a distance since you cannot use your park membership at an affiliated resort within a 125 mile (200-km) radius from your home park.

If you buy-in away from your home area, you can use a variety of affiliated parks close to where you live. However, you can only visit each resort twice a year for seven days at a time with a 30-day break between. Both concepts carry advantages for the buyer but, consider which organization better serves your camping needs. Ask yourself:

♦ Do I want to vacation near my home?
♦ Have I the time to enjoy extended travel away from home?
♦ Do I want to visit a different park for a limited time on each trip?
♦ Should I buy close to home and forfeit the use of other affiliated parks in the area?
♦ If the home park I choose is one of the higher cost parks, will my usage justify the increased cost of this investment?
♦ If I choose a lower cost park away from my home will the number of actual visits to affiliated parks in my area be beneficial?

Just for info, some RVing snowbirds move from one 'free' resort (sister park) to another all winter long; visiting members pay a low nightly fee if they stay in a park other than their own. For the seven-day break between they pay a regular rate at a nearby private park and return for another 'no-cost' two-week period.

Special amenities such as cable TV or use of a health spa may cost a few dollars extra. These expensive extras are not necessary to camping life; therefore, a nominal fee for usage is standard in most resorts.

Again I stress before signing, **shop around** and don't be coerced into buying from high-pressured sales staff – only you can decide where to purchase. Think about what individual parks offer for the price asked. Remember, when visiting other parks, no matter if a member paid $500 or $9,000 to buy into a home park, all members should receive equal treatment.

This system is every bit as good as it sounds. Purchasing a park membership can provide many years of enjoyable and inexpensive camping if, you follow the program operating procedures.

John and I owned a time-share condo before we began RVing, which we were not satisfied with and, because a joint ownership RV park system is very similar, we were hesitant about buying into any club membership. During our beginning years of extensive travel, several rumours about associated problems with these membership parks caused us some concern. But, when we finally took the plunge, within 12 months of becoming a member, we camped more than 150 nights for only $1.00 per night (these days that cost has risen to $6.00 and maybe higher). At times we drove a few extra miles to camp in beautiful surroundings at affordable prices. What costs we saved in camping we put towards sightseeing or to offset the increasing price of fuel, maintenance and food.

Peak Season Travel

During peak season in the southern states, drive-up members (if they can even get in) may only be able to stay two to four days because there is a possibility that the park will be full. However, some parks provide a non-serviced overflow area where members can spend a night. To make sure that you have a site during these busy times, plan to stop early in the day, especially if you prefer to travel without reservations. Expect to spend the occasional night at a private park when the membership parks have no sites available.

> **To enjoy a worry-free vacation during peak holiday periods and long weekends, it is wise to travel with park reservations. Resorts, both private and membership parks, are usually full. Without reservations to guarantee your spot, overnighters may find themselves driving around trying to find a campsite.**

The fascinating Hole in the Rock at Percé, on the Gaspé Peninsula in Quebec, Canada is an outstanding place to stop!

Don't be upset if you're refused an empty spot. Not all sites in a park belong to one system. It's possible for a park to appear empty and staff to refuse you a campsite because your club's allotted sites are occupied. And, by law, each park must keep open sites for their home members who don't need reservations.

Anyone who runs into problems when checking into a membership resort should call the parent park's head office. These parks are regulated and any reported problems will be investigated. Success of this system is solely dependent on happy campers.

Discount Camping Clubs

Judie Riblett of Recreation USA – *'Camp for $10.00 per day'* – 1-850-537-9641, *www.campingandcampgrounds.com* helped with the editing of this section.

The newest cost saving form of camping on the RV horizon is from discount camping clubs. Members pay a low annual fee for the right to camp for 50% off the regular campground price or for $10.00 per night.

One option is **Recreation USA**.[28] The parks in their system have 'NO' blackout dates and each park is $10.00 per night for Rec U.S.A. members instead of the campground standard rate. If the park has a space, you get it for the $10.00 rate. Their annual membership can cover one consecutive year, or 1.5 years where the membership is divided into two 6-month periods over the winter (to accommodate northern snowbirds from the U.S.A. and Canada), or over the summer (for those travelling only in the summer months) – each member chooses the dates to be activated. A 6-month membership is also offered. Rec USA's ever-growing directory of parks are located in most but not all states in the U.S.A.

Another option is to join clubs that offer 50% off a given park's regular price. However, some of these member parks have 'blackout dates' – this means that there are periods when the reduced rate does not apply. In reality it means that a park may give a discount from Sunday to Thursday but not Friday or Saturday. Other parks exclude themselves from providing reduced camping during their high summer season from mid-June to mid-August or peak winter snowbird season from January to March in sun country. Although, this is not all bad; if you take advantage of club rates when you are in an area where reduced camping is in force, over the year you will save much more than the price of the membership. The two most popular clubs following this format are **Passport of America**[29] and **Happy Camper**.[30] Both of these club organizers are very busy and they have recruited numerous member-parks in the U.S.A. plus some in Canada and a few in

---

28 Recreation USA –*'Camp for $10.00 per day'*:
   www.campingandcampgrounds.com 1-850-537-9641.
29 Passport America *U.S.A./Canada/Mexico – 50% off*: *www.passport-america.com*
   1-800-283-7183.
30 Happy Camper – *50% Discount*: *www.camphalfprice.com* 1-866-677-6453.

Mexico. Passport leads the way with the most members and highest number of member-parks.[31]

Members of discount camping clubs sign NO contract agreement and members renew only if and when they wish.

There may be an additional charge for 50-amp service, cable TV, telephone hook-up etc. but the park's regular customers also pay these extra costs. Annual membership fees for most of these clubs range from $40.00 – $90.00 (U.S.) – benefits also differ. Several additional smaller discount camping clubs are available as well; most follow similar programs.

---

31 *More discount camping clubs are listed on the* RV WebLink *page of* www.rvliving.net.

Caravans, Trains And Cruises

RVers who want to travel from South America to Alaska and other parts of North America, but would prefer to travel with other RVers should consider group trips or caravans. Caravans are an organized trip (by a company or experienced RVer) where a number of RVs travel together from Point A to Point B. Caravans should always have a wagonmaster (the leader of the group who maps out routes and makes all necessary travel arrangements) and a tailgunner (who is in the last unit of the group to make sure none of the others become lost) who helps with mechanical difficulties and remains in contact with the wagonmaster. Caravans can seem costly but most include some of the meals for the group, payment for camping sites plus a host of other things. The wagonmaster takes care of reservations, helps sort out needed permits, etc. Many wagonmasters who take caravans into Mexico also speak Spanish and are aware of the different laws and regulations of that country. Check your favourite RV publication for caravan advertisements.

Another dimension to RV travel is by train – we're talking about trains where the RVs are anchored on board like the awesome Copper Canyon 'piggy-back' excursion in Mexico. You and your unit travel to a destination onboard a train and your living accommodation is your RV. Like the Copper Canyon train, this mode of travel can take you into places where there isn't any road access.

In the same vein, RVers can put their units on a cruise ship to sail one way to Alaska or other parts unknown. Many choose to cruise one way and drive back. The newest addition to one-of-a-kind RV adventures is to put your RV on a barge ship and cruise the Mississippi River in New Orleans – additional destinations are also available. Contact caravan companies for more details. To reap maximum travel benefits, join a caravan that includes these escapades as part of their travel schedules; although it is possible to book trips to these destinations on your own.[32]

---

[32] *Caravan companies are listed on the* RV WebLink *page of www.rvliving.net under* Caravans and Cruises.

 ## *RV Clubs*

***Horseshoes and other games are part of the fun at RV club gatherings;
membership and discount camping clubs also host RV rallies.***

Both seasoned travellers and novice RVers have much to gain from an
affiliation in at least one RV club.[33] Numerous local, national and
international organizations provide fellowship and offer assistance to RVers.
They all provide advice, RV information, support, offer RV merchandise
and so much more. Improving the travelling way of life is the primary goal
of these associations.

Many also include a comprehensive magazine in their benefits. Editors
of these club publications, along with volunteers, do extensive research to
find answers to RV-related questions. Technical writers working for various
clubs ensure members understand as much of their RVs as possible. Some
clubs even act as mediators to solve disputes – frequently RV performance –
between businesses and dissatisfied customers.

---

33 *The most popular RV Clubs include*

    Canada – Explorer RV Club*: www.explorer-rvclub.com: 1-800-999-0819.*
        FQCC (Quebec) – *Fédération québécoise de camping et de
        caravanning: www.campingquebec.com/fqcc: 1-514-252-3003.*
    U.S.A. – Family Motor Coach Association (FMCA): *www.fmca.com:
        1-800-543-3622.*
        Good Sam Club*: www.goodsamclub.com: 1-800-234-3450.*
        Escapees (SKP'S): *www.escapees.com: 1-800-976-8377.*

Though these organizations are huge, each has hundreds of chapters (smaller groups) to meet the needs of every RVer. Belonging to and participating in chapter functions and attending rallies are an integral part of this lifestyle to many RVers.

RV club rallies help promote fellowship and provide a venue for informative seminars, new product information, tasty food, campfires, sing-a-longs and lasting friendships. Weekend get-togethers are popular and, sometimes, the agenda covers an entire fun-filled week.

Activities such as seminars, draw prizes, blind auctions, manufacturer plant tours and visits to local and historical attractions headline each rally schedule. To add a competitive touch to these exciting getaways, rally organizers plan games that include horseshoes, beanbag, dominoes, mini-golf, card games or golf and dart tournaments. Frequently, chapter activity schedules include something for every age group of attendees.

It doesn't matter how long the event lasts, the benefits of participating in a rally are numerous for usually a low price. Each club differs and RVers receive excellent value for every chapter dollar spent. For most clubs, there's no restriction on the size and type of your unit, the important thing is that everyone has good, clean and simple fun.

International RV clubs such as FMCA, Good Sam, Escapees, manufacturer clubs and Canada's Explorer RV Club offer a variety of excellent benefits for their members.

Emergency Road Service, RV insurance, contents insurance, out of country medical, air ambulance, discount camping memberships, fuel discounts, MasterCard and Visa credit card programs, vehicle financing, hospital/medical insurance, hotel/car rental discounts are just a few benefits that can be had. They each include an informative magazine in their benefits.

Occasionally some benefits only apply to members of a specific country but it is worth asking about the benefits offered by each club.

During our early years of RVing, John and I belonged to five RV chapters of FMCA (Family Motor Coach Association) but somehow we never managed to make time to attend any rallies. By about our fifth year, we discovered the joys and low-cost benefits of chapter getaways. We found that RV clubs (and there are many) of all sizes not only welcome new members, they depend on increased numbers for growth and input of new ideas.

Several chapter events are conveniently held in cities or towns close to the Canada/U.S. border to ensure easy access for Canadians and Americans to join forces. It's a perfect opportunity for participants to become involved, make new friends plus keep busy and informed.

The chapters send out newsletters and bulletins specific to their activities. Club magazines include events and changes within the organization.

John and I travel extensively in our motorhome and meeting other club chapter members has helped us to understand and adapt to the RV lifestyle. We always feel welcome to join chapter festivities but it is impossible to attend every rally.

Although attending chapter rallies is great fun, the cream of these gatherings – the national conventions – are the most exciting. The majority of RV clubs hold large annual extravaganzas and it'll be worth your while to make a point of attending at least one of these gala events. We have had a ball at national rallies with a 100 RVs and some of FMCA conventions have reached 6000 or 7000 motorhomes. It is awesome to see that many in one spot.

At these large RV conventions – and many clubs host them biannually – dealers, along with manufacturers, promote and sell their products at huge on-site RV marketplaces. Browsing through the plethora of accessories is like shopping in a one big toy store designed just for RVers – the variety of products and choice on display is amazing. You can also explore and dream about owning one of the new showpieces. Of course, they are for sale at rock-bottom prices. The option of attending one of 140 seminars adds to the education value. Each presentation covers a different facet of RVing from technical tips to learning more about the RV lifestyle. I frequently present a 'Travel to Canada' seminar to make the trip easier for Americans to cross the border.

A motorhome chapter caravanning into a large FMCA
(Family Motor Coach Association) convention.

As I've said earlier, we belong to several club chapters and one year we joined other members for a pre-convention gathering in Lynchburg, Virginia. Five days later, as part of a group of 60 coaches, we caravanned 30 miles to the campus of the Polytechnic Institute in Blacksburg, Virginia for the four-day main event. Travelling in a group added to our pleasure as we could enjoy most aspects of the gigantic rally with friends.

All chapters are formed around a common interest or theme. There is at least one available that appeals to everyone such as RVing Singles, Fulltime RVers, Frustrated Maestros (musicians and non-musicians having fun), a specific type of coach and many others. Theme chapters bring together a group of people with a common interest.

Activities and functions are arranged for every age group – from six to 60+ – and include events such as golf, aerobics, roller-skating, swimming, tennis, movies, sightseeing tours as well as a variety of entertainment. Daily coffee and donuts and a mid-week ice cream social, roaming musical interludes and much more bring everyone together and, at most events, babysitting services are offered to ensure that nobody misses out on the activities.

Fun, fellowship and friends are the three exciting and important reasons why so many of us love RVing and each RV trip or chapter rally opens one more door to new adventures. For many of us, time on the road is always too short. Whether fulltiming or on a short vacation, RVers who wish to reap the maximum benefits from their days on the move should definitely join an RV club. It truly is a unique experience and a time of guaranteed fun.

There will always be several RV chapters or organizations located within close proximity to your home. Look for brochures at local RV dealers, nearby campgrounds and RV show exhibitors for the addresses of

157

groups relating to your interests. Ask other RVers if they know of any associations. RV magazines are on sale at bookstands; most are usually published by an RV club.

Decorating For The Holidays

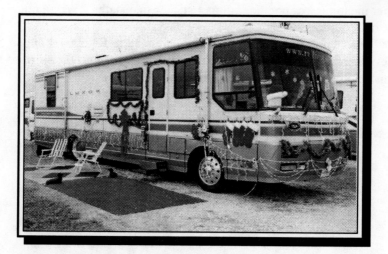

RVers, who will be away over the holidays, especially at Christmas, should bring their favourite decorations with them. Every year I hear new RVers lamenting over the fact that they didn't bring anything to add a holiday touch with them because they thought nobody would decorate when away from home.

To get into the festive spirit, especially at Christmas, pack lightweight holiday trimmings and bring a good supply with you, especially lights, to decorate both the inside and outside of your RV. Large suction cups keep things in place on the outside and the 'S'-shaped drapery hooks keep things secure on valences and curtains. Stick-and-peel window decals also add a nice touch.

Decorating is such fun in the sunny south.

At Christmas time, most campgrounds host tree-trimming and decorating parties, carol singing, craft sales, breakfasts and so much more. One tradition in the southwest is to place *luminaries* around each residence or RV site on Christmas Eve. *Luminaries* are simple candles set in sand inside of paper bags.

Many parks include a Christmas dinner on their activity calendar. Usually park staff provide and cook the turkey, dressing and gravy, and campers bring pot-luck dishes to complete the meal.

One campground that we were visiting set up 'family' tables of 12 guests. Each table provided their own food and decorated their table, much like they would at home. At the end of the meal, all leftovers go on a potluck table for the rest to sample. At some parks the extras are donated to a food kitchen.

Festivities don't stop with Christmas dinner and carol singing. An extravagant New Year's Eve party brings the holiday season to a close and opens the door to another exciting year.

Don't forget other holidays. Bring Valentine decorations, shamrocks for St. Patrick's Day and bunnies and eggs for Easter. Hallowe'en is one more event that is celebrated at many RV parks. If you pack a costume you will be ready for the party your park may be hosting. One of our chapters annually hosts a traditional Hallowe'en rally complete with costumes, decorations, dances, trick-or-treating and more.

Decorating for holidays is fun, with or without the kids, and it adds another meaning to a popular bumper sticker that states, "We're not seniors, we're only recycled teenagers".

Whether you have a young family or are mature RVers, taking part in whatever a resort has to offer adds to the fun. Getting into the spirit of the season helps to make pleasant memories.

PROTECTION PLUS

Breakdowns happen when least expected.
This is us! One day you, too, may need the service of ERS.

Peggi McDonald

Emergency Road Service (ERS)

There are several protection plans that RVers should never travel without. These plans offer a financial cushion for emergency situations and, even though it would be too costly to purchase every plan on the market, one 'must-have' for peace-of-mind travelling is an Emergency Road Service plan.

To date, John and I have logged close to two decades of pleasurable, exciting and usually problem-free travel in our motorhome. Occasionally, however, we experience a period when 'enough is enough'! October 3rd, 1990 was one of those days.

Due to several impromptu side trips we were three days behind our proposed travel schedule. The opportunity to join friends in Fort Lauderdale as planned came and went – we were simply too late to keep several of our promises. Inevitably, those few times we try to run extremely long days together, our journey is cursed with delays and setbacks. Thankfully this frustrating day was not life-threatening or extremely expensive but it was most exasperating, to say the least.

At 7:30 a.m. we left Pigeon Forge, Tennessee (near Dollywood), heading southeast through the foothills of Tennessee's stately Smokey Mountains towards Interstate 40 – a most impressive journey that took us past breathtaking and picturesque terrain. Unfortunately by noon, we'd only covered four miles. Why, you ask, should it take 4.5 hours to drive four miles? You guessed it – the day's fun had begun!

Our coach was equipped with a 'water assist' to heat water *en route*. (Hot radiator coolant travels by hose to the water heater when the engine is running. Water in the heater becomes hot without lighting the propane burner.) Since this water-heating device was already on our motorhome at the time of purchase we never questioned its function or any maintenance that may be required. (Big mistake!)

While climbing a small hill on a narrow road, our coach's heat gauge suddenly lunged into the danger zone. Simultaneously, smoke billowed from under the sink area. Screaming at John to pull over, my first thought was that we were on fire. With extinguisher in hand, I frantically swung open the kitchen cupboards, although, with some relief, I realized that the smoke was in reality steam. A rubber radiator hose had burst near the water heater and hot radiator antifreeze was spewing into every corner of my kitchen. John finally found a safe place to pull over before we did any engine damage.

162

What a mess! Offensive, oily residue clung to everything. It had saturated our new carpet and at least a dozen clean-up hand and bath towels. The excess slowly seeped through the floor – thankfully that coach wasn't a basement model. My first thought was, "I will never be able to remove that slippery radiator liquid from everything".

When the inside problem was under control we called our Emergency Road Service (ERS) number. Larry, the tow truck driver, arrived in less than 30 minutes and temporarily repaired the split hose and filled the rad with water. Guided by his tow truck we cautiously limped to a service centre 10 miles back in Gatlinburg.

At noon, we again commenced our journey, our wallets lighter by only a surprisingly low amount of $46 for the radiator hose repairs and additional antifreeze. Unknown to us these setbacks were only the beginning that day.

Three hours later we decided to end this slow day of creeping through the mountains and stop for the night. Guess what – nine miles from our selected campground – 'bang!' – this time a tire blew, again not life-threatening but certainly more than we needed.

John unhooked the car a second time that day and he stayed with the coach while I drove five miles to call our ERS. Once again, our understanding road service personnel sent a tire repair truck to our rescue. In 45 minutes we were again ready to continue our journey. However, events didn't end there – while I was calling the ERS, I misplaced the duplicate car keys. Now with the new tire in place, we spent the next half-hour searching for my keys. They were on the ground by the pay phone, exactly where I dropped them.

Our chosen campground, four miles away which had received high rating in the directory that we were using was actually little more than a parking place. Not surprising it felt like a five star resort after this horrendous day.

Thankfully we only suffered hours of irritating delays and the monetary cost was, fortunately, rather inexpensive. However, that's not always the case and, although days like this are rare, it's comforting to know that we have our emergency road service to rely on.

ERS plans do work. During most years of RVing, we averaged one to two calls per year on either the car or the coach. On the way to Nova Scotia one year we blew the transmission on our four-year-old unit. On our return both manifolds also had to be replaced. Thankfully these two repairs were covered under warranty but it was the understanding ERS personnel and tow-truck driver that made our transmission experience memorable. During that breakdown the ERS driver made all arrangements for us to spend the night at the GM dealer. He even stopped by several times over the next few days to be sure we had no problem. When our manifold gaskets developed a major leak, we limped into the garage on our own. That GM dealer, too, also looked after us in grand style. Again, thankfully the manufacturer paid for that repair too!

Out-of-pocket costs of only one roadside breakdown will far exceed the price of any road service plan; so even if you have to skimp on other things when planning your travel budget, do not travel without this coverage. The annual fee for these valuable ERS policies ranges between $100.00 and $150.00.

But, before you buy, make sure the price of your ERS plan includes 'no-cost assistance with unlimited towing'. 'No-cost' means that you do not pay the towing fee up front; you simply sign the invoice and drive away. A non-insured tow for an RV is extremely expensive – many hundreds of dollars, in fact. Without an ERS, a towing bill can quickly deplete your cash reserves.

Since your RV is much larger than a family car, make sure that the ERS you contract can provide expert RV towing service. An emergency road service plan that cannot accommodate the special handling of an RV is a waste of money.

Your plan should also provide coverage for emergency gas/fuel (usually about five gallons free – with diesel they will also help re-prime your vehicle), lock-out service, tire changes and jump-starts and the services should be available no matter where you are in Canada or the U.S. Some companies offer 24/7 voice tech support to help RVers deal with problems when you just need to talk to a tech, and a few even reimburse costs for emergency road service in Mexico. Members are responsible for labour charges plus required parts provided by maintenance personnel.

Many plans also include the tow or towed vehicles and other family cars. There should be no restrictions on the number of service calls that you're entitled to – nor should there be a maximum distance an RV can be towed to a repair facility.

Before you go searching for an emergency road service, take a look at what your RV club has to offer. Before purchasing, talk to other RVers and ask what company they would recommend and carefully read advertisements in RV magazines. You'll be amazed at the number of services offered.

Out Of Country Medical
(and dental care in Mexico*)*

*A walk on the ocean floor at low tide is an awesome experience.
Health conscious RVers can include outstanding places in their itinerary
like this stop at Hopewell Rocks, New Brunswick.*

*Within six hours the tide rises approximately 48 feet;
it is an unbelievable transformation.*

RVers visiting a country other than their own should make sure that they have a policy to cover medical emergencies when away from home (you should also have one to cover medical situations at home, too). If you need hospital care or the services of a doctor, without insurance you will be expected to pay up-front. This could be a very expensive proposition. Although in some cases if you get sick in Canada or in Mexico, costs are much less than they may be in the U.S.A. However, lower or not, without insurance you still must pay up-front in any country if you get sick. Required payment will either be by cash or by credit card, even if it rises into the thousands. Be sure you have coverage everywhere you travel.

There are a number of medical insurance programs and policies available to cover those who move from place to place within the U.S.A., check your senior's newspapers and local phone book to begin shopping around for a policy that is affordable.

Canadians heading south should carry enough meds – in their original container – to last their stay.

Many travellers enter another country to buy drugs at a cost less than they would pay at home. At the time this was written, there was a controversy raging about American residents buying lower-priced Canadian prescription drugs (usually through online services). Keep apprised on the legal situations.

However, it should be noted that at the end of 2003, those visiting Canada can purchase prescription drugs if they have a prescription from their own doctor, and if the script was re-written by a Canadian doctor. Ask the pharmacist of major drug stores if they have the name of a local doctor who will rewrite your original script for a nominal fee.

In Mexico, many prescription drugs are available over the counter at a very low cost. Many Americans and Canadians without a drug plan flock to the towns along the Mexican border to purchase both prescription and other medications.

By the way numerous RVers also visit the Mexican border towns to receive all facets of excellent dental work. Costs are very low, waiting time is limited and service is superior. There are also numerous doctors at these border towns offering a long list of services from regular medical procedures to facelifts to tummy tucks and more.

Special Information For Canadians

As Canadians, there are only a few restrictions governing our provincial or territorial health coverage for residents who are travelling. One of the most important is that we need to maintain a permanent residence in our home province or territory.

Each province and territory has individual insurance plans, all with different requirements and regulations. The general rule of thumb is that residents are required to be present in their home province or territory for four to six months per year depending on the province (but 182 -183 days is the general rule). Respect this valuable coverage and treat it as a privilege (not a right) granted to provincial residents.

Every resident can apply for a 'one to two-year' extension periodically from once in a lifetime to time-out every few years; it may or may not be granted depending on the province/territories – apply to your provincial health ministry for this extension. Occasionally, provinces/territories require written notification for absences longer than three months. This includes Snowbirds, even if the allowed absent length of time may be 183 days. Regulations frequently change, be informed, call your provincial health office for details (look in the blue pages in your local telephone book for the number).

Some RVers try to reap the benefits of Canada's generous medical health coverage while working legally in the U.S. (with a green card). Whether you're actually drawing a salary south of the border or not, having a green card in your name could cast some doubt on your residency and your provincial medical coverage. It is not possible to take the best out of both countries – you must decide which country you call home.

> **Before you cross the border for any reason be aware of rules and regulations that pertain to you. Never leave home for travels in another country without insurance coverage – even for a one-day shopping trip.**

Being well-informed and understanding regulations that concern you is your responsibility. Interpret as to how they apply to you. Don't accept word-of-mouth and rumours as fact. If you hear information that is contrary to what you already know; do your research and contact the ministries involved.

Out Of Province Coverage

Each province and territory has its own cap on how much will he paid for medical treatment when you are away from your home base visiting another province. Because of a reciprocal agreement set-up by the federal government, each province or territory honours all health cards but not all procedures; hospital coverages or the amount charged at a doctor's office might be covered. For instance some provinces will NOT cover air ambulance to return you, your vehicle or your remains home. If one province pays $100.00 for a procedure and the one you are visiting charges $250.00 you may be responsible for the difference.

Out of province medical coverage is only pennies a day – it may be an investment worth looking at.

Topping-up with extended coverage can be added to retirement coverage or for a limited number of days for the coverage available on some credit cards (i.e. a Gold card usually offers coverage), but be certain your insurance company understands what you want to do and that they do sell top-up insurance. Without this agreement if you have 40 days 'freebie' retirement insurance and you buy medical coverage to add to this policy but you have a heart attack on the 38th day, it is possible your follow-up insurance may not be effective because you then have pre-existing conditions (the heart attack happened before the top-up coverage kicked in).

Note: At the time this was written (2003), Canadian federal government employees and retirees (including military) can purchase an upgrade to their annual policy of 40-days-per-trip covering out of province/out of country medical from the customary $100,000.00 to $5,000,000.00 (million) per year for a small fee. This can also be 'topped up' by many insurance brokers. Contact your federal insurer for info.

General Medical 'Must-Know' For All RVers

Even if you're just planning to be gone for a day to do some shopping, if anything happens and you require medical attention in a country (or province) other than your own, it is your responsibility to pay expenses. Without supplementary coverage these costs can be excessive – they are much higher in the U.S.A. than in Canada, but any amount in any country can throw a wrench into your travel budget

Always ask about how pre-existing conditions affect your policy. Sometimes it can raise the cost of your coverage. Medications may have to be stable for six months (no change up or down) as well or that situation will not be covered on your supplementary insurance policy. This might not be a problem if it is coverage for a sprained ankle but it can be a big dilemma if there is a change in blood pressure medication. It could be necessary to acquire an additional and more costly policy to cover that medical problem.

Some RVers purchase policies for the exact number of days they plan to be in another country while others choose an annual policy with multi-trip options for 30, 90, or even 180 days. Most seniors' publications have informative write-ups on supplementary insurance coverage – do your research thoroughly before you buy.

In some cases, you must pay the procedure amount directly to the attending physician and send the paid receipt to provincial health service. After the primary reimbursement you then send it to the insurance provider to recoup the balance.

Note: If you need to submit a medical bill for reimbursement, please do so immediately, as there may be time limits.

When buying supplementary insurance, no matter what country you are from, look for policies that cover comprehensive hospital care; out-patient and emergency room services; special duty nursing; prescription drugs in the hospital, and diagnostic services (X-ray, blood work, blood pressure, etc.). You should also find out if your insurance covers ambulance service, including air ambulance; transportation of family to bedside; return of remains; plus whatever else you think is necessary.

Always read the fine print in any insurance policy and ask questions. In some cases, the credit card company, too, will only allow top-up insurance if you purchase it from a specified insurance company.

Air Ambulance Service

Air ambulance service[34] is extremely necessary and it should be part of your supplementary medical plan. If your policy doesn't include this service, purchasing a separate policy is a wise move. Be sure your policy includes repatriation to your home, not just to a better hospital. An emergency flight home can cost many thousands of dollars, depending on how far you are from home when disaster strikes. Because emergency medical flights usually require qualified medical assistance; without insurance, the costs to you are horrendous.

For example: In 1987, when my visually impaired sister fell off a wall in Mexico, the emergency medical flight from Puerto Vallarta to Canada was going to cost $17,000 U.S. Thankfully, she didn't have to use it after all. From various points in the U.S., it ran from $10,000, upwards.

Our previous out of country medical that was in force until John turned age 65 did not include air ambulance service so we purchased a MASA (Medical Air Services Association) policy which included air services back to Toronto (our home base) plus air transportation of organs (for both

---

34 MASA (Medical Air Services Association): *1-800-643-9023*
  Sky Med – *1-800-475-9633*

recipients and those donating them), vehicle return, family and medical escorts, plus much more. It was reassuring to know that, if we needed medical treatment, we could recuperate at home near family and friends.

RV Vehicle Insurance

Information provided by Wayfarer RV Insurance 1-800-461-0318
www.wayfarerrvinsurance.com

Motorhome insurance is basically a motorized vehicle insurance policy. All states, 10 provinces and the two territories in Canada have mandatory vehicle insurance limits and coverages vary according to the different jurisdictions. The mandatory portion of the policy relates to the liability coverage (i.e. personal injury and property damage) and may also include accident benefits, income replacement for the insured person and/or occupants of the vehicle.

Liability is the most important part of the policy. It protects the insured against claims made by other parties that incur injury or property damage. It is recommended that you purchase as high a limit of coverage that is available and as much as you can afford.

Physical damage coverage (i.e. collision, or comprehensive, fire and theft, etc.) are optional coverages and the premiums are usually based on the value of the motorhome.

Most insurance companies will offer coverage for motorhomes, however, there are a few insurers that specialize in RV insurance and offer the enhanced coverages that RVers require.

Guaranteed replacement coverage is available on new motorhomes for original owners; insurance is for the full purchase price including all taxes. In the event of a total loss the insurer will replace the RV with a new current model year of like kind and quality – this is offered usually for a 3 to 7 year period depending on the state or province – an excellent coverage.

Contents coverage is a special added coverage that insures contents usual to the motorhome (i.e. bedding, tools, foods, etc.).

Emergency Vacation Expense: If the RV is rendered unusable due to a claim, expenses for accommodations, meals and/or transportation home are covered up to a specified limit.

Low Deductible: Many companies that offer insurance on motorhomes will insist on high deductibles such as $1,000.00 or even a percentage of the value of the RV. Specialty companies dealing with RVs usually offer low deductibles.

*This bright purple vintage trailer combo was
featured in a Canada Day parade in Elmira, Ontario.*

Trailers And 5th Wheels: This class of RV can be a bit more complex when discussing insurance. You need to make sure whether or not the liability for towing is automatically included with the tow vehicle insurance. This is very important and must be discussed with your agent or broker.

Where permissible some companies that specialize in RV insurance offer a physical damage policy that covers 'all risks' including collision, fire, theft, wind and hail, etc. This is similar to a home property policy. Additional coverages are available for contents and emergency vacation expense.

Replacement coverage or no depreciation policies are also available and some companies will offer this type of policy for 10 or 15 years.

> **Don't take a chance that you have the coverage you need –
> take the time to review your requirements with an RV
> insurance specialist.**

Fulltimer's Policy: An increased number of RVers are now pulling up stakes and choosing to live fulltime 'on the road' in their RV.

Coverage for their personal contents and personal liability were usually extended from the homeowner's policy, but with the home gone you now need a fulltimer's policy. Some insurers will also offer additional coverage for items such as jewellery, computers or sports equipment.

Emergency Nest Egg And Contingency Fund

Maintenance on all vehicles (read this as RVs too) is ongoing. Yes, new RVs are under warranty but wise RVers also set up a **contingency fund** when they first purchase their unit. A contingency fund is when you make regular monthly contributions to a separate bank account every month. Depending on the purchase price of your RV this can be from $100.00 to $500.00 per month. This way when you want to add new amenities (including laptops, cell phones, digital cameras and more) or mechanical repairs need attention, or tires or batteries need upgrading or appliances break down or the RV needs a general 'lift', the cash is readily available.

In addition to this fund every RVer should have an **emergency nest egg**. Any vehicle breakdown quickly consumes ready cash but, with good pre-trip financial planning, it's easy to be prepared for any costly problems that may arise.

No one plans to use their emergency nest egg fund but it's nice to know it's there if you need it. During our first year of extensive travel, a major mechanical repair made it necessary for us to dig very deep into our emergency money. We went into the garage for a tune-up and ended up paying $3,500 U.S. for new brakes, a broken spring, new tires plus many extras before we left. Without our nest egg our RV explorations would have come to an abrupt end.

The incident that started with our broken rad hose several years earlier (see *ERS* chapter) was only the beginning of what turned into a long and very expensive winter. We contended with approximately five months of 'if it could go wrong – it did'. During that unforgettable period, our maintenance expenses rose to over $9,000. Believe me; we were very thankful that we had our emergency nest egg in place. By the way, don't panic – a period of problems such as ours that winter only happens occasionally. We previously enjoyed five years of mainly trouble-free RVing, nevertheless, if you are not prepared, traumatic events can destroy all your plans.

Conscientious RV maintenance records keep you up-to-date on when your engine, tires, brakes, appliances (and everything else) need preventive maintenance. And if, like our so-called tune-up, you find that you need extensive maintenance work or replacement of parts, an emergency fund becomes your most cherished friend. Mechanical set-backs happen to everyone but, with available funds close at hand, they are simply distressing, not disastrous.

If possible, set up your nest egg before you're ready to take to the road. This can be an interest bearing bank account or obtaining a credit card with a high limit. Ask your bank; some offer a low-interest credit card or a line of credit that you only use for emergencies. If you choose the credit card, keep the balance at zero and only use it for unexpected RV repairs and maintenance.

A well-invested nest egg continues to grow until you need it (hopefully never!). Several financial institutions (especially trust companies) offer many benefits if you deposit over $5,000 in their investment package. When your balance drops below $5,000, all benefits stop. Wise RVers make a concentrated effort to keep their emergency fund accessible.

Shop around to find a banking facility with group benefits that suits you. Developing a nest egg is not mandatory but it is something you should really consider during your planning stage. Emergencies do happen – when they're least expected.

TOWING

RVers find a tow or towed vehicle necessary to get around.

 ## *Weighing Your RV*

The new ultra-modern RVs have a number of neat places to pack those items you know you simply can't live without. Motorhomes come with basements, fifth wheels have large storage compartments under the overhang and most cubicles are easily accessible with the help of slide-out drawers. Some of the larger RVs even have all-in-one washer/dryer units and freezers stashed in the under-floor compartments. Most have storage under the beds plus many come with extra slide-out rooms. There are even units featuring built-in 'garages'. Every addition contributes to the overall weight.

If your RV isn't equipped with extra places to put additional gear, there are numerous add-on storage cubicles available from RV supply stores. Pods are designed to attach on to the roof of trailers and motorhomes or cling on to the back end of an RV – along with chairs and bikes.

There's only one problem to having all this extra storage – overloaded RVs. Overloading your RV is very dangerous. Too much weight or an improperly balance load decreases handling capabilities and braking efficiency. An overloaded condition can cause cracks in the sidewalls of your tires or resulting in uneven treads. The extra weight also takes its toll on brake shoes/pads, the suspension system and the frame.

When the engine and transmission (in both your RV and towing vehicle) works harder to carry an overloaded RV, excessive heat is generated. Engine and transmission failure could result – been there done that.

Keeping within the weight limits of today's lighter and fuel-efficient RVs is extremely important. RVers who follow a few simple guidelines within load limits will discover that their RV remains in top shape for a longer period of time, providing more reliable service.

To ensure that your RV is carrying a proper load, look at the plate attached to your unit for the **Gross Vehicle Weight Rating (GVWR)** and the **Gross Axle Weight Rating (GAWR)** of the chassis. The GVWR is what your RV can safely carry with the chassis it is sitting on and the Gross Axle Weight Rating GAWR tells you the amount of weight-carrying capacity each axle can sustain. Most labels also give you the **Carrying Capacity (CC)** weight allowance.

There is a company called 'Aweigh We Go'[35] that was formed simply to make it easy for RVers to be weighed – they have now joined the RV Safety network. This knowledgeable team is equipped with four DOT (Department of Transport) scales and they are present at many RV rallies to weigh the units either coming or going – cost is minimal. Those who do not have the opportunity to be weighed using these individual scales at rallies and other RV events should look for a scrap yard, RV dealership or a feed mill with a truck scale. Some truck stops also provide weigh scales but on some scales it is difficult to weigh each axle as outlined below. Government operated truck weigh scales (located on the highway) are another option but, one word of caution, if the scale is open and your RV is overweight you may have to off-load before leaving the weigh scale. Although after hours when these scales are closed to trucks some of the highway stations will still give a reading as to the weight of each axle even when staff is not there. Public scales are still your best alternative.

To Obtain An Accurate Weight

Make sure that the sides of the scale are flat. First weigh the entire coach (record the reading).

For motorhome weighing: Locate the centre of gravity and mark it with tape. Move the front of motorhome off the scale and re-weigh the back end of the unit. Subtract the rear weight from the total weight to get your front axle weight ratio.

To weigh each tire individually, move your RV 50 percent to the right of the scale and to the front of the centre of gravity and record the weight. Back up your RV so that the centre of gravity is off the scale and re-weigh the unit. Repeat this procedure for the left side. Compare the weights to those listed in the manufacturer's specifications to ensure that you are not overloaded.

For trailer weighing (compliments of www.rverscorner.com): Drive both the fully loaded tow vehicle (include passengers) and trailer onto the scales. If possible record the weight reading as each axle or axle group comes on to the scale.

1. The first reading will be the load on the tow vehicle front axle.
2. The second reading is the total tow vehicle weight including the trailer tongue weight.
3. Subtract the first reading from the second – this gives you the loading on the tow vehicle rear axle.

---

35 *Contact* Aweigh We Go *at* www.rvsafety.com *1-321-453-7673 to enquire if you will be attending one of the rallies where they are weighing coaches.*

4. Drive both the tow vehicle and the trailer onto the scales. This reading is the total combined towing weight.
5. Subtract the second scale reading from this combined weight – this is the weight carried by the trailer axles.

If you are overweight, remove items from inside the RV. If one side of your RV weighs considerably more than the other, redistribute contents more evenly for safer highway travel, improved braking and overall vehicle control.

Always weigh your RV packed the way you will be driving it – this includes water, fuel and propane tanks filled to the usual capacity and all items on board, including passengers. An overloaded unit will cost you plenty in repairs plus reduced handling and performance. To protect your unit, try to keep within manufacturer's specifications. These specs are posted near an entrance of your RV.

 ## *Car In Tow*

To tow a car behind your motorhome, be aware that the brakes on your coach are only designed to stop the **Gross Vehicle Weight Rating (GVWR)** set by the motorhome manufacturer plus a built-in margin of 1000 –1500 lbs. The **Gross Combination Weight Rating (GCWR)** is the maximum combined weight determined by the chassis manufacturer (the chassis is the base your motorhome is built on). The GCWR includes the real weight of the motorhome plus the weight of your towed vehicle or dolly. The towed weight allowed is the difference between the manufacturer's chassis weight rating (GVWR) and the combination weight (GCWR). The gross combination weight is the amount that the motorhome can safely handle. Never exceed the GCWR – you will add stress to the chassis plus create dangerous driving and handling conditions.

Once you have figured out how much weight your motorhome can tow, you will have to decide how to tow your car. That depends a lot on what kind of car you have. Most manual shift transmissions can be towed four-wheels down, plus several cars with automatic transmissions can also be towed without sustaining damage to the transmission. However, be sure the manufacturer rates your new car for four-wheels down towing to avoid warranty problems.

Flat towing is the most convenient way to go.

Four-Wheels Down

Sometimes called 'flat towing', towing this way means that all four wheels of the car are on the ground. To use this method a 'Y'-shaped tow bar must be attached to your car via a baseplate. Usually a professional service mechanic installs the base plate to the car chassis. The receptacles at the wide end of the 'Y' are located near the bumper – the coupler may or may not protrude outwards. Some of the attachments on newer models of base plates are not visible when the hitch is removed. The more advanced tow bars remain on the motorhome when you disconnect. Rather than the ball style connection, these tow bars have a square end that fits snug into the motorhome receptacle so there is less chance of the hitch disconnecting.

If you have a folding, self-aligning tow bar, connect the hitch, attach the safety chains and electrical connections then drive your motorhome a few feet forward and from side-to-side to lock the tow bar arms in place.

Failure to do this simple procedure could result in damage to both your car and tow bar system. You could also even lose your car. Check your lights to be sure they are working.

> **Backing up your motorhome with your towed vehicle attached using a tow bar is dangerous and should not be done.**

Several passenger vehicles with automatic transmissions have been rated for four-wheels down towing. Towing mileage no longer accumulates on late model vehicles either because one-to-three fuses are pulled as part of the hook-up procedure. An upgraded list of towable cars is featured each spring in several RV magazines including *Motorhome* and *Family Motor Coaching* (FMCA); these publications can be found on bookstore shelves or received by subscription.

Note: Vehicles can be rated differently for the Canadian and U.S. markets. In some cases, a vehicle built for the U.S. market with a four-wheels down towing rating may not apply to the same vehicle built for the Canadian market.

If you tow a vehicle not rated for towing, you are responsible for all mechanical problems. Another vehicle option to look into are those with four-wheel drive. If the vehicle has a built-in manual-lever transfer case, it may be able to be towed four-wheels down when shifted into neutral. If your vehicle has electronic shift-on-the-fly, it is programmed differently and cannot be towed four-wheels down.

Note: Remco Towing is the expert in the field of modification – they offer a variety of available options. Upgrades such as lube pumps, axle locks and drive shaft couplings can transform most automatic cars into flat towable vehicles. Remco also promote breaking devices. [36]

Vehicle Braking

For peace-of-mind travel, the experts suggest all motorhome owners towing vehicles four-wheels down should install some kind of braking system on their towed car (toad). Adding these accessories is not yet law in most places but some states and provinces are in the process of trying to implement the use of braking devices. At the time of writing (2003), British Columbia is the only one that enforces supplementary brakes if the tow car is over 2000-kg or 4400 pounds.

In a panic stop, the motorhome brakes take much longer to stop the combination than the motorhome alone because the brakes are only designed to stop the weight of the RV, not both vehicles. Many units are available, using a variety of braking system designs and each contribute to a more efficient safe stop. Some of these systems are permanently installed; others are transferable from vehicle to vehicle.

Supplementary vehicle braking covers four basic systems including air, surge, hydraulic and vacuum models. A breakaway device that stops the vehicle if it becomes separated from the motorhome is standard on most of these devices – providing one more form of security. It is recommended that braking be applied to all four wheels.

The **air** system uses a source from the air compressor on the coach and it either pushes or pulls the vehicle pedal brake down. If your unit does not have air brakes, it is possible to add an air cylinder to the master cylinder of the towed vehicle to use this system. The **surge** works on the premise that the towed pushes the coach. This mechanical brake has no wiring except the warning light in the coach. Applying the brake of the lead vehicle prompts the towed to push the surge brake into the receiver of the hitch. Due to an intricate system of pulleys and cables, the harder the coach brakes are applied, the faster the surge brake stops the car. In the **hydraulic** system, a brake cylinder on the tow car taps into the vehicle brakes when the motorhome braking is applied; this causes the towed to surge forward. The **vacuum** assisted supplemental brake creates a vacuum from the master cylinder of the towed vehicle, or you can add a pump that supplies vacuum to this cylinder. The towed vehicle brake pedal acts as an assisted pedal.

Braking Regulations

As of 2003, there is only one province enforcing these braking devices and that is in British Columbia. In that province tow vehicles where the gross vehicle weight (GVW) is less than 4400 lbs (2000-kg) or less than 40% of the GVW of the motorhome, no supplemental braking is required. Several states have launched changes to their braking laws that will enforce the use of these supplementary braking devices – as yet there are none where the law enforces the use of a braking device.[36]

Reps who sell these devices use the premise that having one on your towed vehicle gives you peace-of-mind travel and if you get into a situation where you need a panic stop you will be very happy you have one. This choice is definitely up to you. Do your research, talk to many manufacturers of these devices and decide on your own if you want to add one. Then decide on the type best suited to your situation.

Tow Dolly

Using a tow dolly is another way to tow your car behind your motorhome. A tow dolly has two wheels joined by a bar with two short ramps for your car to sit on. Most have a built-in braking system. When the tow dolly is hooked up to your motorhome, you drive or back (rear-wheel drive) your car on to the ramps. One set of wheels is on the road and the other set is lifted up. Although the tow dolly can carry both manual and automatic cars, those with rear-wheel drive are usually not recommended for towing this way.

When using a rear-wheel drive, it's difficult to align your tow vehicle to the ramps when backing it on to the dolly. Also, when driving, the front wheels of your car will be constantly rotating backwards which could result in the front end wearing out too quickly and other damage.

Your car must be secured to the dolly with chains or other applicable strapping. It works well for short occasional trips when you want to take along a special vehicle. However, the connection set-up can become an unwelcome hassle before long.

---

36 Companies specializing in braking devices are listed under Towing and Safety section on the RV WebLink page of *www.rvliving.net*. State and provincial laws constantly change; so it is important to do your own research.

Tow dollies may solve one problem but if you tow using a dolly, you also must find a place to store it when you arrive at your destination campground, plus licence and insure it. Part of securing the car on the dolly will be done on your knees. As a result dollies are not the choice of seasoned RVers; however, they do have a purpose for transporting a special vehicle. Backing up your motorhome with a car on a tow dolly is difficult but not impossible.

Tow Trailers

These come covered and uncovered but they are still the least popular because they are so bulky and difficult to store. The advantage to these is the car is completely off the road; this may be a necessity for special or classic vehicles.

Tow-Lifts

A tow-lift literally lifts the front or rear end of a vehicle off the ground by a special lifting device. Using this system eliminates mileage accumulation and it doesn't matter if your towed car is equipped with an automatic or manual transmission. Unlike using tow bars and dollies, it is relatively easy to back up with this system.

Unfortunately, the tow lift is very expensive, places a heavy tongue weight on the motorhome hitch and hitching is rather elaborate and time-consuming. Tow lifts aren't transferable from one make of vehicle to another.

Safety Chains

Safety chains are a must for all types of towing! When connecting safety chains, always attach them criss-crossed underneath the hitch receptacle before securing them from the frame of the tow vehicle to the frame of the towed vehicle. Take my word for it; the ball does work loose.

While travelling south to our Mexican hideaway during our fifth year on the road, we ignored an occasional thud we kept hearing. Eventually John looked back and reacted with a shout. Our car was being towed with the nose nudging the curb-side rear bumper of our motorhome. Our tow ball had worked itself loose when we had executed some extremely sharp turns. Only one hook of the safety chain was all that kept our car connected to our motorhome.

When hitching the two vehicles together, we had not criss-crossed our safety chains beneath the hitch. Criss-crossing creates a cradle to support the hitch at the coupler end. Fortunately, for safety's sake and our pocketbook, the car never catapulted on to the tow bar when it hit the ground. We learn well from our mistakes, now for peace-of-mind towing we always connect our safety chains properly.

Precautions

Always check that your hitch is secure when it is first connected to be certain there are no weak spots. Several years ago one welded connection on our collapsible tow bar broke loose as we pulled out of the campground. That was the first time in a long time that I had not completed a final check by lifting on several areas of our hitch before I entered our motorhome. Make sure that the arms are extended and all is secure. We felt very fortunate that this break in the weld happened in the campground and NOT on the highway.

Brake And Hazard Lights, Turn Signals

Proper lighting on your tow vehicle is just as important as using tow chains. There are several ways to hook up lights from sticking them on with suction cups to wiring into a light fixture from each vehicle.

No matter what method you choose, you must equip your towed vehicle with brake and signal and hazard lights compatible to your motorhome lights. On our Honda in the early 90s, our electrician attached three-way lights (stop, turn and running lights similar to the suction cup variety) permanently to our back bumper. They were brighter and easier to connect than it would have been if he had directly wired into our car lights.

On our present car and our previous 'R Go 4' (our licence plate on our towed vehicle), the car lights that connected to Kastle #3 were never bright enough. Recently our RV dealer rewired our motorhome directly into the 12-volt starting battery. Finally we can be seen by everyone because our car lights shine as they should.

When connected, on and off controls are controlled by the lead vehicle. We use a coil styled electric cable that is more efficient than the straight cable we originally used. The coil prevents the cord from dragging on the ground but on the side of safety we still secure the cord to the hitch with a couple of bungees.

Tow-riffics

Tow-riffics are a one-of-a-kind special accessory that consists of four 18" wands with a circular illuminated head on one end – the other attaches to the vehicle. There are no wires attached. One wand attaches to each rear side of the motorhome and another on each rear car fender. When they are set-up for towing, the ones on the car drop down to a 90° perpendicular angle. The car wands intersect with the ones installed on the motorhome in the form of a 'cross'; this 'cross' shows-up in the side mirrors. If a tire is low or you have a hitch problem the 'cross' shifts in position alerting the driver to a possible problem. When you un-hook your towed, the wands are again raised to a perpendicular state.

We used these on our first two motorhomes for about five years. They provided great peace-of-mind, especially from the viewpoint of the co-pilot. I always knew what our tow car was doing. Our Luxor amenities included a back-up camera so we gave up our Tow-riffics when we changed coaches. We now keep track of the car through our camera lens.[37]

Tire Monitor

A tire monitor is available that informs the motorhome operator if the air pressure in the tires of the tow vehicle changes. If something happens to one of the towed tires the driver may not be aware of the situation without this indicator. Ask your RV dealer for information about this product.

Back-up Camera

Some more expensive motorhomes are equipped with a back-up camera (they are also available as aftermarket add-on accessories as well). Our first camera was part of the standard options on our Luxor. These cameras make it so easy to see what is behind your unit as well as beside you. Some RVers only turn this accessory on when they are backing up. John and I prefer to always drive with ours turned on. This practice is also recommended by towing experts. The camera allows the driver to be aware of the location of other vehicles beside and behind us when we are on the highways. It is one of our most valuable accessories and although we didn't have one for the first 14 years we hope we never have to be without this helpful amenity.

---

37 *Contact* Tow-riffics *at* www.tow-riffic.com *1-800-465-8694.*

Points To Remember

♦ Repeat tip – Always double check that the electric cord connecting the lights to the towed vehicle is plugged securely into the sockets. Secure it in place with a bungee. You do not want it to come apart and then drive over it.

♦ Because most vehicles being towed four-wheels down require a key in the ignition, make sure that you always carry an extra set of keys for the towed vehicle. It's a real pain to have to break into your own car (or call your ERS) before you can disconnect. Trust me I've been there.

♦ If stopping for the night, without unhitching your car, it is a good idea to take the keys out of the car's ignition for security sake. Depending on your ignition set-up, having the key turned on for prolonged periods could drain your battery. This may not be the case if you remove fuses as part of the towing set-up: but why take a chance?

♦ Before unhooking a towed vehicle always activate the emergency brakes, especially if you're parked on an incline.

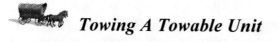

Towing A Towable Unit

***RVers flock to beachfront utopias like this one on Florida's
panhandle. Tow vehicle are convenient
for exploring the surroundings.***

Since the original purchase price of a towable RV is usually lower than
that of a motorized unit, towables are quite appealing to many buyers.
Owners never have to worry about costly transmission and engine repairs.
Towables enjoy a low rate of depreciation (excellent for trade-in value) and,
because a tow vehicle is required to transport the unit from point A to point
B, after unhitching a separate run-around vehicle is always on hand.

Even though the lower price of a towable seems to fit your pocketbook,
before choosing a towable, make sure that your present family car can
properly tow your RV. If the RV you fall in love with weighs 4,000 pounds
and your existing family car can pull up to a maximum of 2,000 pounds, you
will have the additional purchase expense of a new vehicle. (If you buy a
fifth wheel and don't already have a heavy-duty pickup truck to install a
fifth wheel hitch onto, then you will definitely have to buy a new vehicle.)

For optimum safety and performance, towables should only be hitched
to tow vehicles that have been built and rated by the manufacturer for that
purpose. The amount allowed by the manufacturer, according to frame
construction, engine power and transmission strength, is known as the
towing capacity.

Along with the towing capacity, another point to consider when determining if your tow vehicle can handle the job of towing an RV is the **axle ratio**. It determines the **torque** (or pulling power) of a tow vehicle. This designation is always shown as a ratio (i.e. 4.00:1 means that the pinion gear or torque is rotating four times for every one revolution of the ring gear or differential which controls the rotation of the vehicle's wheels). Your tow vehicle should have a low axle ratio because, the lower the axle ratio, the better the acceleration capability and pulling power of the car. What is confusing about axle ratios is that the lower the ratio, the higher the number (2.50:1 is a higher axle ratio than 4.00:1).

When choosing a tow vehicle, you also have to keep in mind the **Gross Vehicle Weight Rating** (maximum amount that can be carried by the chassis of the car) and the **Gross Combination Weight Rating** (maximum combined loaded weight of both car and trailer).

To determine if your car can tow your trailer, add the **Gross Trailer Weight** (total weight of your trailer when fully loaded) and the **Tongue Weight** (the downward force of the hitch ball). The Tongue Weight is about 10 but no more than 15 percent of the Gross Vehicle Weight Rating. These two, added together, should not exceed the Gross Combination Weight Rating of your tow car.

Other factors that contribute to easier towing are having both your tow vehicle and trailer level and evenly distributing the hitch weight. To see if your hitch weight is evenly distributed you can perform this simple exercise:

Park your car and trailer in a straight line. Make sure the parking area is smooth and flat. Unhitch the car and trailer. Don't move the car and make sure that there isn't any weight of the trailer touching the car. Measure your car from the ground to a predetermined spot on each side of the front bumper and to the middle of the back bumper. Mark all three spots and note the measurements on a piece of paper.

Now hitch up your car and trailer. When you've done that, re-measure the three spots on your car. Your car will be lower and that's okay. What is important is that your car should be lower by the same amount at all three points. (For example: If the two points on the front bumper have gone down 1/2-inch, then the back bumper should also be lower by 1/2-inch.) If there is a difference then your weight isn't being evenly distributed and your towing performance will be sluggish. To correct this problem, adjust your torsion bars until all spots are equal.

Trailer Hitches

Contrary to popular opinion – and, wouldn't it be nice if we could? – you can't use just one hitch for any towing situation. Hitches are rated by class, and each class is rated by the amount of weight it will pull. Before you buy a hitch for your RV, make sure that you've selected the right one for the **Gross Trailer Weight AND Tongue Weight**. Hitches are also divided into two categories – <u>weight carrying</u> and <u>weight distributing</u>. A weight-distributing hitch is normally used for heavier trailers with a high tongue weight.

Hitches come in four classes: Class I, up to 2,000 pounds; Class II, from 2,000 to 3,500 pounds; Class III, 3,500 to 5,000 pounds and, for heavier trailers, a Class IV that handles from 5,000 to 10,000 pounds. You will also want to install some kind of sway control device. These come in several models – see your dealer for the correct one for your unit.

If you have carefully chosen your tow vehicle to match your trailer (or vice versa) and followed all towing instructions from your dealer, then towing a trailer can be a very pleasant way to enjoy the RV lifestyle.

Hitches for fifth wheels have a different design than those used for travel trailers. Fifth wheel hitches are fitted onto the bed of a pickup truck and, as with travel trailers, there are different designs for the size of the pickup's bed. Some of these designs feature side-pivots (for easier hitching and unhitching).

Fifth wheel hitches are mounted in the bed of the pickup truck. The hitch weight is directly over or slightly ahead of the rear axle centre line. With the fifth wheel design, more of the weight of the trailer is carried by the tow vehicle. Although it used to be that fifth wheel hitches weren't recommended for short bed trucks (this is because a fifth wheel hitch needs to be mounted two to four inches ahead of the axle which is hard to do with a short bed), a sliding hitch is available for short bed pickup trucks so that when manoeuvring in tight spaces the hitch may be slid rearward to allow for more clearance between the trailer front and the truck cab (for tighter turning ability). The hitch should always be placed back in the regular towing position for road travel. Talk to your RV dealer to find the hitch that is suitable for your truck and fifth wheel trailer.

HEALTH AND SAFETY

*RV travel takes you to serene locations. We left our footprints
in the sand at Lo De Marcos, Nayarit, Mexico.*

 *Security Tips*

Whether you use your RV on occasion or to travel extensively, finding that your RV has been vandalized by a break-in destroys carefree travel memories in a hurry. It also adds unwanted and unpleasant thoughts to future vacations.

During rallies, I've attended several entertaining and informative security seminars presented by the Hillsborough County sheriff's office in Tampa, Florida.

We are living in a world of security alarms. However, if you choose not to install one of these sophisticated accessories, below are a few highlights from various pamphlets that were distributed at the seminars. They just may reduce the risk of a break-in, and help protect your home and your RV. I've added several more noteworthy points to emphasize what we learned from RVers we met over the years.

On Vacation

Never discuss your proposed trips in public and don't give information about your vacation to the newspapers, etc. It's safer and more interesting to provide the colourful details on your return.

Depending on the community you live in it may be wise to inform the local police that you are leaving. Provide them with a name of a neighbour or relative to contact in case of an emergency. If you belong to a neighbourhood watch, make sure other members know when and for how long you're going to be away.

Ask the post office to hold your mail and place a stop order on your newspaper subscription. Arrange with a neighbour to pick up any pamphlets and flyers left at your doorway.

Have a reliable person cut and water the grass in the summer or during the winter, shovel your driveway and sidewalk. Ask them to walk up to your door and back to leave footprints in the snow. It's important that your home looks lived in.

Don't leave valuables in the house. Always put them in a safety deposit box; extra cash belongs in your bank account.

Any attractive objects that can be observed from the front window should be moved out of sight. Keep a list of serial and model numbers of each appliance in a safe place. Etch some form of ID (such as the last digits of your Social Insurance number but never your name or address) on to each item. Some police stations even loan electronic markers for etching. (Note: An electric etcher is not expensive and can be picked up at most hardware stores.)

Repair any broken windowpanes, plus add locks to doors and windows. Dead bolts are the only effective locks, so update if necessary. Replacing windows on doors with break-resistant glass also deters burglars from gaining access.

Put 'toys' such as bicycles, lawn furniture, skis or sleighs out of sight. Left in view (even when locked), these items make easy targets for thieves looking for quick money. This is a good idea even when you're not on vacation.

Hire a house sitter or ask a neighbour to regularly visit your home. Give them your approximate itinerary, your vehicle description, licence number plus a phone number of someone to call in an emergency.

> **In case of a break-in, the neighbour or house sitter should know how to reach you and your insurance agent. Your contact person should also give this information to the investigating police officer when they report a suspected burglary or emergency.**

A continuously ringing phone is a tip off that there's no one home. If you subscribe to a call forwarding service from your phone company, all calls are directed to a number where someone will answer them.

Note: Adding a voice message to your phone also works well – change your message occasionally to make it appear that you are at home. This is also a great way to stay in touch when you are on the move. Call in and pick up your messages once a day.

Use electrical timers to turn both the inside and outside lights off and on. Have the person checking your house rearrange the time controls to prevent a set 'time' pattern from developing.

Unplug all electrical appliances, such as radios, TVs, irons, washers/dryers, etc., to lessen the chance of damage during electrical storms. If the pilot light on a gas appliance must stay ignited, be sure it's in good working order.

Turn off the water at the source to prevent disasters if lines break in the summer or freeze in the winter. (To reduce the risk of pipes freezing in the winter, leave the heat turned on at a very low setting.)

Ask a neighbour to put one of their garbage cans in your driveway on collection day. Lock the garage and, if it's accessible from the house, secure the door(s) from the inside. Adding a deadbolt to all entrances offers one more form of protection.

Our local police recommend you leave the window shades in normal day-time position and arrange all main floor drapes, shades and curtains so neighbours and police can see what's going on in and around your house. Closed drapes (if it is a change from your normal) advertise an empty house.

> **Do a security walk around before leaving your home and ensure all doors and windows are secure.**

Be sure the vehicle left in your driveway is locked. If you're taking the car, ask a neighbour to park one of their cars in your driveway to make your house appear lived in.

People looking after your house should look for more than vandalism. Not all problems occur from intruders or outside sources. Before we began RVing, during a freak weather system one January, a horrendous rainstorm preceded freezing temperatures followed by a heavy snowfall. A prolonged thaw in February melted the ice under the snow and the newly developed 'lake' worked its way through a roof joint into our fireplace and furnace area. We woke up at 5:00 a.m. to a waterfall flooding two of the four floors in our home. Our immediate solution was to remove the water from the roof as soon as possible. If our home had been unattended for several days, I'd hate to think of the damage we would have come home to.

Installing a security alarm monitored by the police or security agency deters most burglars but it may not be the cheapest way to go. Costs vary according to how elaborate the system. Some programs are basic but others include motion sensors or closed-circuit TV. Installing an alarm may or may not reduce your insurance premium.

For more hints, look at the travel sections of the newspaper (especially senior's newspapers) for articles on pre-travel security preparation. Senior's newspapers are also available from most banks and convenience stores.

Security information is available from a number of sources. For instance, the Toronto-based Canadian office of Florida tourism offers these suggestions:

♦ Don't carry excessive cash – use traveller's cheques or ATMs; leave jewellery at home;

♦ Don't lock valuables in your vehicle. If you're travelling in a strange city and not sure where you're heading, go to a business place such as a restaurant or hotel and ask staff for directions;

♦ Park as close to your destination as possible on well-lit streets;

♦ Drive with your car doors locked, even in the daytime. Always fill your gas tank when it reads half full and have a mechanic check the car before starting your trip.

General Safety

If you have a mechanical problem on the highway, authorities suggest you put your hood up and wait inside the locked vehicle for police to come by. Do not open the window other than a crack for anyone. If someone stops to assist, give them a note and ask them to phone the police or better yet, your emergency road service (ERS), for help.

> **The International 'Call for Help' in any country is to honk your horn three times in quick succession, take a break, and honk three more times followed by another break. Continue till help arrives. Turn on headlights and flashing lights.**
> **Even if you have never heard of this signal most people will come to see what the problem is.**

Officials also warn about the importance of being cautious when using Channel 9 on your CB when problems occur. Some police (in states and provinces) no longer monitor this channel. Although REACT volunteers (Ham radio operators) do listen for CB help calls and contact authorities in emergencies, be careful, not-so-nice people also monitor CB conversations in search for victims. A cell phone, on the other hand, allows you the freedom and convenience to call your ERS service (if your phone is not in dead air).

Vehicle drivers should be wary of where to take a break. One sheriff's seminar I attended suggested to always carry a small amount of cash ($10 to $20) into public rest rooms; especially those at Interstate rest areas during quiet hours. Vagrants may strongly insist on a 'donation' even if you don't feel that generous.

The law enforcers also suggest that you carry just enough cash to pay for gas or restaurant meals. Avoid waving around a wallet stuffed with cash anywhere others can see you.

If you must carry excess cash on the road, wear a money belt. A fanny pack, located in front, allows more freedom than a purse. We each only carry one credit card in our wallets, excess cash and/or cards are stowed in a secure place. That way, if a purse or wallet disappears, we are temporarily inconvenienced, not incapacitated and our trip can continue.

There are several credit card control services available although these companies do charge a fee. We don't need them because it is so easy to cancel one card. John and I keep a list of credit cards in a secure area of our unit; our power of attorney also has one for safekeeping. Our personal control is free and more effective than a service. Always remember that crowded areas, no matter where you are, are a paradise for light-fingered people.

Parking or camping in lonely out-of-the-way places in your RV is extremely unwise and risky, especially in some non-busy rest areas. This applies in any country, however, in some states and provinces RVs are permitted to gather in out-of-the-way places such as a special lake in British Columbia or at a gravel pit like they do in Newfoundland or on the beaches in south Texas or in the southwest deserts of Arizona and California. It is not wise to stop on your own anywhere but there is safety in numbers.

Unoccupied RVs in parking lots make inviting targets day or night. It's actually quite simple to enter an RV illegally; don't put yourself in a position to become the next victim. We simply do not stop if we are the only RV.

Safe 'Free' Stopping Spots

Some of our friends feel safe camped in hospital parking lots (although these are not always free these days); others choose 24-hour shopping centres such as Wal*Mart shopping centres as overnight stopping spots. A word of caution, always ask first at Wal*Mart and mall parking lots because in some areas bylaws restrict overnight parking.

Most truck stops in general welcome RVers to spend the night. However the Flying J Travel Plazas cater to RVers with special RV parking and a separate island that features fuel/gas/propane, dump, air and fresh water among other amenities. More recently TravelCenters of America have become RV friendly stopping spots as well.

Both these truck stops also offer secure parking, restaurants, stores, discount gas/fuel and so much more. John and I overnight at these facilities occasionally but we still prefer the security and the comforts of a campground.

> **One word of caution, always park with your door facing the people – not to the secluded grassy area that surrounds the parking area.**

New RVers may not be aware that there are quite a few 'free' places to camp, all within the security of a campground setting. There are several books listing free or low-cost campgrounds available from bookstores, RV dealers as well as information on-line. [38]

---

38 *More safe stopping spots listings are on the* RV WebLink *page of* www.rvliving.net.

197

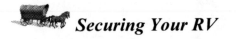

Securing Your RV

It is important to always secure your unit, even in manicured resorts like this one at Holiday Park in Kelowna, BC.

We learned to take safety precautions – the hard way – during the first year of our travels when we became the victims in two separate break-ins six months apart. In the first incident, we made so many mistakes due to our trusting natures that, inadvertently, we probably told the crooks every detail of our plans.

Beginning with a leisurely RV excursion from Ontario to Florida we spent two enjoyable weeks at our timeshare condo. Our RV vacation continued for another month of exploring the sunny south. We planned on flying to Ontario in early January and return to Florida in late March (this was the period when we thought our money well was bottomless) to continue the second phase of our exciting travels.

A great plan, except that I explained our plans to too many people as we shopped by phone searching for a secure place to leave our Kruisin' Kastle. Our biggest mistake was that we were proud of our soon to be fulltime travelling lifestyle and simply wanted to share our experiences with everyone (actually to anyone who would listen to me). Eventually we found a place secure enough (we thought) to leave our motorhome.

When the first phase of this vacation was over we hopped in a taxi, suitcases in hand, from the storage unit to the airport. In an enthusiastic manner we not only telegraphed the fact that we were leaving the RV unoccupied, it was obvious that we wouldn't be back for at least a few days. Who knows, the taxi driver could have been part of the intended robbery plan; if so the crooks knew we would be gone for at least several months.

On our return in March, big gaping holes stared at us from where the appliances once sat. One thing we were happy with, the crooks were careful. They removed things without destroying anything. We provided security (blinds were down), tools, lights and a no-rush timetable – great working conditions. They did break one sliding window lock by tapping a screwdriver at the corner – providing easy access to come and go as they wished. In our honest and trusting manner, we asked to be robbed.

A difficult lesson to learn but our RV living education didn't stop there. Our contents insurance coverage for our motorhome was part of our homeowner's policy and, according to our policy, we were only covered when we were on vacation with our motorhome. Because we left the motorhome 'on vacation' while we returned home, our coverage for RV contents was voided. Something good did come out of all this – we discovered that vehicle insurance covered all items permanently attached to the motorhome such as the microwave, CB and stereo. Unfortunately, this didn't include appliances such as the coffee pot and toaster oven plus clothes and other valuables. The price tag of that expensive but effective lesson totalled approximately $3,000.

Six months later we experienced our second intrusion. This time we parked the motorhome directly in front of our timeshare condo office in Pompano Beach, Florida. At four o'clock in the afternoon sunshine, some young people entered the locked motorhome through the escape hatch in our shower. This time the loss was minimal because most of our valuables had been moved into our condo. However, I forgot to remove some jewellery, much of it sentimental pieces that belonged to my late mother. We surprised the burglars as they were leaving, but they still managed to get away.

Because this second loss occurred before we found an RV contents insurance policy (and we no longer owned a house or homeowner's policy to fall back on), we were out another $1,000. Small, clear handprints all over our dusty coach provided excellent training for the fingerprint division of the Florida police department but they never even tried to locate our missing items.

The most secure place to leave your RV is in a storage area in a campground. This even includes the time you spend at home. An RV in the driveway is most convenient but, when you drive it away for a holiday or a weekend getaway, it sends a clear signal to all that there is no one home.

Note: If you are considering parking your RV in your driveway, become aware of your municipal bylaws. Most do not allow vehicles over a certain size to remain in a residential area.

When we were at our dealership shortly after we bought our first unit, an RV couple from London, Ontario was there recovering after their home had been robbed. Their keys to a new Class A motorhome hung proudly in their kitchen. The crooks unloaded their house contents into the motorhome and simply drove it off. The abandoned motorhome was found in poor condition five miles away. The fate of this RV might have been different if it had not been parked in the driveway.

Museum visits are another favourite pastime of RVers.
The Dinosaur Museum in Drumheller, Alberta is awesome.
Be sure to take extra security precautions
if your RV is left in ANY parking lot.

Baffling The Burglars

There are many ways to create out-of-sight hideaways to stash your valuables. Unfortunately, since most crooks know more than you ever will about 'safe' hiding spots, I can share the ideas with you. However, even if you use an idea, the location of your safe spots should only remain with you.

Even if crooks know how you plan on keeping safe, it's hard to steal something quickly when you don't know where it is located.

Very common hiding places include stashing small bottles containing valuables packed inside food packages such as cereal or cracker boxes, containers of coffee, sugar or rice. The only problem with this method is that it is so common that any 'self-respecting' thief will know about it and will simply dump all of the contents out to locate the hidden goodies.

Attach small bottle lids to the hidden underside of a cupboard, place valuables in bottles and screw on to the secured lids. This method, too, is standard but more time-consuming for a thief who prefers to get in and out with the minimum amount of time.

Install, hide or camouflage a fire-resistant safe. You can also buy an inexpensive (under $30) California safe from discount or department stores. These safes are replicas of brand name cleaning containers or spray cans. They look exactly like the actual product but the bottom removes to access an empty chamber. Place these cans with other cleaning supplies to keep your valuables safely out of sight. Unless you give your burglar ample time in which to rob you, most crooks won't take the time to find out which container is fake.

Place a lidded container in a cupboard with other similar containers. Use one of them to store valuable 'stuff'.

Attach a storage tray to hold valuables behind the plate of an electric plug-in socket assembly. Place this storage tray and plate into a pre-cut hole in a wall panel. Your valuables are again out of sight and hard to find.

Use the area behind a false panel, under a drawer or some other hard to reach place for a larger secret hide-away.

It is OK to share ideas for securing your valuables but never share the location of your makeshift safes or hiding places. Even in idle conversation, the information could unintentionally be passed on to those with questionable intentions.

Always lock the RV door when leaving your unit. In one campground, an RVer stepped out for a short visit to a neighbour and, you guessed it, some young kids watching for an opportunity jumped the fence and entered his unit. They quickly found his wallet plus some cash on the night table and were gone in seconds. Since he felt secure in his surroundings he neglected to lock his door.

Cut wooden or metal dowels to fit inside the tracks of sliding windows and doors. The dowels will make it more difficult and even stop intruders from forcing the doors and windows open.

Commercial locking devices, the removable screw-on kind available for patio doors, also work well to secure your RV's sliding windows.

The last and most expensive security measure is to install an alarm system. These range from the less expensive window alarms to elaborate systems with motion detectors. Alarms may be a nuisance but they do provide much needed peace-of-mind for some people.

The bottom line is that keeping your RV secure begins with being cautious and using common sense.

Fire Protection

Unfortunately fires do happen, even in RVs, but most fires are preventable and, with a little conscientious pre-planning and 'fire-proofing', you can reduce the risk of this disaster.

Caution and common sense are the two main ingredients in fire prevention. One thing that never ceases to amaze me is the number of people who are so off-handed about their propane supply on board. Whether to travel with your propane turned on or off is one of the biggest controversies between RVers. Half think it is OK to drive with it turned on and the other half think that propane should always be turned off. John and I fall into the second category.

Most RVers are concerned that their fridge may not stay cold. Even though your RV refrigerator requires propane or power to function, **it is OK to drive with your propane turned off.** So long as no one stands with the door wide open for longer than necessary, an RV fridge will stay cool for six to eight hours. We have never had food spoil, even on a long day the interior temperature drops only a few degrees. During hot driving days, we turn the fridge up a few degrees the night before we plan to leave.

> **Adopting specific emergency procedures in your RV could save your life.**

We, along with many RVers, feel there is real danger in leaving your propane turned on during your travels. RVs move and sway, roads twist and turn, and the motion may cause the copper tubing to crack allowing propane to escape – you will not even smell it because as you drive the odour will dissipate behind you.

Even if your tubing doesn't crack and propane doesn't leak, every vehicle on the road is at risk for an accident. If your propane is turned on when travelling and you are involved in an accident – even a fender bender – you may not have the time (or ability) to turn off your propane. The jarring from an accident could cause propane to leak on to leak putting everybody at risk.

I still can't believe it when I hear of someone trying to light the pilot light on a stove when travelling. Take note: Every time that you think it's important to cook a meal so you can eat as soon as you arrive at your destination, think again. You are risking a fire. If you're that hungry, go to McDonald's – and I don't mean our place!

While on the move, the combination of motion and drafts can extinguish the propane flame, causing gas to leak into your RV without you even being aware of it happening. **During one routine propane leak check**, unbeknown to us, the tech discovered that our water heater was leaking. If we had stopped for fuel a problem or a fire could have resulted. Yes, today's RVs include many safety shut off features but, although propane has an odour, the smell of the gas often dissipates with the airflow as you are driving. Your sense of smell may not alert you to a possible problem.

Never leave your propane stove unattended (or any stove, for that matter). If the flame goes out, the gas will continue to seep into the air and a small spark can cause an explosion. Be careful and use common sense when cooking, especially in the confined space of an RV galley. Keep paper towels, curtains and all combustibles away from the stove area.

> **Consider all pros and cons plus the reasons for leaving your propane turned on during travels. In the interest of safety, many seasoned RVers turn theirs off before each trip.**

Always buy an RV unit approved by the **Canadian Standards Association (CSA) or the Recreational Vehicle Association (RVIA) in the U.S.** RVs that have been approved display a seal as your guarantee that propane, plumbing and electrical components meet rigid safety requirements. Be sure a competent licensed electrician completes all aftermarket electrical wiring.

Using electricity incorrectly can also put you at risk for fire. When connecting to campground power, **NEVER use a small, yellow/orange 14-gauge, 15-amp extension cord** to connect the electric power between the receptacle and your RV. These cords are not heavy enough to support the heat generated by RV appliances, especially air conditioners and heaters. They will catch fire.

All hoses, especially the radiator hose, should be looked at on a regular basis. Look for cracking, hardness, extreme softness, swelling and improper routing. Antifreeze (ethylene glycol) won't burn until the water in the solution boils away leaving a volatile concentration that will burst into flames if it drips on to an extremely hot manifold.

When you're travelling in hot weather at high altitudes, your gas engine could quit due to a **vapour lock**. Park your RV and try to keep your engine idling. If that's not possible, stop and sit until your engine cools down before trying to start it up again.

Don't forget the tires and brakes when taking steps to prevent fires, Always check the air pressure in the dual or tandem tires. The friction caused by the low air pressure in these tires can ignite a spark and begin burning long before you notice that you have a problem. A dragging brake also causes friction that can set fire to tires or brake fluid.

Keep mirrors, magnifiers and binoculars out of the path of direct sunlight. Remember how easy it was when you were a kid to start a fire when the rays of the sun reflected through a piece of glass? On the same note, those gorgeous crystal drops that hang in a window to capture the fire of the sun may also burn holes in any fabric in the path of their reflection.

To prepare your family in the event of a fire, **hold periodic fire drills**. Immediate and calm action will save lives. Don't forget to establish an outside meeting point to count heads and ensure that everyone is safe. If your RV does happen to catch fire, get out immediately. Unlike your home with different rooms, an RV is one big rectangular room and flames won't find anything to stop them from sweeping through.

Store valuables in fire-resistant containers. We put important but not especially valuable papers in our freezer. Not for security reasons but because it will be the last place to burn. If your wallet or purse is in fingertip reach and you have time, grab it. If you have to go fetch it, forget it.

Fight the fire from a safe distance. Never, ever, under any circumstances, re-enter a burning unit because RVs have a tendency to 'melt' as they burn and the walls collapse. Items can be replaced, people can't.

If John and I have a fire emergency when we're travelling, the **escape plan** in our motorhome includes a fast stop as soon as it's safe without endangering others. John exits by the driver's door and grabs one of the fire extinguishers mounted beside each exit. I'm responsible for the dogs, their leashes, my purse and camera (all are ready at the door) and head for the towed car. I keep a spare set of car keys in my pocket while we're in transit. Depending on the fire location I put the dogs in the 'towed'; hopefully I will be able to disconnect the car from the RV and move it away to a safe distance. John will do what he can to control the fire with the fire extinguisher from outside of the motorhome. A quick exit from a tow vehicle (of a towable unit) that is on fire is an easier situation to deal with.

205

You should always keep several **fire extinguishers** on board, especially one at each exit and another in the kitchen. Don't forget to put one in your tow/towed vehicle as well. Familiarize yourself with the escape windows in the bedroom (not all the windows are escape windows). A fast exit through these windows may work better if you roll out, bum first. But again I stress never re-enter a burning RV. A fire drill at the campground is a good idea; practising a fast exit may save the life of you and your family.

All extinguishers should be **rated for B and C type fires.** B-rated extinguishers are effective on grease and oil fires while C-rated extinguishers are for electrical fires. They must be approved by ULC (Underwriter's Laboratories of Canada) or UL (Underwriter's Laboratories for U.S. ratings). When in doubt, ask your fire department.

Take a look at your gauges regularly. Your local fire-department will be able to tell you if your extinguisher is working properly.

Though **Halon-type cylinders** have been effectively used in the past, they are destructive to the ozone layer and no longer available.

Familiarize yourself with your fire extinguisher before having to use it in an emergency. Always aim your extinguisher at the flames but, do so only from a safe distance through the door when you are outside of your RV. Be sure to leave the fire area because the fumes from burning material are toxic.

Always store aerosol cans away from all heat sources. An RVing neighbour several years ago left a spray can of no-stick cooking oil beside her RV stove. The resulting loud explosion left a horrendous mess to clean up. Fortunately for everyone, no injuries resulted.

Don't store objects in front of your RV's electrical/fuse boxes, either. This practice restricts quick access to fuses or to wiring that may need attention.

Incorrect portable gas containers are also a fire hazard. **Only approved portable gas containers can be filled at gas pumps.** (This rule includes marinas.) No container manufactured before 1973 meets CSA standards, similar regulations are in force in the U.S.A. Don't forget, most fires are preventable but only if you take the necessary steps to stop a fire from happening.

Propane Tanks And OPD Valves

All containers must be in good condition with the required gasket and closure in place. Portable tanks must be fitted with an OPD (Overflow Protection Device) to ensure your tanks cannot be overfilled. As of 2002 this valve is required before a tank can be refilled in the U.S.A. This is not a federal U.S. law, it is a provision contained in a standard published by the

National Fire Protection Association (NFPA). It may and may not be in force in all states but this listing of compliant states change constantly. It is not required to refill a tank in Canada.

If you do not have a valve on your tank you can go to the 'exchange cabinet' found at various retails stores (including Wal*Mart) in the U.S.A. It may cost a bit more but your tank will comply for refilling. All size cylinders can be refitted but not all can be exchanged.

Horizontal cylinders manufactured prior to October 1st, 1998 are exempt because they cannot be retrofitted due to the design of the tank. Horizontal cylinders made after September 30th, 1998 should already be fitted with an OPD and are included in the Code. These OPD valves are only required for travel in the U.S.A.

✎ *Life Saving Detectors*

Every RV should have an approved **smoke alarm** as well as propane and carbon monoxide detectors. It is important that your fire alarm be sensitive to smoke. Usually before a fire takes hold, it will smoke, the alarm will sound and provide you with an early warning. Smoke is also deadly. Smoke inhalation is the number one killer in a fire.

Unfortunately, in the confined RV space, cooking on the stove, a toaster or even a hot shower can trigger these sensitive alarms. Although you may be tempted to disconnect the alarms or remove the batteries – don't. The annoyance is not worth your life if you forget to reconnect. We stop the noise of false alarms by blowing on the smoke detector or by fanning the air around it. Temporarily covering the alarm with a plastic sandwich bag also works but be sure to remove it as soon as possible. If you absolutely can't live with false alarms when showering or cooking, put the batteries in a conspicuous place and replace as soon as you finish.

For safety sake **propane detectors** are also a must for all RVs. These life-saving devices should be installed two feet above the floor – gas is heavier than air. In its compressed state, propane is a liquid gas but when it hits the air it turns into vapour gas. Both forms are extremely volatile – for instance, turning on a light switch always creates a spark and if there is a build-up of gas, even that simple act can ignite an explosion.

Propane does have an offensive odour. Under the law, Ethyl Mercaptan has been added to the liquid gas so that the smell of rotten eggs will alert users that gas is leaking. Although air movement can take away this particular smell, sometimes when we have a cold or allergies, we just can't smell scents properly. A detector protects you against a 'faulty' nose by sounding an alarm when the first trace of gas is detected.

If you smell propane, immediately move everyone outside leaving the door open and turn off the gas at its source. When the odour is gone, open all windows and roof vents plus shut off all automatic ignitions. Have a qualified service technician locate the leak and repair the problem before turning the gas on again.

Before we installed our first propane detector in the early 90s, during a routine propane check it was discovered that we had a leak in our stovetop and one outside in the water heater. Because the windows were open and fans were on, we didn't notice the smell. We had no idea that there was a problem with our propane appliances. Luckily, we are in the habit of always turning our propane off. If we had been driving with ours turned on, something as simple as a gas fill-up or a cigarette being tossed out a window by a passing motorist may have sparked a fire.

Always shut off each pilot light, propane appliance and automatic igniters when you are filling your RV's gas/fuel/propane tank. When refilling the propane cylinder, shut off the cylinder's supply and only fill the propane tank to a maximum of 80 percent. Any excess should be bled off through the pressure release valve.

Never allow anyone to tamper with or seal this release valve. If the pressure in your tank changes because of temperature fluctuations, the release valve regulates the tank or cylinder pressure. In a properly filled tank there should be no reason to release gas, even if you have travelled from the cold north to the sunny south.

There are different types of detectors on the market. Some only sound an alarm when gas or liquid is present while others have a solenoid valve to shut off the flow of gas. Most units operate on the 12-volt system.

Hand-held propane detectors, operated by rechargeable or standard D-cell batteries, are also available. Though costly, these small devices are very handy in detecting small leaks throughout the system.

Carbon monoxide (CO) gas is an insidious killer that lulls you into a sleep from which you never wake. It's odourless, colourless, tasteless – totally invisible. It collects in enclosed places and is a result of gas or fuel powered appliances and, unless you have a detector, you don't know that it's there. Don't be its next victim.

For instance, if the furnace/heater is running and you are awake in an enclosed RV, car or, even a house, and you feel a headache coming on, or you are drowsy, sick to your stomach, weak, vomiting or you experience heart palpitations, immediately open a window and get out into the fresh air! Because carbon monoxide poisoning robs you of common sense and causes disorientation, you may not even be aware that you have become a victim. A coma, heart attack and death usually will result. Because the symptoms mimic the flu, motion sickness, food poisoning, etc., you may be tempted to just pass off the feeling and curl up in bed.

Don't do it. Carbon monoxide can take a while to build up and, because it is the same weight as air, it mixes easily and freely moves around. A CO detector should be installed four feet off the floor and be placed in your main living area as well as your sleeping area.

Some carbon monoxide and propane detectors are so sensitive that they will react to hair spray, alcohol, exhaust fumes, paint cleaners, sewer gases, glue and, even the chemical treatment on new carpeting. Although it can become tiresome, never assume that your alarm is being triggered by something harmless. Follow your evacuation procedures until you can safely sound an all clear.

Don't park so that your exhaust pipe faces towards a wall or fence – the fumes will bounce back into your coach. Never run your engine or generator in an enclosed area such as a service centre or garage. You're asking for trouble if you keep your generator running while sleeping.

Furnace fumes, exhaust fumes from a generator and vapours from other vehicles all contribute to the accumulation of carbon monoxide. Parking too close to idling vehicles in rest areas or camped next to an RV running a generator can also put you at risk for carbon monoxide poisoning.

If you can't avoid the later two situations, keep all doors and window closed and turn coach exhaust vents on to minimize the risk of CO poisoning. Spend the money and cut the risk – install a carbon monoxide (CO) detector now.

When using the stove or oven, turn on the fan to remove gases. Never use the stove to heat the unit – carbon monoxide is released from the propane burners. **Don't bet your life on 'just this time it'll be okay'. Carbon monoxide kills**.

How To Avoid CO Poisoning

Before setting out on a trip examine your exhaust system and generator to make sure all are running properly. The tip of your exhaust pipe should extend beyond the outer wall of your RV. If there is damage, replace the exhaust pipe. Do not use flexible piping as it can leak.

Note: When using your generator, close all windows above or near this power source.

All propane appliances should have bright blue flames. If the flame is red or yellow there is insufficient combustion, which creates a high level of CO.

210

Many seasoned RVers add a specially designed attachment to their GenSet exhaust pipe to disperse CO gases upwards and away from their neighbours living areas. The 'Gen-Turi' by Camco seems to be the attachment of choice.

Don't place objects directly in front of the furnace vents and inspect the walls and floors of your RV for openings that could allow fumes to enter. When you are travelling, always keep your rear windows and vents closed. While the RV is moving, a low pressure is created drawing gas fumes into your RV. When travelling in heavy traffic or going through a tunnel, the exhaust fumes of other vehicles may be seeping into your unit. If you or your passengers begin to feel woozy or exhibit the symptoms mentioned above, immediately pull over and get out into the fresh air. If symptoms remain present or worsen, seek medical help.

 **First Aid**

One perfect, sunny February afternoon in Texas, while swimming with new-found RVing friends, a wasp landed on my back and stung me, leaving me in terrible pain mainly because I couldn't reach it. That winter my blood pressure was somewhat erratic and this situation didn't help.

When I felt my heart racing and the beginning of palpitations, I was close to panic. Several swimmers suggested home remedies and since I had no known allergies to insect stings, my neighbour drove me home instead of to a hospital.

As we travel, many RVers pass on hints for situations such as this; however, I tend to forget them as fast as I hear them. As the immediate shock subsided, my blood pressure settled down but, my back was still very sore. I reached for our medical reference book to find a simple way to relieve my discomfort. We carry *The Doctors Book Of Home Remedies*, published by Preventive Magazine Health Books, Emmaus, PA, 18098, just for this type of situation.

This book is filled with hints that work well when dealing with minor medical problems. Although it's a great book to have on hand, fortunately, we haven't had to use it that often.

Our book suggested that the way to lessen the discomfort of stings from jellyfish, bees and wasps was to put a paste of baking soda or sand on the sting and after several minutes, take a plastic card or a flat table knife and scrape the top of the bite to remove the stinger.

Amazing, but it worked. Almost immediately after John scraped the sting area, all pain went away. I guess he removed the last traces of the stinger.

Whether you choose this manual or some other one, RVers should carry some form of medical reference book, plus a well-stocked first-aid kit. Many hints and suggestions on how to handle minor medical situations are especially beneficial when doctors and medical clinics are a distance away from your campsite.

Your first-aid kit should be easy accessible and, ideally, a large kit belongs in your RV and a smaller one in your tow car. A properly stocked kit should contain a basic first-aid manual, scissors, tweezers, bandages (strip and butterfly), gauze (both strip and pre-cut packaged dressings), adhesive tape, no-stick burn dressing, pressure pads, slings and an assortment of different size safety pins. Medications should include an antiseptic cream for minor cuts and wounds, sunburn ointment and your family's analgesic for pain. A personalized supply of antihistamine (capsules and/or Benadryl) should be included in case of a reaction from a sting. Anyone who suffers from anaphylactic shock should always carry his or her epinephrine (Epi-pen, ephedrine) kit with them. Special note: Never share over-the-counter or your prescription medications with anyone. Your prescription may be poison to someone else.

Though no one anticipates an emergency, it's comforting to have basic supplies close at hand. Besides knowing to scrape a sting and to never pull the stinger out with tweezers, there are a few other basic first-aid points to keep in mind.

If a victim has fallen (or in a car accident) and it is safe to leave them where they are, do not move the person – there may be spinal injuries. Call an ambulance and let trained paramedics take over.

Never, ever administer medication to an accident victim. You have no way of knowing if they have allergies and your so-called 'helpful' treatment may kill them.

Anyone who has suffered a trauma is subject to shock. Keep patient warm and watch carefully. Shock victims can become confused and often start wandering.

Try to control bleeding, by applying pressure directly to the wound. If the pad becomes soaked, apply another one right over it – do not remove the first one. If bleeding persists, seek medical help.

Nosebleeds, though fairly common, can become severe. If your nose begins to bleed, never tilt your head back. Tilt your head forward and lightly pinch the bridge of the nose – a couple of seconds at a time. Apply a cold compress to the back of the neck. If the bleeding doesn't stop or the flow is heavier or there is clotting, seek medical help.

Burns should not be treated with grease. Do not rub butter on a burn either. Instead, cool the burn with cold (not ice) water. Use a sterile burn pad and do not cover the affected area with a tight bandage.

Apply wet dressings to cuts, scrapes, burns, etc. The moisture in the dressing cools and soothes the burn.

Learn the basics of blood pressure monitoring (carry one on board), CPR (Cardiac Pulmonary Resuscitation) and artificial resuscitation. Knowing how to perform CPR could, one day, save the life of a loved one.

213

St. John's Ambulance in Canada plus some high schools, community colleges and fire departments in many communities in most countries offer these lifesaving courses. Take the time to learn the techniques or to keep your training current.

Snake Bites

As children, many of us were Cubs, Scouts, Brownies or Girl Guides and we learned to always 'be prepared'. RVers should follow this same practice. Before you begin tramping through the wilds or into an unknown area, visit the local library, stop at local tourist welcome centres, talk to RVers camped nearby and/or to staff members at the provincial, state or national park office(s). Learn what you can about the habits and lifestyles of local wildlife. When you know what to expect, you'll see more because you'll be alert to small tell-tale signs that signify what creatures live beyond the trail.

One procedure all travellers should become familiar with is what to do about snakebite. Since most of us don't know the difference between a poisonous and non-poisonous snake, if you get bitten wash the bite with soap and water. Keep the victim quiet and still and immediately call an ambulance or get to a hospital.

If possible, kill or capture the snake (without risking a second bite) to bring along for identification. If you can't kill or catch the snake, take a good look at what it looked like.

Don't think about playing hero by cutting into the snakebite to suck out the poison. This practice is dangerous to both the victim and the 'hero'. Doing this or applying an ice-pack is extremely traumatic to the body's natural defence and it raises the chance of infection.

Do not apply a tourniquet either. Tourniquets can cause far more damage than the snakebite. Improperly applied, they can cause loss of blood flow and possibly gangrene, resulting in required amputation of the limb. The best help is to immediately transport the victim to a medical facility or call an ambulance.

Feeding Folly In The Wild

Every year we hear of people attacked or mauled by bears, wolves and other wild animals. In real life, wild animals are not pets so, forget Yogi the Bear and Bambi, do not approach an animal that does not belong to you. Never stand too close to any animal or reptile – this could violate their territorial rights, especially if the young are present – you will be attacked.

In the same vein, do not feed wild animals. They will become dependent on handouts and, when food supplies stop, they will become aggressive and terrorize a campsite to get at the 'free' goodies.

When you are out of your element and in theirs, respect the fact that you are in their home and treat it as such. Don't create a situation that could endanger your life.

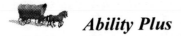 **Ability Plus**

As John and I travel the countryside we meet many warm and friendly people and, although each person is special, occasionally we meet someone who is simply unforgettable.

Such was the case when a 40-foot motorhome settled into the site next to ours in a Louisiana campground. Nothing appeared unusual until the driver turned off the engine and climbed from his motorhome to sit in his wheelchair.

This American RVer lost his legs in Vietnam and he and his wife decided that instead of sitting around feeling sorry for themselves, they would get on with the art of living. And, part of their new life was travelling in their RV with a car in tow

It sounded almost unbelievable when he told us how inexpensive and easy it was to modify their RV. Immediately after purchasing their motorhome, the couple ordered their modified operating equipment. Three days later a hand-control system arrived and, shortly after, their coach was ready and waiting for a test ride.[39]

Using only a hand lever, our new friend has full control of his vehicle brake and his accelerator – each operates separately. He can also use both 'pedals' at the same time when necessary (for parking, going up a hill from a stop, etc.).

His driving modifications fit a particular vehicle by year, make and model. Most conversion equipment is not transferable to alternate vehicles without additional parts supplied by the manufacturer. Driving aids and conversions assist disabled drivers to independently operate their vehicle. A

---

39 *The renovation company these disabled friends used is no longer in business but several others are listed under* Ability and Disability *on the* RV WebLinks *page of* www.rvliving.net. *You may also find RV Renovating companies in your local phone book.*

number of RV modifications are available for people who can't walk to enjoy travels away from their homes. Vans, specially designed with similar conversion can carry several wheelchairs to provide transport for physically challenged people on short trips.

Since our first encounter with a physically challenged RVer, we've talked to several others who have taken to the road against all odds. One fall, while touring the southwest, John and I met another physically challenged RVer and his wife who were also experiencing the joys of RV living. When this RVer lost use of his legs, he had a new RV sitting in their driveway. Instead of sitting back and letting the world go by, this adventurous couple searched to find a way to accommodate their new lifestyle. They had places to go and things to see and, with conversions, his medical problems were only an inconvenience, not an obstacle.

At one of our national motorhome conventions, John and I talked to various members from a chapter called the 'Achievers'. This chapter is made up of members with disabilities and their partners. The members of this chapter routinely deal with a variety of medical problems; however, nothing deters them from participating in the many pleasures associated with life on the road. The Achievers chapter is part of FMCA (Family Motor Coach Association) but Good Sam and Escapee clubs and maybe others also have chapters devoted to physically challenged RVers.

We also met another RVer and his wife (also members of the Achievers) who turned their disabilities into abilities. At times their RV fantasy followed a rough and rocky road, depending on their health of the moment.

He was diagnosed with post-polio syndrome several years before, an ailment that attacks an adult who suffered from polio as a child. In time, this latent polio disease restricts breathing plus slowly decreases most leg muscle control. The periodic assistance of a respirator sometimes helped his breathing.

His wife's health, too, was less than perfect. She has MS, a disabling illness that causes abnormal hardening of body tissue. This couple loved RVing but they prefer to dry camp so that they can participate first hand in all aspects of nature. Because of the vast amount of equipment necessary to cope with their everyday living, their motorhome doubles as a car. It's easier for them than pulling a separate vehicle.

After the wife became a proud owner of a mobility scooter, these two wanderers explored each destination – she simply towed her husband's wheelchair around their campground behind her 'freedom machine'. Mobility scooters provide another dimension of independence for physically challenged RVers, especially the compact models that fold to fit into the trunk of a car or RV storage pods. This adventuresome pair installed a series of on-board batteries plus a heavy-duty generator to power the scooter and required respirators.

Her mother also liked exploring RV hideaways. She, too, didn't let her heart and asthma problems interfere with tagging along. She simply packed her breathing machine along with her clothes, and she was ready for any on-the-road experiences.

RVers with disabilities don't waste time thinking about what isn't available to them, nor do they allow anything to disrupt their RV travels – they just do it their way.

Each year, more and more tourist attractions, national monuments, private campgrounds plus provincial and state parks add wheelchair accessibility to their facilities.

In Canada and the U.S., there are many companies that offer conversion service for RVers with disabilities. As well as providing hand-controls for driving, these companies can install hydraulic lifts, widen doorways (for wheelchair access) and provide a number of adjustments to make an RV handicap accessible.

Campgrounds, too, are making facilities available to people who are physically challenged. Many are upgrading washrooms and showers to 'wheelchair user friendly' facilities. They're also installing ramps into buildings and creating sites that offer easy access for the physically challenged RVers. When choosing a campsite, look for the universal handicap symbol.

All the RVers with disabilities who we've met on the course of our travels have found a way to turn their fantasy into a reality and each one offered the same message...

"Life is too precious to waste any of it. Sitting around while opportunities pass you by is not living, it's only existing. Don't wait for someday...do what you want to now while you're able. If following your dream means travelling in an RV, find a way and just do it!"

Appreciate North America's natural beauty at your convenience – turn your disability into ability. Follow your heart and, with a little luck and a lot of determination, we may see you in one of North America's interesting campgrounds.

FULLTIMING

*Since fulltimers have no need to return to a home base, picturesque settings
like Saugeen Cedars Campground in Hanover, Ontario
can become part of your newest backyard.*

Budgeting For The Good Life

Some time ago, I received a letter in response to one of my columns suggesting that John and I must be rich to travel the way we do. I can assure the writer (and anyone else who thinks the same) that not too many RVers (including ourselves) on the road today are what could be described as rich, or even remotely wealthy. Most of us have simply discovered how to live comfortably within whatever retirement income we receive.

Our logo from our early days of, 'Goodbye Tension, Hello Pension', says it all. Once we learned that the 'money well' had a bottom to it and each month there's only a fixed amount to fill it up again, we adjusted our lifestyle accordingly and living on a pension became an acceptable way of life. The last week of each month the well, at times is pretty dry.

We also realize that many RVers can only use their RVs for weekend excursions and during vacations. The following money saving tips applies equally to 'fulltimers' and 'part-timers' too. Just weed out anything not applicable to your lifestyle.

This information guideline is based on two people enjoying an extended trip. When you draw up your budget consider your personal lifestyle, hobbies, interests and the number of people travelling in your unit – these factors will alter your living expenses. Every situation is unique and, although some RVers exist on a monetary output of Old Age Pension or Social Security, others need $5,000.00 or more each month. The average RVer finds a happy medium between those two figures.

Don't assume that because the couple in the unit next to you has a very elaborate Class A motorhome, they must be rolling in dough to be able to afford that and a house somewhere else. Many retired RVers liquidate all material assets, including the house, before buying (or mortgaging) their RV. Instead of an extra luxury, their RV may be their only home.

When John and I retired, we sold our house and with the stroke of a pen we eliminated $13,000 of annual expenses. Over the years we have learned to fine-tune our living expenditures even more.

For us, many costs such as property taxes, home insurance, the second car, cable TV (now we pay for satellite service), heating, water and so on became obsolete. Dry cleaning expenses were also history since casual and washable clothing is much better for the relaxed lifestyle of RV travelling. One amount that remains fairly constant is the cost of food – after all; no matter where you live you have to eat. Our biggest change was cutting back on the times we ate out – dining in expensive restaurants does not go well with a fixed pension income.

If you have RV loan payments, include them in your budget just as you would a mortgage on a house and, if you have always been an avid golfer or have any other costly hobbies, add those in as well. Quite a few RVers choose to scale down those types of hobbies or substitute them for free ones such as hiking, fishing, bird watching and other nature related alternatives. A number of campgrounds also help RVers stretch their budget with free activities such as movie nights, card games, bingos, craft classes, billiard tables and shuffleboard.

There are two expenses that are not possible to eliminate – gas/fuel and camping fees. Nevertheless, with a little pre-planning, you can reduce these costs to a liveable range.

For instance, John and I budget $400 to $500 Cdn. or ($300 to $350 U.S.) monthly for camping costs (but you can spend much more). These days we have less control over fuel costs. But by travelling shorter days with longer stops between we can limit our fuel costs.

Because we don't pay high camping fees when travelling (we use discount camping clubs – see that chapter for info), and we don't pay for RV fuel when stopping for extended periods, the two costs balance each other making this expense an either/or situation.

Early in our travels we used membership park systems with overnight rates from $4.00 to $10.00. This definitely kept our camping fees low and in control. These days our discount rates are between $10.00 U.S. and 50 percent off the cost of regular camping rates.

In contrast, because we stay for a longer time at destination parks – we reserve from one to six months in Canada during the summer and three to four months during the busy winter season in sun country – the monthly rate is much lower than the daily (per night) fee.

RVers on vacation may not be able to enjoy a leisurely pace but all RVers should try to tour a bit of each area during a stopover. By cooking and eating your meals in the comfort of your home-on-wheels, it saves 'restaurant' money to use for more interesting pursuits.

Another way to save money is to learn to give each other a haircut. The only difference between a good and bad hair cut is three days. An added bonus – it costs you nothing,

During our first years of extensive travelling, the Cdn./U.S. exchange rate was acceptable and we didn't bother with excessive budgeting. So every dollar we spent bought almost a dollar's worth of goods. However, during our first seven years on the road, we had no pay increases, so learning how to stretch each dollar was necessary to continue our lifestyle in comfort. It was a challenge at times but mostly fun to see how many corners we could cut and still enjoy ourselves. This practice has become our way of life since.

Every RVer has different needs. In this chapter we've included a sample of our on-the-road living expenses. Although at times we travel on a tight budget (and sometimes have to dig into our reserve), we try not to travel on a tight schedule.

This is only a guideline for budgeting expenses – add and subtract your own costs to determine your overall expenses. I am not adding any figures because the amount you spend on an item may be different than we spend on ours. The topic is added so you can decide the amount you need for life on the road.

Budget Overview

The general consensus of how much is needed to fulltime RV is a minimum of $30,000.00 a year, but that amount is so vague. Your expenses on the road will be the same or higher than they are now. Fulltiming is not meant to live like a pauper. The amount of your costs will be such a personal choice. You should also have a plan for phase two (such as a move to an apartment, etc.) if you, or your partner becomes ill.

Where you spend your time will depend on which country you call home, but most fulltimers spend winters in the south. To convert currency...

♦ While in Canada, <u>to obtain the 'approximate' two-digit exchange rate</u> - divide $1.00 by the posted three-digit Cdn. exchange rate promoted on the TV or radio (Example: $1.00 divided by $1.42 = $.70).

♦ While in the U.S.A. exchange rate is listed as a two-digit amount. <u>To obtain the 'approximate' three-digit exchange rate</u> – divide $1.00 by the two-digit exchange rate (Example: $1.00 divided by $.70 = $1.42).

♦ To convert (approximate) U.S.$ to Cdn.$ - <u>multiply the U.S.$ amount x the three digit exchange rate</u> = Cdn.$. (Example: $10.00 U.S.$ x $1.42 = $14.20 Cdn.$).

♦ To convert (approximate) Cdn.$ to U.S.$ - <u>multiply the Cdn.$ times the two digit exchange rate</u> = U.S.$. (Example: $14.00 Cdn.$ x $.70= $10.00 U.S.$).

♦ OR, to convert (approximate) Cdn.$ to U.S.$ - <u>divide the Cdn.$ by the three digit exchange rate</u> = U.S.$ (Example: $14.00 Cdn.$ divided by $1.42 = $10.00 U.S.$).

Note: When the dollar exchange is bad for Canadians heading to the sunny south, it's a real bargain for Americans who want to explore the friendly country to the north.

General Costs

There is no set amount required to live on the road fulltime. General costs are as follow:

* Camping in the U.S.A. will routinely run between $250.00 to $800.00 per month, plus tax, depending what state or area you are visiting, length of visit, the location to attractions, what camping clubs you belong to and if you pay full price.

♦ Seasonal Canadian monthly rates average between $200.00 Cdn. and $500.00 Cdn. for a 6-month stay, higher for individual months. In both the U.S.A. and Canada the longer you're in one spot, the lower the monthly rate. Most seasonal rates in the U.S.A. are for 3 to 4 months – although longer stays are also available.

♦ Daily rates routinely range from $25 to $35.00 (Cdn. or U.S.). Most parks that are part of discount camping clubs charge $10.00 U.S. per night or 50% off regular rates, plus tax. Membership clubs charge less per night, but that is after you pay big money to buy into a system.[40] Members of large RV clubs may also receive 10% discount from numerous parks throughout North America – as a benefit of that organization.

♦ Weekly rates may include one free day.

♦ Our groceries run from $450.00 to $600.00 per month (U.S. or Cdn.) for everything we buy in the grocery store.

♦ We eat out about 4 to 6 times per month – $20.00 to $25.00 (2 meals) (Cdn. or U.S.) for lunches (higher for dinners) – times the number of meals.

Note: As close as we can figure our total monthly living costs are similar in Canada or U.S.A. and they range between $1000.00 to $1200.00 per month, plus camping (at every opportunity we travel by discount camping clubs at an approximate cost of $300 per month, plus tax) and gas/fuel. (For exact amounts Canadians must add the conversion rate – Americans deduct it.)

♦ Annual maintenance for both vehicles is extra ($4000 to $8000 Cdn. or $2800 to $5600 U.S. – see below)…

---

40 *More info about membership campgrounds is in the free downloadable e-book* called RV Living: Facts, Tips, Hints and More – Volume One – *see* www.rvliving.net *for details.*

- Plus upgrades
- And new equipment such as a computer, etc.

♦ <u>Expensive hobbies</u> such as golf or tennis, etc. plus if you smoke or drink your costs will be much higher.

♦ Allowance <u>for gas/fuel costs</u> – average RV combo gets 9 to 14 miles per gallon for diesel, less for gas. Costs vary; to determine your expenses, simply multiply your distance times the cost of gas/fuel at the time. Total amount depends on where you plan to drive and how many miles you accumulate.

♦ When we started RVing, propane was relatively inexpensive but its price has steadily been rising, both in the U.S. and Canada. We try, when possible, to fill up at Flying J truck stops because they are frequently more economical.

♦ Whether you're from Canada or the U.S., you will want from $300.00 to $400.00 <u>to be a tourist and to buy things</u>.

♦ You should have access to about $5000.00 (Cdn. or U.S.) in <u>an emergency fund</u>. We choose not to have cash sitting around collecting dust, instead we set aside a zero balanced credit card to take care of the emergency and we rearrange funds when we return to our home location.

♦ Other items that need to be addressed are listed in the table below. I may have missed some things but this overview will give you the idea.

-phone cards	-insurance (vehicle,	-clothing
-cell phones	RV, house, medical)	(purchase/upkeep)
-Internet ISP	-Emergency Road	-discount club dues
-mail forwarding	Service (ERS)	-RV club dues
-tax consultant	-mortgage payments	-RV chapter costs
-driver's licence	-health care	-accumulating
-vehicle licensing	-Air ambulance	costs from keeping
-prescription meds	-dental	the house

<u>To determine your costs</u> use the above expenses as a guide and fill in the blanks that pertain to your lifestyle. We know American RVers who fulltime solely on social security OR Canadians who have not much more than Old Age Pensions plus Canada Pension Plan (CPP). Other friends can't exist on $5 to $6K per month. It seems no matter how much John and I have coming into the bank every month, the last week before payday, the money well is very low in available cash.

Some fulltimers add to their cash flow as working campers (<u>work while they travel</u>).[41] Many RVers do menial work at parks in exchange for rent. Even in our case, I present seminars and write articles. I declare all monies received as part of my worldwide income. We will never get rich from these extras but it does help to cover some of our travel expenses. The future belongs to those who believe in the beauty of their dreams.

Now it is time to pull out the paper and pencil to determine how much it will cost you to hit the road fulltime. These Budget Guidelines are the items we consider important; your list may include different things.

Budget Guidelines $$$

Possible expenses to consider for life on the move.
- Fluctuating Monthly Expenses
    - Camping
    - Fuel (distance times the cost per litre or gallons)
    - Food/groceries/cleaning supplies, etc.
    - Entertainment
    - Clothes/miscellaneous
    - Hobbies
- Fixed Monthly Expenses
    - RV/car payments
    - Insurance (car, RV, RV contents)
    - Storage unit
    - Life insurance
    - Occasional landline phone
    - Long distance rates/calling cards
    - Cell phone service
    - Internet service provider (ISP)
    - Secondary ISP (if required during an extended stay)
    - Satellite service
    - Calling cards, etc.
    - Mail forwarding service and postage
    - Banking fees (telephone service)

---

41 Part-time work links are listed on the RV WebLink *page of* <u>www.rvliving.net</u> *under* Working on the Road *section.*

◆ Optional Annual Club/Association Fees
  National/international RV clubs
  Manufacturer clubs
  RV club chapter dues
  Membership/discount camping fees
  Associations — military, Elks etc.
◆ Miscellaneous Living Costs
  Medical insurance
  Out of country/province medical for Canadians (variable)
  Dental Plan
  Prescription drug plan
  Eyeglass replacement
  Tax preparation (2)
  Credit card fees
  Pets – shots/medical
  Driver's licence
  Vehicle and/or RV registration/licensing (2)
  Air brake course if required (renewed with licensing)
  Banking power of attorney
  Mail forwarding assistance and postage costs
  RV vehicle maintenance ($3000 to $8000 –
      including laptops/digital cameras/cell phones etc.
    see *Maintenance Costs* below)
  Unexpected breakdown (emergency nest egg of $5000.00)
  Emergency Road Service (ERS)

We keep a modest reserve contingency fund of approximately $5000.00 for unplanned surprises. In our case this emergency fund is a zero balanced credit card for 'just in case' problems. We rearrange funds when we return to Canada in the summer. Our annual vehicle maintenance expenses vary but it's better to be prepared than to be sorry.

Maintenance Costs

When we had our gas engine motorhomes we used to budget approximately $3500 Cdn. annually for both car and motorhome and we frequently came up less than that. However, in 1991 with our 1983 Pace Arrow gas motorhome we had to replace the rad, the fridge, the toilet, an A/C, awning fabric, tires, manifold and a lot of other things; that year we spent over $9000.00 Cdn. That was a very unusual year but, keep in mind that maintenance and breakdowns do happen. If you're a handy tech-type person, you could reduce some of these expenses considerably, but we are not that handy. Appliances do wear out and some carry a high price to replace.

John and I now are driving a high-end diesel pusher motorhome. Several years after purchasing our pre-owned dream machine, it still has a value close to $140,000.Cdn. but her house part is showing signs of wear, so upkeep is constant if we want to stay on the road. Diesel engines last in the range of 400,000 to 450,000 miles and for us this will be our lifetime coach. Maintenance is more costly than a gas engine although it does occur less often; for instance it takes 27 litres of oil for a routine oil change on our unit and seven on our gas engine units.

The following facts about maintenance should help with planning for this budget area. It was written in response to several e-mail requests about budgeting for maintenance items.

ANNUAL MAINTENANCE COSTS (Summer 2003)

I receive many questions on our website about our maintenance costs. RVing good times always outnumber the bad in this lifestyle but not every day is perfect and some may be a bit costly. This is the reason I strongly urge every RVer to have a $5000.00 emergency fund is so that you do not have to use your travel funds for emergencies – ours is a zero balance credit card that we can deal with when we return home in the summer.

Some years, like this one for us, can be exceptionally costly, BUT most are not. When we drove gas motorhomes, we budgeted $3500.00 Cdn. ($2500.00 U.S.) per year for both vehicles and frequently came in well under that. Last year our motorhome maintenance was $3000.00 Cdn. ($2100. U.S.); $174.00 Cdn. ($123.00 U.S.) for the car – no one thing in particular stood out. Most of the past four years have been similar amounts. (Note: We did spend $4200.00 Cdn. on our renovations last summer.) [42]

In the spring of 2003 we updated our tow car, that meant purchasing a new baseplate and adding car lighting. (All costs given are in Canadian dollars, the rate of exchange was 71 cents U.S. for each dollar.) The baseplate and lighting cost us $1300.00. During that period the furnace quit on our 95 Luxor, as well as a check-valve on the water pump plus other

[42] *Those who have access to a computer can see the full details of our renovations and detailing on www.rvliving.net.*

miscellaneous things which added up to $1100.00. One week later the check-valve on our water heater quit ($100.00) and then the ballast on two 18" 'Thin-Lites' stopped functioning at an approximate replacement cost of $70 and $80.00 each. Routine class B maintenance (oil change and fuel filters, lubrication and visual check), along with a few additional parts plus a regular tune-up with parts on our generator added another $1300.00. The hourly rate at that service centre was definitely on the low side of things and not much was wrong or had to be changed but this service call contributed to the year's maintenance costs. Prices may appear to be lower in the U.S.A. but after tax, conversion rate and living costs most things equal out.

Our windshield cracked in April with a deductible of $300.00. This meant we needed new website lettering (plus the same company added an Invisible Bra on the tow car to help combat stone chips) for another $250.00.

While dry camping at an FMCA convention, our four year-old batteries would no longer hold a charge, so four new 6-volt (golf cart) house batteries added another $580.00. (I was shocked when the techs told us that most batteries can only expect a lifespan of four years.)

We still weren't done. When we had the oxidization professionally removed from the skin of our Luxor, (approximately $550.00 for service and miracle products), John used this time for his bi-monthly cleaning of the wheel wells and the tires. He discovered the cracks on the sidewalls of our four-year old front tires were becoming deeper and he no longer was confident driving our motorhome. (RV tires have a life between 4 to 5 years.) So two front tires at a cost of $409.00 each plus tax added another $956.00 towards maintenance (the other four are slated for replacement next year). From the middle of April to the beginning of August, our maintenance for both vehicles sat at approximately $6500.00 – total costs for the year – $7200.00 Cdn.

Look at the big picture to understand your overall cost of RVing. On the days when things look a little black don't forget there really is no journey as joyful as seeing North America in an RV. What better way to explore this great continent? Most yearly maintenance is well within affordable means.

Tip: If you set up a separate maintenance contingency fund and add a few hundred to it each month, money will be available to cover the expense of most unexpected repairs and upkeep

One of our biggest costs was renovating the interior of our Luxor. The renovations gave us more room and by removing the couch, we now have 'the space of a slide'. It was worth EVERY penny.

I can't stress enough how important it is to have an emergency fund. Heavy maintenance or replacement does not happen often, but when it does, it can be costly. Buying a unit several years old may be less costly than purchasing new and they do depreciate much slower than those just off the assembly line but keeping it up is a must. Even so, it still may be less costly than buying new.

This is a great lifestyle and so rewarding but it is not a bargain basement way to travel. With a little research and budgeting you can have a wonderful life on the road. **Remember many RVers who go fulltime work for a season to accumulate funds so they can travel from one great destination to another**. If RVing is what you want to do 'GO FOR IT'. With advance planning you will find a way…just go in with your eyes wide open.

"The future belongs to those who believe in the beauty of their dreams".

Peggi McDonald

General Budgeting Information

Use the above ideas to design your personalized budget.

> **Most grocery costs are similar dollar for dollar in both the U.S.A. and Canada. Only after converting at the current exchange rate will costs differ.**

Our budget is set for our lifestyle, not yours. Keep in mind that your insurance rates, mortgage payments, out of country medical, etc. will change your expenses. Our stated club affiliations or our cell phone costs or some of our other expenses may not apply to you. On the other hand, if you play expensive sports such as golf or tennis, or like to eat out, take in a stage show or go on shopping sprees, your costs may be higher than ours. All travel styles differ.

Note: My writing, seminars and book sales are declared as part of my worldwide income on our income tax. Whatever I make from my craft sales go towards buying more craft supplies.

Credit Applications

Most people don't have the cash to plunk down to pay for an RV. Even if you've sold your house, you may want to invest a majority of the amount received so it can grow. Unfortunately, lending institutions have traditionally frowned on financing 'mobile' purchases, especially if that purchase is going to be your home and can be moved at will. Essentially, the collateral can literally drive away and it's difficult to recoup in the event of default.

Another reason why it's difficult to obtain financing is because of certain questions you must answer on any credit application pertaining to residence status.

Even though we keep a room in a relative's house, we do not pay rent. So, every time we were faced with answering "Do you own your home?" or "Do you rent (an apartment or room)?" and "How much do you pay?", we were thrown into a tail-spin because we didn't know how to answer. We simply don't fit the mould of owning a house on a foundation with a white picket fence that so many non-RVers find necessary.

Our RV is our home (to us, not a bank) and our room is also part of our residence but, because we don't pay rent, the bank doesn't consider it such. We have always avoided approaching any financial institutions for credit because of these questions.

Most bank employees do not even know what an RV is. When we applied for a bank loan to purchase Kastle #2, the young loan officer's comment said it all, "The RV you want costs more than a house so we have to say no". So much for being a loyal bank customer for 35 years.

During this purchase we discovered the value of using dealer financing, the amount was competitive and the dealer worked with us to obtain the best deal.

Note: In Canada RV dealers have agreements with many financial and banking institutions. The banks want customers and the dealers hope to deliver good rates for their buyers. So a Conditional Sales Agreement is the mortgage of choice of Canadian RV dealers.

A Conditional Sales Agreement is like a low interest mortgage style loan, amortized up to 20 years depending on the cost of the unit and it can be paid in full at any time without penalties. Life insurance is also available on these agreements. Interest rate may remain low for the initial 3 to 5 year period or even longer. At a recent dealer open house where I presented seminars, interest on new RVs was 0%. The financial situation of each RVer is very personal, it pays to shop around and look at all options.

One year, during the Motorhome and Trailer Show (near Toronto, Ontario), we talked to representatives from a large Canadian bank. They were offering a very low interest loan for show buyers. They didn't know who we were so we could be very honest about our fulltime status. The reps listened and, after I said that we didn't know how to respond to the questions and qualify for a loan, they informed us that the additional part to the above-stated questions was, "Do you live with parents?" or "Other?". Finally, a category we fall under – we are definitely 'other'.

According to the definition of the 'other' category, we do own a home – with wheels and, we do pay rent – to campgrounds. What a relief to finally come out in the open and, once again, qualify, for a mortgage or loan.

American RVers should take a look at what's offered by major RV clubs before going to a bank. Additional options are also listed in international magazines. Most U.S. financial institutions have some of the same concerns as Canadian banks do about financing a 'moving' object. However, many of the larger U.S.-based RV clubs have teamed up with several companies that offer extremely low RV financing. Definitely check all financing options from your dealer, your bank and with clubs such as

FMCA (Family Motor Coach Association), Good Sam and Escapees, etc. It is your money, shop for the best deal for you.

More For The Money

While John and I were working, our two substantial and steady salaries allowed us to buy what we wanted. However, living on our two adequate, but somewhat limited, military pension incomes, things changed. Yes, our expenses are lower but, so is the cash restocking our bank account each month.

During our first year of extensive travel we spent whatever we wished on 'toys' for ourselves plus many gift and souvenirs for everyone back home.

We soon realized if we wanted to continue exploring this way, we had to find ways to make every dollar count. The following dollar stretchers helped us to cut daily living expenses and some of these may be helpful to you.

♦ When we visit a place, we like to savour the flavour of the area by enjoying the different cuisine from local restaurants. A lot of these places include early dinner specials and buffets, so dining out gives us a treat without emptying our bank account. Having lunch at an expensive restaurant is more affordable than dinner. Mid-day meals are also more casual so the relaxed dress of most RVers is perfectly acceptable.

♦ When it is practical, visit popular 'hot spots' during the off or fringe seasons. The restaurants, campgrounds and attractions offer discounts up to 50 percent simply because it's a slow time of year.

♦ For example, Florida's warm and sunny climate is beautiful in the winter but also in November or in April, especially on the panhandle beaches. These two off-season months are a perfect time to visit most winter utopias without crowds of tourists or extremely hot weather.

♦ If you can't save dollars, collect your nickels or quarters. Empty your pockets and purse of your loose change every night and treat yourself to a special meal or unique gift with your savings.

♦ In this wash-and-wear age, there really is no need to buy 'dry clean only' clothes. Read the labels carefully because some blends, especially cotton and rayon usually need professional care. On the other hand, many silks and woollens are now washable.

♦ Look for large shopping malls promoting a wide range of bargain merchandise. These shopping meccas may simply be discount stores in a mall, factory outlet stores, or at the immense diversified pottery factories (popular stopping spots throughout the U.S.).

Note: Williamsburg, Virginia, the home of the 'queen' of pottery factories is an immense shopping facility. An endless variety of merchandise and a vast amount of stock is available at extremely low prices. This particular (135-acre) complex resembles a giant flea market – only here all merchandise is new.

You can find everything from silk flowers and craft supplies to Christmas decorations, kitchen stuff and linens. Fabric, household accessories, hardware, plants, plus so much more, highlight the inventory and every item is reasonably priced. It's a fun and interesting place to visit.

♦ Outlet malls are the latest form of discount shopping. Manufacturers use this marketing method to off-load first quality products of last year's designs, overruns, over-stocked merchandise, samples, seconds, irregulars and discounted articles – all at very low prices.

♦ Be sure to shop around and become aware of regular prices of the items you plan to buy at outlet malls. Although many name brands do sell below retail price, all outlet mall merchandise is not a bargain.

♦ These discount havens are usually located near major highways and, sometimes, the only form of advertising may be an extra-large billboard indicating which exit to take to reach the store.

♦ In the U.S., RV discount stores, such as Camping World, stock an extensive line of RV accessories at attractive low prices. Located throughout the U.S., the Camping World chain performs general repair service and RV warranty service plus provides installation of all items sold at the stores. Several RV dealers on both sides of the border offer competitive prices in their stores as well. But many RVers prefer to shop at home in familiar territory.

♦ Using credit cards adds convenience to shopping excursions but if possible avoid cards that carry an annual fee. Paying the balance in full eliminates costly interest charges. However, be aware that some small businesses such as campgrounds or out of the way gas stations may charge an extra fee for credit card sales. These stations may offer discount for cash.

♦ Check the pumps carefully before filling up; if you're paying in cash and accidentally use the credit card-designated pump, you will have to pay that price not the lower cash amount. More and more stations require payment before filling up your gas tank.

Peggi McDonald

- Don't assume you must be 65 years old to enjoy senior's benefits. Some discounts begin when you reach 50, others start at 55 or 60. In several restaurants if the senior member pays, all members of the party may benefit from the discount. Ask, ask, and ask – you'll never know who offers discounts to seniors unless you ask.
- To see as much as we can we take inexpensive sightseeing tours plus we look for self-explanatory CDs and cassette tapes that play in our vehicle's player. These CDs and cassettes offer a very comfortable and informative way to explore an area at your own pace and in your own vehicle. They are available for rent in many tourist areas; they may even be free with your camping fees.

   Note: The most interesting pre-recorded auto-tapes that we've used were Gettysburg, Pennsylvania and during an excursion from Banff to Jasper in Alberta and one that related the history and sites of Lafayette, Louisiana's Cajun country. Some government-run parks also promote cassette tapes to explain wildlife.

- In both Canada and the U.S., several welcome centres and tourist bureaus have coupon books for travellers. At each information office ask the staff if they have any area coupon promotions – the savings may range from minimal to '2 for 1' to substantial.
- From Monday to Thursday, provincial and state parks may offer discounts to senior campers; however, in some areas to reap benefits you must be a resident of that state or province. At several places this discounted price bonus continues on weekends, especially during the off-season. Camping rates may be lower than private parks although, in many of these beautiful places visitors may have to pay an extra day-use fee in addition to camping costs.

> **Special Note: Several states don't allow pets into the state parks. Tourist bureaus and camping directories can provide info as to the location of these 'no pet' areas are located.**

- Most campgrounds offer 'one day free' if you camp for a week – you pay for six nights and the seventh one is complimentary. The monthly rate is usually 30 to 40 percent lower than a daily fee – seasonal or extended stays are even less.
- Numerous large RV clubs on both sides of the border have put together a selection of member parks that offer discounts to card-carrying

234

members. Campground directories are part of club benefit packages.[43] In most areas, reservations during off-season are unnecessary, however, this is not the case for peak travel periods such as long weekends and January to March in all sun country states.

I'm aware that quite a few RVers like the freedom to roam and travel without reservations. You will probably find a spot to stay but, unless you want to be turned away from many popular destination parks, or spend time boondocking in fields behind park walls, making a reservation guarantees you a site during busy periods. Vacations will be much more enjoyable if you don't waste time looking for a campsite.

The above are only a few of the many ways we extend our pension cheques. To find your special dollar stretchers, talk to other RVers you meet. Most of us love to share our secrets and find out all about yours.

Bookkeeping

Keeping a record of all your expenditures is extremely important for both short vacations and for extensive explorations. Whether you simply make notes in a small booklet for each day or week on the road or you keep records much as I have since our early years of RVing, it is very important to know what you're spending your money on and how much you will need for a later excursion. It doesn't matter whether your destinations are next door or someplace far away, good records make follow-up trip planning a lot easier.

I kept my early records by entries hand-written into a ledger; then I moved all my recorded information to the computer. After several computer crashes (and with limited back-up) I have again reverted to hand-written notes. There is no right way so no matter which route you follow it helps to have records to fall back on. Using a ledger with expense columns works great for us to keep track of weekly and monthly expenses. John has set-up several binders to record vehicle maintenance for our tow car and motorhome, fixed expenses (include due dates) plus gas and unexpected costs are some of the other things we record. Investments, appliance warranties and taxes fill the pages of a few more binders. Add any other information pertinent to your lifestyle. Don't forget to include dollar exchange rates to your home currency no matter which country you are travelling in. We totally rely on these records at tax time.

RVers receiving fixed incomes find it a challenge to cope with rising costs. Good record keeping helps to stretch your money to the maximum. Be

---

43 *Contact information for many RV clubs can be found on the* RV WebLink *page of www.rvliving.net.*

thorough, but keep your records as simple as possible. After all, your main objective is to enjoy your travels not be bogged down with enough work to challenge an accountant. 🛩

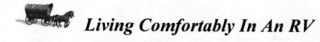 *Living Comfortably In An RV*

A simple stroll over the bridge at the border between Texas and Mexico is a perfect place to find unique crafts. This is where we had our satellite dish painted to match our mural.

After living in a spacious house or apartment, many people wonder about coping in a confined area of an RV. Don't worry, if you travel extensively or live fulltime in your unit, you will soon discover that adapting to a smaller space isn't really a big problem.

When we stopped working, John and I moved from a four-bedroom house to our 32-foot motorhome. The transition was challenging because, for three months, we had military uniforms, job-related articles, large clock alarms, make-up mirror and so many extras packed into our home-on-wheels. Although these were important items for our military life, we didn't need them for our road life and it was a big relief to finally off-load those extras.

The day we offloaded our alarm clocks and extra stuff at my sister's for storage, our tension went with it. Yes, as fulltimers we do continue to get up early to attend certain events but, now our internal clock kicks in. Other items that we discovered we could live without were my makeup mirror, John's eight pairs of dress pants, two suits and accessories plus my evening clothes. Although we still dress up for special functions, it's no problem to wear the same outfit two times in row. As we move to different locations we meet new friends who have never before seen our wardrobe.

The easiest way to become comfortable in your RV is to eliminate excesses. After years of a life of travel we find most houses have an excess of wasted space. In a house, instead of having to eliminate things, it's easier to hide them in the back of a closet or crawl space. After all, who knows when you might need that treasure again? In our garage sale extravaganza two decades ago we sold $1,700 of valuable junk that we spent 25 years collecting.

Most RVers are experts at extending space and each one of us is only too happy to share these travel tips with anyone who will listen. The following are some other ways to ease your transition from a house to your home-on-wheels.

♦ At RV shows listen to as many product demonstrations as time allows. It's to your benefit to learn every detailed fact about RVs – both inside and out.

♦ Study all information you can get your hands on with the same intensity as you would a promotional course at your work place. Ask dealers and the people conducting seminars what everything does and how it works.

♦ Include questions on such things as weight limits, RV appliances and operation of the levelling devices.

♦ Add personal touches to your unit.

♦ Luxuries and extras make your RV a special place. If your house had lace and frills, carry that décor into your RV. For instance, I have silk flowers displayed everywhere (real flowers do NOT move easily across the border – see the section on *Customs*), silver candleholders on my dinette table and silver wine goblets in the cupboard. These travel well in our motorhome and they were very much a part of our life in our house. Do whatever is necessary to be comfortable and cosy, albeit on a smaller scale.

Although an RV is compact, it's not necessary to live without the comforts of home. Carrying favourite 'toys' and appliances on board enhances RV travel, just find easy-to-reach places to stow them. Don't forget there is probably space underneath for appliances you may only use occasionally such as a blender, etc. When you bury things that you must dig for, it doesn't take long to discover it's easy to live without it.

RVers who join RV club chapters and attend rallies benefit ten-fold from the fellowship and knowledge of the other attendees. Friendships emerge as RVers take part in area tours, potlucks, catered meals, campfires and entertainment. Besides keeping busy, everyone has a good time.

At large rallies and conventions, activities include numerous seminars covering all facets of RVing. You can learn so much about the RV lifestyle and your RV from these informative sessions. Speakers discuss engine performance plus talk about and demonstrate accessories such as propane appliances, your 6 or 12-volt battery system or converters or inverters or sani-system or security or, or, or. The more you learn, the more you're able to share with others; and, the more you will enjoy RVing.

Read and understand all literature received with your unit. Comprehending RV warranties reduces possible problems you may experience during a breakdown. Stressful situations are easier to handle when setbacks don't become overwhelming. Knowing exactly what insurance you have or what each warranty covers will prevent disasters when trying to obtain reimbursements later.

New RVers should travel and live in their RV as much as possible – look for campgrounds close to home. Learning the idiosyncrasies of your unit can be an enlightening yet somewhat frustrating experience. The year before John and I retired we spent most of the summer living in our motorhome. What an education that was!

I mention this next point quite frequently but it's extremely wise for both pilot and co-pilot to be comfortable driving the unit. On one trip south, we met a couple in Amarillo, Texas, who, due to a non-life threatening medical problem, had to frequently change drivers. Up to that point, the husband had done most of the driving but he had developed problems with his legs, which prevented him from sitting in one position for extended periods. Since both were adept at handling their motorhome, they simply traded places every few hours and continued their journey. The trip would have ended abruptly if Mary hadn't felt comfortable driving their coach. Excellent places to practise are shopping centre parking lots – after hours and on holidays, of course.

One thing is certain; when life in your RV becomes commonplace you will never miss the spacious comforts of your other house. In the beginning, when we parked in the driveway of friends or relatives, they frequently asked us to come inside to sleep in a 'real bed'. Our reply was, "We have a real bed, a real shower, a real bath and a real home." Over the years, although some people still can't understand our lifestyle, most no longer ask us to leave our RV home.

Our visits are more enjoyable when we live in our comfortable home-on-wheels in our hosts' driveway and simply spend time socializing in their spacious houses. Before long you, too, can be extremely content living in an RV and maybe even wonder why anyone really needs two homes. This just may be the time to join the thousands of us who call ourselves fulltimers.

The House Dilemma

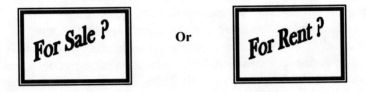

Now that you have your RV, travelling on a whim is fun. The thought of becoming a fulltimer appeals to your sense of freedom but most of us question if it is wise to sell the house or rent it out 'just in case'. That decision is yours alone and, whatever you decide, neither choice is hassle free and each one carries painful decisions.

To discover the option most suited to both you and your family try to consider realistic economic factors; don't let emotional memories of happy times cloud your decision.

Remember, when a natural disaster such as a flood, fire or tornado destroys a home, finding everyone safe and sound is all that is important. As a result, to objectively dispose of personal acquisitions, think of your home, car, furniture and 'can't live without' treasures as inanimate objects.

The following is a list of the pros and cons of renting versus selling.

Renting

Advantages – Renting out your home keeps your original investment intact and the extra monthly income helps, too. Rent payments should be sufficient to cover mortgage payments (if applicable), property taxes, maintenance, management fees plus any repairs caused by tenants. Of course, it would be ideal if you had some of the rent money left over. Treat rental property as a business. It provides a beneficial tax break. Yes, you must declare the rent received as income but as long as the house remains a rental property, all expenses should become tax write-offs.

Disadvantages – Absentee landlords need someone to assume responsibility on their behalf and relying on a friend or relative to keep an eye on your investment may not be the smartest move. Managing a rental property for someone else can turn into a big responsibility.

Overview – Since this is a business hire a professional broker to handle the job. Unless you have excellent tenants, costly management fees may dig deep into any rental income you plan to receive.

For instance, if your tenants vacate early or get behind in rent, finding new occupants or dealing with the eviction process costs money. It may even require your personal input or participation. Usually repairs or redecorating are also necessary before new tenants move in.

When John and I faced the sell or rent dilemma it was a surprise to learn that, even if professionals did manage our house as a rental property, we must be part of all decisions, including evictions and screening new tenants. Although every tenant won't cause trouble, one bad experience can easily tarnish your dream.

No one likes to think that situations such as these occur, let alone coping with them from a distance. Problems are aggravating, a nuisance and a huge irritation especially if all you want is to enjoy your new-found freedom of the RV lifestyle. During our early adventures, maintaining an accurate balance in our chequebook was difficult. If we'd chosen to become absentee landlords, the thought of dealing with potential problems from distance places would have been horrendous.

Selling

Advantages – The most important point in your decision is the market value of your house. Generally speaking, real estate will always be a profitable investment and you should end up with a large chunk of disposable income.

Disadvantages – The decision to sell may not be easy, especially when you've lived in your home a long time. Before deciding, learn the current selling price of houses in your area. Ask yourself if real estate property is on a rise or in a decline.

Overview – Most RVers realize that wisely invested resale dollars can supplement monthly pension income. Although investments fluctuate from high to low, a well-invested portfolio can provide extra dollars at regular intervals. Investment income is a sure way to add to your travel pleasures without the problems or concerns of long-distance property ownership. When the most beneficial route to follow is uncertain, consider retaining the services of a financial advisor or a broker of any large insurance company. These professionals usually don't charge fees to advise you about investment options, instead they receive payment from the companies where they place your money.

No One's At Home

Advantages – This is another choice – just simply lock the doors and go. This way you do not gain monthly equity, however, you also do not pay for any damage caused by unruly tenants.

Disadvantages – Even though you're away, you must pay for utilities, snow removal, mail-forwarding and much more. Ensuring that an empty house appears lived in takes creativity. If a house looks unoccupied, it sends out an open invitation and a challenge for vandals to gain access. During your absence, routine security checks on your residence are a must. Asking someone to keep on top of what is happening is not only an insurance requirement; it adds tremendous peace-of-mind while you're exploring North America.

Overview – On the other hand, if your empty home is an apartment situated above the second floor or possibly a park model in a secure campground, you could lock the door and walk away after a few minor preparations. Maybe this is the time to downsize your home; keep your treasures but move to a smaller place.

Decisions, decisions, decisions – each situation is unique and individual, only you can make a personalized choice. It's not easy to decide what to do, however, try to remain focussed on your new lifestyle. Most definitely, eliminate emotional ties from your final conclusion. Maybe your dilemma will be solved by the answer to this very pertinent question, "Do I need the equity from the sale of my home to finance my RV purchase?" When John and I retired, the resale market was booming and this positive economic fact influenced our decision to let the house go. Ultimately, it was a wise decision.

Another point to consider before making up your mind to sell or rent. Selling our house while we still lived in it ensured that our home entered the market in show condition. This might not have been the case if tenants had occupied our home for a period of time. We received a good price and, although the market continued to increase after we sold, a wise long-term investment made up for any loss. Even now we are still happy we made this decision and we have never looked back.

Should It Stay Or Should It Go?

> ## I brake for
> ## Garage Sales

One of my favourite signs – I shop till I drop and come home with nothing because I have no room to put new things.

Now that you've bought your RV and have decided what to do about your house, the next big question is what to do with important stuff that you've accumulated over the years.

The answer to that question depends whether you plan to simply downsize your residence to allow time for extensive travels or whether you've decided to take the bull by the horns and head out fulltime. In either case, there's no painless way to accomplish the overwhelming task of weeding out your prize possessions. And then there's the daunting task of deciding what to do with your furniture.

First, accept the fact that all furniture and treasures are actually inanimate objects. Whether you decide to keep your collectibles in a storage facility, sell them at a garage sale or give them to the kids, don't despair – you won't eliminate your memories because the memories will stay with you forever.

With these thoughts in mind, the disposal of acquisitions accumulated over the years becomes easier. I realize no major decision is simple, however, when parting with the furniture and accessories that complemented your home, not all choices must be disastrous or heart-wrenching.

If downsizing to a smaller retirement home, a condo or a park model in a campground, simply take valuables to your new home. The collectibles and souvenirs stored at the back of the crawl space in the basement make interesting garage sale items. That is, if the kids or your favourite charity can't use them. Your junk may become somebody else's treasure.

243

When dismantling a lifetime of memories, many RVers with families ask their kids to choose their favourite things. This way your special mementoes remain family keepsakes. The kids care for them and you can enjoy them as you explain related history during your visits.

In preparation for our new and exciting retirement lifestyle, John and I held a two-day garage sale extravaganza in our driveway when we sold our house. This enjoyable occasion never seemed to end. Since many mementoes were from my single days, it was fun to watch others appreciate and purchase the treasures I had found irresistible years earlier.

John and I have no children and were only married four years when we both retired. Shortly into our marriage, new furniture graced our home. On retirement, everything was too new to let it go as used and selling our wedding gifts and valuable keepsakes didn't appeal to us either. We weren't ready to part with new acquisitions such as sheets, blankets, dishes and crystal. There was always the chance that fulltime living in our motorhome wouldn't appeal to us in a few years down the road. So, for the time being, all cherished items went into storage.

We packed keepsakes in well-labelled boxes and found new homes for everything else. Even with all of our planning, John and I made one huge mistake. During the first two years we placed our belongings in an inaccessible long-term storage facility. The main problem with this enclosure is that we had no access to add or subtract anything. When we moved the contents a second time into a self-storage unit, several items from the long-term facility had simply vanished. Yes, they were insured but now we no longer owned those particular (cherished enough to keep) household valuables.

Eventually our things were moved to a 'U-Lock-it' storage unit where only John and I had a key. This allowed us easy access to dishes, bedding, clothing and other necessities. Simply for the sake of change, it was fun to add new items (from our household cache) to our coach each summer.

This move into a self-storage facility provided us with one more benefit; with easy access we no longer travelled in an overloaded state. We now store or dispose of every item on board our coach we haven't used during the previous year. If I have a favourite special something in the coach then I'd better find a use for it by springtime or it goes.

Originally our plans included spending two years of life on the road before settling into one place. We stored sufficient furniture to ensure any future two-bedroom apartment would be comfortable. A wise thought at the time, although in retrospect – for us – this was a bad move (our planned two years has grown into nearly 20).

Our first self-storage compartment was large and spacious; however, paying the increasing monthly costs soon became an excessive and unnecessary expense. These costs equalled an amount similar to condominium fees on a small apartment outside of a high-cost-of-living area.

Those wanting to experience fulltime travel in their RV may decide that storing valuables for a few years is the answer. You should, though, liquidate large furniture pieces. When wood and fabric is piled high and sits unused and uncared for over several years, it depreciates very quickly. In time, long-term storage is actually destructive.

Our advice: Don't hang on to your furniture. Sell it and replace it as required. Liquidating bedroom, dining room and living room suites displayed in their proper household settings is so much easier than selling the same items from a storage unit several years later. Trust me, we've tried it!

John and I thoroughly enjoy our travelling lifestyle but, unfortunately, the longer our explorations continued, the more our furniture suffered. Although used furniture is popular, as a resale item it's always an extremely poor investment. Whether you sell in a consignment shop, flea market, newspaper advertisement or at an auction, most owners feel that, even if the pieces are in excellent condition, they just about give away their precious pre-owned home furnishings.

When we finally eliminated a few large pieces of our furniture, we chose to sell. I can't say that we actually sold it because the price we received was equal to accepting a small fee from someone who paid us so they could take it away. (Don't forget, not only must you consider the original price, you also have to calculate the amount that you've paid for moving your furniture and storage fees over the years. Very rarely will you recoup even a portion of your costs.)

The auction did, however, scale down our possessions so we could fit everything (stacked up high) into a smaller and less costly storage unit. Even with fewer possessions our storage irritations didn't end. Heavy snow during the 93/94 winter damaged the roof of our storage unit. In less than two years, due to the horrendous winter and construction of the storage complex, our contents moved five times.

Each move added more stress to our furniture and it was time to let everything go. John and I had no plans to settle anywhere in the foreseeable future and, when we do decide to stop travelling, we'll replace stuff as needed unless, of course, our next home is a fully furnished RV park model.

Against our better judgement, we decided to sell the balance of our beautiful furniture at another auction. (It really was our only choice.) We knew that our expensive and quality furniture was becoming slightly tired-looking from long-term storage. However, once again, the low and inappropriate price we received for the three room settings was less than a modest donation to charity. Selling at an auction (with unsealed bids) was and still is a very upsetting experience.

One thing we did learn from this is that these buyers take your prized possessions home with them for practically nothing. Forget about receiving a fair market value at any auction – you take what you get. On the other hand, if we must replace any furnishings in the future, a visit to a small town auction may be our most economical shopping spot. Something good did come out of this. We no longer worry about our furniture wasting away in storage.

Everyone's situation is different. A close friend included their house furniture and contents in the price of their home. Two years later they had no regrets with their decision.

Many fulltimers feel a self-storage facility is the only way to go. Other travellers use a room in their kids' house instead of a rented self-storage unit. This works especially well as they can also use that address for a homeowner's insurance policy. (Note: It is difficult to buy insurance to cover contents in storage.)

John and I need an area to keep household items such as clothes, linens and treasures close at hand and some place to store our photos, my wedding dress, diplomas and awards as well as our lead crystal, sterling silver serving pieces and more. We couldn't part with these costly treasures then – now two decades later many have really have become quite unimportant but since we have room to keep them they will probably stay where they are till we hang up the keys. And we do need a storage utility for day-to-day stuff that we offload from time to time to reduce the weight of our motorhome.

Our present storage unit is the smallest one available but, it works well for us; we have room to move around plus we can sort through things when necessary.

Look carefully at all options. Be aware that nothing in this life stays the same. Ideas on what is important change rapidly as you live or travel on the road. At each stage, simply take one day at a time and deal with difficult decisions as they happen. Rest assured, no problem associated with the 'good life' is so overwhelming that it should prevent you from enjoying this interesting RV lifestyle.

Residency – Where To Call Home

Legally no one can visit any country for longer than six months without special visas. (Visas can take considerable time for processing.) From a tax point of view, visitors who remain in another country (U.S., Canada or Mexico) longer than six months are considered residents and should be paying taxes. The host country expects tax money from every resident.

Canada's economy is similar to the U.S. As a result it's not easy for a Canadian or Americans to emigrate from one country to another but it's not impossible either. Before you decide to make a change in your country of residence, look into all facts such as medical costs, residency requirements, vehicle registration and licensing plus tax rules – pension money may be taxed as well as long-term investment benefits.

Moving to another country may seem to be a perfect solution, however, after you discover all the facts occasionally the initial incentives may lose some of their lustre. Contact lawyers, embassies or consulates on both sides of the border to obtain the most up-to-date information available.

The big consideration for Canadians is medical coverage. This means becoming a resident of a province where you can spend four to six months per year. Exact times will vary but a special 'time-out' for travel from once in a lifetime to a period every few years is available – the rules of each province and territory differ. In all cases you do have to declare a specific permanent residence or address home; a campground or post office box usually will not qualify as your official home. If you shorten your time in the south and take an occasional time out, you can still find lots of time to explore our great country.

American RVers will find some states friendlier to fulltimers than others with reference to taxes, required time in the state, vehicle licensing and registration, etc. South Dakota has extended a very warm welcome to fulltimers looking for a home state. Florida, Texas, Arizona, Oregon. Nevada, Alaska and Tennessee are also additional favourites. Do your research, become aware of all pertinent details before deciding the best location for you. You have to be a legal resident somewhere so find the most advantageous place for your situation. Even having vehicles tagged (licensed) in two states can send up red flags if you plan to cross the border. Select a place to call home, be aware of the regulations affecting time required to be in state and travel where you choose.[44]

---

44 *Contact phone numbers and state websites that welcome fulltimers are listed under the* Resource *section on the* RV WebLink *page of www.rvliving.net. Phone numbers of government departments of each state are listed in local phone books.*

The Homesick Blues

12-year-old Kayla feeding the goat at a
unique shopping stop **en route** *east.*

Deciding that extended RV travel is for you is all well and good but, when it comes down to the crunch, inevitably there's a cry, "But I don't want to leave my family!" The homesick blues have struck even before you've left the driveway.[45]

Most fulltiming RVers and long-term travellers reluctantly leave the grandkids when they retire to 'play on the road'. But, leaving for your new

---

45 *For information about family camping log onto* www.familiesontheroad.com

life doesn't mean that you have to cut all ties with the folks back home. Instead, look for unique ways to stay in contact.

Several RVers we've met plan their winter travel destinations to places suggested by children and grandchildren and all parties make arrangements to meet for their own family holidays. That way everyone enjoys a vacation in the sunny south while spending precious time together. Texas, Arizona, Florida, California and Mexico are popular winter getaways. During Christmas and spring break the southern RV parks change from primarily an adult campground to a family reunion party site.

The American Thanksgiving holiday period in late November serves as an alternate time to celebrate an early Christmas for American RVers. Although Canada's Thanksgiving takes place mid-October, many families also use this time of togetherness as a substitute for Christmas gatherings before Grandma and Grandpa take off on their travels. They share gifts with visiting family members, decorate a tree with all the trimmings and indulge in the usual Christmas feast. This preliminary sociable family gathering frees the kids to spend leisurely time with the other side of the family on Christmas day, or to celebrate on their own.

A trip home during the holiday season is another option. Since supplementary medical coverage is changing, habits of extended travellers are too. Several Canadian medical insurance companies offering out of country medical coverage now include an inexpensive annual policy for trips that don't exceed a specific amount of continuous days per trip (35 or 40 or 90 days). This type of insurance provides a perfect excuse to fly home at Christmas and break up the time spent out of the country.

We live in a time of mass mobility and frequently kids move because of careers and other employment opportunities. They (and the grandchildren) may work anywhere from one coast to the other. For these grandparents, RV travel can be a lifesaver. It provides a perfect opportunity to visit the children and their families when *en route* to other exciting destinations. When there is room to park your RV in their driveway, your visit takes on a new dimension since everyone can enjoy their personal space and family routines don't change much.

Consequently, RVers who live in their unit during family visits place less strain on the lifestyle of both families and, having your own home to retreat to, also provides time for a little rest to recover from the exuberance of active grandchildren.

Whether fulltiming or simply living a distance away from the grandkids, several RVing grandparents invite one child at a time to travel with them during a short vacation. When only one grandchild is with you the event becomes exciting and you can cater to their every wish with undivided attention.

Although we don't have children, John and I are surrounded by a large family of siblings. When we started RVing I had five sisters (two are now deceased), along with brothers-in-law, nine nieces and nephews plus great nieces and nephews scattered from Ontario to Nova Scotia. John's sister and brother-in-law and their children and grandkids live in northwest Chicago. During summers in the early 90s we spent as much time as possible camped near John's aunt (now deceased) who lived in a senior's complex north of Toronto.

Our flexible RV travel schedule affords us the perfect opportunity to visit with family more frequently now than ever was remotely possible while we were working or living in a house on a foundation. Since beginning our RV travels, family visits are more leisurely and, because we're not always rushing from here to there, a joy. When we park in our hosts' driveway we are close to the action but not so close that we're intruding into their home routine.

Several years ago we added an exciting twist to our travel adventures. Many family members and friends matched their travel destinations with ours. One year we stopped for a visit with John's sister in Chicago then we travelled to Tennessee for a week's stopover in Nashville. There, my sister and her husband joined us to see the sights of Opryland. John and I then headed for Pompano Beach, Florida where we met another sister and her husband who wanted to enjoy a little relaxation and a lot of sunshine.

That winter, a third sister travelled with us for two months of RV explorations up the west coast of Mexico, into Arizona and southern California. Along the way, several other impromptu reunions with long-time RVing friends complemented this wonderful season.

Kids also enjoy exciting RV adventures. Our niece, Kayla, gets acquainted with the horses during a covered wagon ride near Brandon, Manitoba.

251

A few years ago our 12-year-old niece Kayla flew to Kelowna, British Columbia to travel back east with us in our motorhome to Ottawa, Ontario. It was her trip and we let her plan our destinations and stops to make this a memorable adventure although she did have to deal with being homesick occasionally. However, if we hadn't been RVing none of us would have been able to enjoy that great experience.

Not all years blended so well with travels of our friends and family but, if we hadn't been RVing, that season wouldn't be etched in our cache of our most pleasant memories. As experienced RVers we find it fun to share our adventures and, like most RVers, spend more time now with our families than we ever thought possible.

The following few hints are used by grandparents on the move to ensure that the grandkids don't forget them. They send small trinkets to each child from the area they are visiting – just to let the kids 'see' where they are. Providing each child with a map before you leave home is another way to stay in touch. Follow this by sending postcards from each stopping spot so the kids know why you want to go there.

Gifts don't have to be expensive. For instance, younger children will enjoy hearing their own personalized bedtime story. Every region has some kind of legend so make a recording of a story by either reading it directly from a book you've bought or paraphrase the story in your own words to their level of understanding. Older kids may like to read the historical brochures you pick up along the way.

Large-hole plastic craft webbing is a fun medium for young kids from which to make a variety of things. With a magic marker, trace comic books patterns on the mesh and send it to the kids along with coloured yarn and a large-eye needle. The kids can sew around the design with the thread to create their own special artwork. In an accompanying letter, give simple instructions for them to follow, including the basic cross-stitch pattern.

Another option for younger children is to cut a variety of shapes out of cardboard. Punch holes around the outside edge and enclose colourful shoelaces so they can lace through the holes. As well as learning dexterity and simple sewing stitches, they'll also be learning about the different shapes. A set of punch-out cardboard letters from a stationery store is a great learning tool and punch-out numbers can help with basic math.

Most kids like to put stickers on everything. If the grandkids are young, make them a personalized sticker book. Place a line of stickers on a piece of cardboard, leaving room for a second row for the kids to match. Send the left over stickers with a note accompanying your gift.

Take a photo of an unusual tree or flower you see on your travels and explain in a letter its unique characteristics. If possible, include a dried leaf or a few dried petals to illustrate your description.

Collecting sea shells is always fun, but carrying around a vast amount of them may be too heavy to store in an RV. But, a photo of Grandma and Grandpa on the beach with seashore treasures is a lasting memento. Send the kids samples of the different shells with a short note of where you were when you found them. If they still have show-and-tell in their class-rooms, suggest that they take the collection to show their classmates. Visit the many craft stores to pick up unusual treasures as well.

Search the discount bins in Wal*Mart and dollar stores for end-of-the-line items such as post-it notes, pencils or colourful pin-on buttons that fit inside of a legal size envelope. If you look for easily mailed items that only cost a few dollars, you can enjoy sending these treasures more frequently.

Potato chip tubes make great mailing tubes to send small items to the kids. Postage for odd-shaped objects may cost more than the item but it is the thought that counts.

It really makes no difference what you send home, it's hearing from you that matters. Unusual postcards, short letters, small activity crafts, photos or just a note to say "Hi" will ensure that you will always be remembered. They will also take a delightful interest in your travels.

To leave your family for an extended journey or as a fulltimer is a big decision only you can make. However, on many occasions, children and grandchildren (not to mention the grandparents themselves) are happier with frequent visits for short periods. RVs are one of a few forms of travel that contribute to this type of togetherness.

Peggi McDonald

MAIL CALL AND CYBERSPACE

Keeping In Touch By Post Or E-mail
(See also **Keeping In Touch By Voice Contact)**

These days there are so many ways to keep in touch with family, friends and those 'back home'. Message services and cell phones make it easy to stay in voice contact but another option is through the old fashioned way – regular mail. Of course, before the Internet, we received all correspondence and paid our bills using the postal service. Thanks to the many mail-forwarding services, RVers who move from place to place now routinely receive their 'snail' mail without too much difficulty.

Our permanent mailing address in Canada is through Mail Boxes Etc. (their outlets are also available internationally). My sister usually picks up our mail but if for some reason she can't, Mail Boxes Etc. will send our mail to any address and by whatever means requested – from courier service to postal service. They do add a slight handling fee. Staff will go through our mail to search for, and even read, a special letter if we ask.

For a higher fee, Canadian and U.S. postal services will also forward mail to one particular address but they will not go through your mail to decide what you want to receive.

John and I take advantage of a free U.S.A. mail forwarding service from one of our RV clubs. A number of these groups (including many RV manufacturer and discount camping clubs) offer similar mail forwarding services as part of their benefit package. Some charge an upfront fee while others take regular withdrawals from your credit card to pay for postage required to send the mail on to your destination.

Several businesses advertised in international RV magazines[46] and newspapers on both sides of the border also forward mail at regular

---

46 *Major RV magazines include*
      Family Motor Coaching *published by FMCA:* www.fmca.com,
       1-800-545-3622;
      Highways *published by Good Sam Club:* www.goodsamclub.com,
       1-800-234-3450;
      Escapees *published by SKP:* www.escapees.com, *1-888-757- 2582;*
      RV gazette *published by the Explorer RV Club:* www.explorer-rvcub.com,
       1-800-999-0819;
      RV Lifestyle *magazine:* www.rvlifemag.com, *1-905-624-8218;*
      RV Times *based in British Columbia:* www.rvtimes.com, *1-604-857-8828;*

intervals. The policies of the majority of these services are similar but, as an example, I'll explain how our service works:

As we move from one location to another, we call our club's head office by a toll-free number to provide the address of where we want mail sent. Our mail forwarding address includes our name and membership number along with the club address. Because our last name begins with the letter M, our mail leaves the mail-forwarding department every Thursday as long as we provide a new location before 5:00 p.m. on Wednesday. When we are in the U.S. our mail is waiting for us the following Monday.

In the summer our U.S. mail forwarding service sends our mail to general delivery to wherever we are in Canada. We allow 10 to 14 days for it to come north (however, after 9/11 it took 20 to 23 days for forwarded mail sent by airmail to go south – apparently every piece was being scanned at the border. When that package was sent at the more expensive 'global priority' it reached us in seven days). The reverse will work for visitors who plan to spend time in Canada, especially between U.S.A. and Canada.

Redirection can be arranged for either a multiple or one-time mailing or we can request it stay put 'until further notice'. By using such a service we know that our mail will reach us every week that we're on the move. If we modify our itinerary and don't connect with our package, it's automatically returned to sender after 15 days.

We leave FMCA's mail forwarding service (located in Ohio) in place year-round; but due to low volume we usually only have mail forwarded every two weeks. Our continual U.S. address is a great convenience for us (or any fulltiming Canadian), especially when applying for a service or product warranty that requires a U.S. address. It also works well for mail-in rebates on purchases; as an added bonus, American camping club mailings plus RV magazines reach us faster.

Memberships in some clubs, such as Camping World's President Club, are more expensive for Canadians, mostly because of postage costs to send literature across the border. With a U.S. address, we avoid these extra costs. Mail forwarding service is available from several U.S.A. RV clubs plus additional options are advertised in the classifieds of international RV magazines.[46]

(46 con't) Camping Caravanning *published by the FQCC (Quebec):*
www.campingquebec.com/fqcc/information.shtml; 1-514-252-3333;
Motorhome*: www.motorhomemagazine.com, 1-800-678-1201;*
Trailer Life*: www.trailerlife.com, 1-800-825-6861.*
Additional RV magazines *are listed on the* RV WebLinks *page of*
www.rvliving.net.

Americans visiting Canada can use general delivery at any post office or if you return every year you can open an account at places like Mail Boxes Etc. They will forward your mail to wherever you wish for a small fee plus postage costs. Canadian Xpresspost envelopes reach destinations within Canada in 2 to 3 days as does Priority Mail in the U.S.A. General delivery postal codes and ZIP codes are available from any post office.[47] Of course, to keep that information close at hand, you can always purchase the cumbersome postal or ZIP code directories.

In The Past

We didn't use a mail forwarding system during our first years and, due to delays at the post office, our plans frequently changed while we waited for mail. For instance, we were in Texas for a month and a priority post package along with three redirected magazines left an Ontario post office in the same mailing. The magazines arrived in three days and the priority package took 23 days. This was our most exasperating delay but not the only one that upset us. Another time all that reached us was an empty envelope. The contents 'fell' out of the envelope and slowly made their way back to our Canadian address. Obviously someone decided to play football with our mail.

Thankfully times have changed. Receiving mail on regular intervals is no longer a big problem for RVers. During our early travels we spent many months in Mexico, mail didn't always arrive as expected but we were fortunate that over the years my sister flew in to spend several extended stays with us and she hand-carried important mail to us. Mail delivery has improved over the years. One winter in the mid-nineties while we were stationary on the beach in Mexico for three months, we received our forwarded mail from Ohio every week. My sister in Canada sent our Canadian mail to Ohio and we received it 10 to 14 days later.

Many RV parks throughout North America will not accept mail sent to campers. However they will provide the address of the nearest post office for mail sent in care of 'General Delivery' – you can obtain a ZIP code from any post office.

---

47 *To find a* US Post Office *log onto* www.mapsonus.com/db/USPS.

In Touch Electronically

Electronic mail (e-mail) is a product of the computer age. To use this system you need a computer, a modem and a telephone. Those with expertise in this field know what I mean, those who do not have a computer on board can learn the ins and outs by going to a library or a Cyber Café to access the net and pick up e-mail. It is really easy to subscribe to a free e-mail address from Hotmail, Yahoo or Netscape. If you are computer illiterate ask a friend or grandkid to help if needed. Many RV resorts in sun-country include 'computer clubs' so everyone can learn from each other.

My computer station/dinette in the Luxor.

Using a laptop is more convenient but numerous RVers prefer a desktop. Many RVers who settle into a park for a seasonal getaway of three to six months will connect to a landline and subscribe to a local ISP (Internet Service Provider).

➢ *PocketMail*

A very simple way for non-computer users to stay in touch is with a handy device called PocketMail. This battery-operated device looks like a mini computer (3" x 6" – about the size of an organizer) complete with keyboard that operates without wires or phone line connections. It works worldwide and connection is made by calling a toll-free number in the

U.S.A. and Canada plus in several other countries. You type your e-mail message and hit 'send', go to a phone (pay phones too), dial the access number, put the device up to the receiver, push the PocketMail button and your e-mail is on the way to the addressee. At the same time e-mail messages addressed to you come in as text message, without attachments. It is possible to consolidate PocketMail e-mail with your computer so messages can be downloaded through your regular e-mail program as well as on the PocketMail device.

A wide range of devices, are available but the 'Composer' unit functions with many cell phones as well as regular phones. These units are available in the U.S.A. from stationery stores, and Camping World; in Canada from Radio Shack and BatteryPlus. It is also available from many online sources including our site and from numerous RVers you meet on the road. Look for signs such as 'E-mail without a computer' or 'E-mail at your fingertips' or 'E-mail in your pocket' plus more. The RVers who sell PocketMail devices can set up your service in minutes. If you want to stay in touch without a computer, PocketMail can be the answer.

> ➢ *Ositech*
The influx of cell phones has made it so easy to stay in voice contact, but to go 'on-line' many RVers still carry their computer to a public access modem (phone jack). Since we can't move from place to place with a phone line attached like an umbilical cord we must rely on available phone hook-ups in campground offices, airports, truck stops, and several stationery/office supply stores. In some locations Cyber Cafés and city libraries or other such businesses offer computers for use (usually there are no hook-ups for laptops) – and cost may be minimal or even free, but it can be a hassle locating this form of access. As a result we frequently searched for campgrounds with on-site phone hook-ups simply because connecting without leaving our rolling home seemed like heaven.

That was before I was privileged to test special PC cards using CellFlex technology from Ositech Communications based in Guelph, Ontario, Canada. With these versatile PC cards and my cell phone, equipped with data/text messaging, I am able to pick up and send e-mail plus surf the 'Net from the comfort of my motorhome. This amazing CellFlex technology provides a simple 'in-touch' solution for many cell phone users.

Most popular dual mode cell phones have voice and data capabilities that function in both analogue and digital coverage areas, the PC card/software promoted by cell companies usually connect in one OR the other. As a result when your phone/PC card modem wants to work in digital and you are in an analogue area you will not be able to 'log on'.

However, Ositech PC cards connect in both areas. When we are in analogue coverage areas, access is slow as is typical with a cell phone, but while retrieving digital data the connection speed definitely increases but it is still not as fast as the traditional landline.

Ositech PC cards, by default, choose digital data connection when it is available, if not it moves to analogue without interruption. Analogue service has been around longer, it remains much more widespread than digital service although some metropolitan areas do operate on both systems. Many RVers (and travellers in general) flock to less populated places where analogue rules, but Ositech CellFlex PC cards make connecting easy even in these secluded utopias.

Ositech's CellFlex products can be used with laptops and PDAs (handheld computers) as well as any device that contains a PCMCIA slot. Ositech products are available worldwide. CellFlex technology is designed to work with the phones of today and those of the future, too.

Your phone plan should be 'one-rate roaming' that includes long distance, airtime and roaming in each minute of use. The system works better if your phone connects in digital data. No matter where we are to go on-line, I simply dial my Canadian ISP access number in Ontario, Canada by long distance rather than searching for a local dial-up number – subscribing to an ISP close to where we are camped is also no longer a necessity. However, the occasional times I post updates on my website or access some secure complex websites such as my on-line banking I take my computer to a modem because the cell is too slow for this. If I do not have a local dial-up access number I use the toll-free access number for my ISP.

Ositech's helpful tech support will work with you at each step of the way. Ask them if your present phone works with this amazing device[48] – most do. Just for info: Even though I am Canadian, I am using the Verizon cell phone service from the U.S.A. mainly because my plan includes unlimited after-hour one-rate calls when I am south of the border. I no longer need to install a landline for the winter or subscribe to a local ISP.

Using Ositech PC cards makes connecting so convenient even if it is quite slow (14400 BPS). However, if you subscribe to a phone plan with sufficient phone minutes to support Internet usage this system is a joy to use.

---

48 More details and contact info for Ositech are listed on www.rvliving.net under
Advice and How-to page. A story about Ositech can be reached from the direct link
on our home page or call 1-888-OSITECH for more info.

➤ *WIFI, Air Cards*   *And Much More*

Wireless technology is constantly changing and it is impossible to stay on top of it in a printed publication. The following processes are new and as they become more accessible for our lifestyle, I will add them to our website.

Air cards provide high-speed connections in specific areas without a phone line. These tiny antenna/PC cards show a lot of promise but they are still in their infancy and they are not available in many areas as yet.

WIFI (802.11b) allows wireless Internet connection from various 'hot spots' without being connected by a wire leading from a telephone/TV cable jack to your computer. These are becoming common for home users and can be found in some campgrounds, McDonald's restaurants and Flying J's, etc. If you have a special PC card/modem you can access the 'Net by highspeed within a certain distance from the main connection, even in your RV at a campsite. The special PC card picks up the signal from a main receiver box located in your house or your unit. The receiver is connected with your Internet service of choice (i.e. telephone line, cable TV, etc.). With a wireless connection, you can take your laptop outside or in different rooms and still connect to the Internet. All you need is a unique PC card (in some laptops the software may already be built in) and a main receiver within signal range. Expect wireless connections to be a more viable source in the future but it, too, is just beginning. This technology is still in its infancy, but so far connecting fees are reasonable; payment is monthly when you subscribe to a particular provider or by the hour as a visitor.

♦ Cell phone technology is moving towards high speed Internet as well but at this point it can be quite costly.

♦ Satellite system also work well but the ones that access the Internet without phone lines cost several thousands to install and the monthly fee is approximately $100.00 (U.S.). Prices are coming down so in a few years this may be another option.

Connecting to the Internet is only in the beginning stages for RVers. Expect many more exciting techniques to surface in the near future. Keep your eyes and ears open and if you attend RV rallies with seminars on these subjects be sure to attend. It should be interesting time ahead as technology and our unique lifestyle move closer together.[49]

---

49 *As technology evolves, current updated info will be featured on www.rvliving.net.*

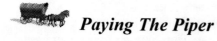 *Paying The Piper*

With a little financial planning RVers can enjoy sightseeing trips like this at the impressive 'Eye of the Needle' on Needles Highway – Part of our Mt Rushmore, SD bus tour.

Thanks to telephone banking, paying bills has become easy for those of us who live on the road. For a small monthly fee (seniors may enjoy banking with reduced or no fees) we can now do everything from transferring funds to obtain balances, establish exchange rates, apply for a loan, pay bills and so much more by calling a toll-free number. To make it even easier, a friendly computer 'voice' assists you with helpful prompts. Press zero to talk to a real person.

Internet banking is also so easy and it is free. This process simplifies keeping on top of your finances to another degree. To enjoy the benefits of online banking, visit your bank's website and register. You will need your client card and will have to supply a password. When the information is in place, most banks require that you call a toll-free number for voice confirmation to activate your online account. With online banking capabilities you can pay bills, transfer money from one account to another and send e-mail money orders (a small fee will be charged for e-mail money orders).

The longer we enjoy our extended travels, the less mail we receive. RVers going away for a season can decrease some of their bills by pre-paying pro-rated amounts on water, electric and telephone statements. Bills can also be paid automatically by a credit card.

Most banks will also set up a program to pay your bills each month – for a small fee. You set the amount, provide the dates and account numbers and the payment automatically comes out of your account. Banks will also pay a credit card from your accounts as well or you can pay it yourself by telephone banking or through Internet banking.

Using cash from ATMs eliminates credit card charges all together. Stop all newspaper and magazine subscriptions and ask the post office or a relative to eliminate all flyers and other junk mail.

Many businesses, especially insurance companies, offer pre-authorized payment deductions taken directly out of your account. You send a voided cheque to the company you owe money to and that company, in turn, forwards the information to the bank to be filed; when the bank receives notification of the bill, payment automatically is deducted from your account.

Banking Power Of Attorney

During our early days of travel we asked a brother-in-law to be our banking power of attorney. He picked up our mail, paid our bills and deposited cheques. He was also close at hand if we had a problem when we were a far distance from home. As our main contact with the bank when we were not in Canada he interceded several times. One occasion in particular he was the only one who was available to sort out a major banking problem. At that time we were in Mexico; each month the bank withdrew money (in error) from our account without our knowledge. I had tried to stop this withdrawal several times before we entered Mexico. Thanks to this helpful relative, he convinced the bank to take full responsibility to cover an overdue NSF cheque, plus associated costs both locally at the bank and in Mexico. We had written the cheque in good faith for campground payment, expecting the cash to be in the account. Writing an NSF cheque in Mexico can mean a jail term but thanks to our power of attorney, he was able to sort the problem out plus insist the bank pay all costs.

Since it is a necessity to have a legal resident/address for vehicle registration, driver's licences, insurances, investments, income tax, voter's list and passports, etc., this same relative allowed us to share his home, address and phone number. To keep everything in one neat package, he was also our executor of our estate.

My sister is our present banking power of attorney with access to our savings and checking accounts. Since I can't deposit cheques I receive by mail for my writing, etc. while I am in the U.S.A. she takes care of that as well. However, with the Internet and telephone banking the times she must intercede is becoming less every year. When we are out of Canada our banking power of attorney opens and deals with our 'official' mail before she forwards everything to us via our U.S.A. mail-forwarding address in Cincinnati, Ohio. We receive our mail at the local U.S. address we provide within a few days later.

The only stipulation from the bank on the required banking power of attorney permission letter is that, if we die and she writes any cheques after our death, she is responsible for repaying the money to our estate.

Having someone at home to fill in when we are not there provides peace-of-mind to our travels. It is easier to talk in person rather than trying to 'fix' things from a distance.

Filing Income Tax

When we began fulltiming, our power of attorney prepared our tax returns. He would mail everything to us for signatures and we'd return the forms for final preparation and submission. We then switched to a private tax consultant service; now he forwards a prepared return that we signed and returned by registered mail for submission. At present, our tax service sometimes files our returns by e-mail.

Another option is to file your own income tax, either using written forms or by purchasing a CD tax program for the applicable year. If you have been issued an electronic registration number (for Canadians, the number can be found on the address labels sent to you), government-approved tax programs allow your return to be electronically filed (e-file) through the Internet.

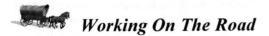

Working On The Road

To work in a country other than your own you must have a work visa or, in the U.S., a green card. Although these are not impossible to obtain, before you apply for a work visa or green card, check out the details. There may be some ramifications that affect your country status, such as medical benefits for Canadians or pensions that don't travel across the border, etc. These regulations are similar for Americans wanting to work in Canada. It is also not always easy for Canadians, Americans or international visitors to obtain these work visas in countries other than their own. Be aware when employed or retired in another country, it becomes your place of residence for income tax purposes.

Although many RVers do earn money on the road by becoming creative, holding a job in its true sense is not feasible. It is easier to work in your home.

Creating and selling crafts is a favourite way to make extra pocket money.

Adding To The Cash Flow

To help pay for their next big getaway, some RVers work in their own country for a season. I am one of many who send stories to several magazines about our interesting travels. Others exchange services such as general park maintenance for free camping. They run errands, cut grass, do electrical repairs and keep up with building maintenance. No money changes hands so, technically, you're not employed. But Revenue Canada (maybe the IRS too) could consider this payment as bartering – your pay may be taxable with reference to income tax. Most RVers who work for services or under the table cash, keep the details to themselves.

One friend is a bookkeeper. She works two afternoons a week in exchange for a portion of her campsite rent. Others fill in at the campground gift shop for a similar agreement.

Some RVers bake for a hobby, so they take orders for special pies or cakes from fellow campers. Ask if you can sell fresh bread or pastries in the campground store. You might even enquire if it's possible to use the clubhouse kitchen to do your baking during the off-hours.

Occasionally park management may exchange camping fees for a ready supply of sweets to sell to park residents with morning coffee. The park supplies ingredients and receives the profits, you camp several months for 'free'. One Arizona resort that we stayed in is very busy. Since the park manager doesn't live on-site, the campground owners employ two host couples. Although they alternate weeks, one couple is always on call to answer park phones, respond to after-hours emergencies and to make sure that late arrivals have sites. These people are also paid with rent-free camping sites.

This same park also employs a winter resident to run the kitchen. Several times a week, the resort hosts special meals such as Saturday morning breakfasts, special dinners, snacks for dances and provides donuts and muffins for morning coffee. The kitchen has many volunteers to help in the preparation for these functions but the overall planning and co-ordinating is handled by one key person in exchange for campsite rent. She happens to be a Canadian but very few RVers are aware of her 'payment' circumstances.

U.S. national, state and provincial parks as well as the Bureau of Land Management facilities all employ RVers as on-site hosts. Duties and hours of work are minimal and payment is free camping. Even though many are 'working' this way, if you are doing so without visas do not broadcast it to the world.

Workamper News and Workers on Wheels are two U.S. publications that list seasonable employment opportunities for RVers. WorkKamper Canada is a new division for Canadians.[50]

Other tips to earn money include a gift-wrapping service (especially lucrative during the Christmas season), power washing and waxing vehicles to protect them from the sun's harmful rays and, even yard care at resorts where seasonal renters are responsible to keep things neat and manicured. If payment is forthcoming make it for cash.

Of course, there are always odd jobs such as pet sitting and walking animals or, if you have a computer, teaching techniques to new users or preparing letters and documents.

One person we know is very knowledgeable about RV repair. As a favour to park members, he performs in-park RV service. This is a hobby for him and any payment he receives for his inexpensive charges is 'cash only' without receipts. When we asked how much we owed he stated, "I can't charge a fee but I normally receive a $20.00 tip for this service." This RVer has managed to establish a prosperous non-business that adds considerably to his travelling funds.

We've met RVers who perfected the art of window tinting, upholstering and carpet installation. These crafts provide additional income during their travels. Doing favours by adding extras such as this and updating unit interiors for RVers in some parks is one more way to supplement travel expenses.

Another RVer friend accomplishes chores that others may hate. For instance, he earns pocket money by washing RVs and awnings. Detailing RVs or power polishing is one more way of earning money. Other RVers use their cars to deliver the 5:00 a.m. papers to subscribers throughout the resorts.

One RVing friend is a retired dressmaker who utilizes her skill to create designer jackets. Making and selling her creations keeps her busy and supplements her living budget.

My sewing machine also receives a good work-out during our travels. In my early days I designed a special line of hand-painted sun clothes plus reproduced unusual crafts. Frequently, these items are for personal use but they also serve as fun gifts for family and friends. If I have any extras, I sell them at craft sales.

---

50 *Although, many cross border work opportunities do not apply to non-residents, it's worth a one-year subscription to obtain some idea of what is available. Subscription details and websites for* Working on the Road *are listed on the* RV WebLink *page on* www.rvliving.net.

Numerous campers at RV resorts in the sunny south create exquisite crafts to sell from rented tables at area flea markets and craft shows. Most full-service parks hold monthly craft sale days for both local residents and visitors.

Many RVers make jewellery from the beautiful shells, stones and semi-precious gems they collect along the way. Not only do they sell well at resort craft sales, quite often they are in demand at campgrounds everywhere.

Those planning to stay in an area for an extended time or return to the same area each year, could arrange to sell their creations at a local shop on consignment. Although no one we have met has become wealthy by selling crafts, making the items is a satisfying and enjoyable way to fill the quiet hours plus add a bit of play money.

It's difficult for RVers to find time to do everything they would like to do. Many mornings I begin writing at 5:00 a.m. because this time frame doesn't interfere with our busy retirement schedule. Some hobbies and tasks are extremely time-consuming but, even the small amount of cash you receive could make the difference between exploring North America or filling each day up with a dead-end job. Although, in most cases, working on the road tops up a travelling budget, it's difficult to earn a sufficient amount to live on.

Work, as you previously knew it, might not be possible while travelling. However, some enjoyable activities can add small amounts of cash to the budget and give you 'free' camping with full hookups.

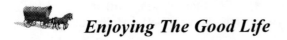 *Enjoying The Good Life*

Ultimate form of relaxation! John and the dogs at El Caracol
campground in Lo de Marcos, Nayarit, Mexico.

Our family and friends who haven't had the opportunity to enjoy the RV lifestyle are always asking us if we get bored. Bored! I just wish that we had the time to fit our busy schedules into a 24-hour day.

We spend most of our time moving around and exploring new and exciting destinations. We've enjoyed the sights in winter hot spots – Arizona, California, Florida, Texas and Mexico– as well as in the vast and beautiful country of Canada during the summer. In the spring and fall we explore points *en route* to the next destination.

Although some parks only provide basic facilities, others are five-star resorts overflowing with amenities such as weight rooms, billiard tables, pools, hot tubs, saunas, clubhouses, sport facilities and fully-equipped wood-working rooms. To avoid the winter rush to sun country, we simply find a park that we think will suit us from a campground directory and book early for a three-month reservation. Booking for an extended stay is more economical than daily, weekly or monthly rates.

Each summer we try to spend an extended season someplace in Canada. Since long-term or seasonal rent is usually low we feel justified to take trips away once or twice a month. Once we arrive at the park, we set up house and have a phone installed. It's like a holiday for us where we can relax and stretch out.

Canada is a great place for worldwide summer visitors and Canadians can explore the U.S.A. during the winter. Climate is usually pleasant during these timeframes. Americans and international visitors reap an additional benefit of a great conversion rate for the U.S. dollar while Canadians can receive a benefit of campgrounds and major attractions that are priced at par.

Most southern parks provide regular activity schedules and newsletters to let campers know what events are taking place in the park and surrounding area. A full calendar of events may include golf, shuffleboard, aerobics, aqua-fit, dance lessons and card games and crafts, etc. plus a whole host of special theme nights. Depending on the park, activities in the north range from laid-back with no planned activities to resorts with full recreational schedules.

The busy snowbird parks are our usual choice of a winter getaway but, one year, we and many of our RV friends changed destinations every one or two weeks. Some evenings, groups get together for impromptu music fests or a tail-gate pizza party. As well, most overnight-style parks also plan activities such as dances, potlucks and special dinners.

I could go on and on about the extensive array of park activities. Each resort differs from the next but, in most cases, it's absolutely impossible to participate in everything. We've found that when RVers are new retirees or, are on their first extended vacation, they take to the road and try to see everything at once. It's difficult to accept the idea that returning to work in two weeks is a thing of the past. Most of us 'run' during our early getaways. Eventually, everyone slows down but two decades later, we still find the lack of time to do everything is our biggest problem.

There are so many things RVers like to do in retirement, from reading a book there was never time for in the 'old' life, to enjoying leisure hours by the pool, taking long hikes, biking or walking throughout the park. Just plain socializing with others not confined to a schedule is another benefit of RV living. And, it's certainly not boring.

RVers moving from park to park can enjoy long forgotten hobbies or take the time to learn a special craft. Each area they visit caters to different interests so, whatever your wants, there will be something perfect for you.

The most common complaint we hear from full and part-time retirees is, "I don't know how I ever found the time to work eight hours every day." Life is so full when everything you do is enjoyable.

Keeping busy doing what you wish to do is why RVing seniors remain so young. There are people in their 80s still roaming and calling all of North America their home. However, by that time, many RVers trade their home-on-wheels for a home on some kind of foundation but they still continue to enjoy life – they just choose local festivities without travelling to new horizons.

*Zion National Park in southwest Utah is one of
my top 10 all-time favourite places.*

What Is An RVer?

During our years in the military every job had a description. I like to think the following applies to most RVers:

Skills
- ♦ Must have the ability to trip plan exciting and scenic routes between destinations.
- ♦ Stretch a week's allowance to include attractions *en route* but never go over budget.
- ♦ The ability to be a friend and goodwill ambassador representing your country and the RV world.

Duties
- ♦ Take part in every interesting event your present resort offers. Join RV clubs/chapters and participate in events.

♦ With the balance of each day, you will explore the surrounding area as well as trying to discover and visit all available bargain or shopping areas. Be extra careful not to miss important sights along the way.

Benefits Package

♦ In the evening, you have earned the time to relax and enjoy a little TV, visit friends, play cards or read. You can also indulge in toe-tappin' music or any other miscellaneous activity that strikes your fancy.

♦ If the RVing lifestyle appeals to you, don't wait to follow your dreams. RVers we meet who now spend many months on the road can't understand why it took them so long to begin the adventure.

Recap Of Our Years On The Road

When John and I began RVing, no one was greener or as inexperienced as we were. We found a campground 20 minutes from work and spent as much time as possible in our motorhome.

Fortunately, for us, our neighbours, Jack and Eunice McCleary from Florida, were seasoned RVers. They took us under their wing while they explained, coddled, protected and educated us on many facets of RVing. They also shared their hints and secrets to successful living and travelling in an RV. Their hospitality set a precedent for us to do the same for inexperienced RVers we meet on our travels.

Over the years John and I have spent so much time explaining the basics to new RVers and, as our first year rolled into many, we decided that the simplest way for us to reach the maximum amount of people was to include everything in a guidebook.

Completing *Spirit of the Open Road* and now *RV Living in the 21st Century* were both a long haul over a very rocky road but, nevertheless, I count these challenges as my finest accomplishments – other than marrying my best friend, John, four years before we retired.

Without the help, encouragement and the never-ending patience of John and other staunch supporters, these publications may never have become a reality.

This updated version of *Spirit* should answer most of the questions that you may have or, at least how to obtain information when required. For your convenience I've included footnotes with phone numbers, website and research information plus other tidbits to help you on your way.

When seeking information, call an office several times to talk to different officials (especially from a government office). Do this anonymously, if you wish, and if you receive (like I do) a variety of explanations for the same question, ask why. Assess the information and decide how each situation applies to you.

With a little planning and preparation for the unexpected, you'll prevent upsetting surprises. Preparation is the first step to exciting RV travels. And, if you travel informed, emergencies and problems become less traumatic.

John and I proudly display a highway mural (cover photo) on the back of our coach – our motorhome licence (tag) spells out R DREEM and our car reads R GO 4 and, on the road, we tune in to Channel 14 and 19 on the CB. When our paths cross, honk your horn and give a wave to say "Hi!"

During one of our trips we saw a sign on a billboard outside a small Ontario town. Though I can't remember the name of the town, the words on the sign stuck in my mind. They were a perfect description of the RV lifestyle.

"We meet, we part until we meet again." Happy travelling.

From this...

  the first RV.

    to this...
    our Luxor and latest towed, our Grand Am.

INDEX

walkie-talkies help to park, 58
washer/dryer, 16, 80
water filters - in line style, 53
water hose – for winter camping, 85
water hose – safe for drinking, 52, 54, 138
water leaks, 48, 50
water pump – turn off while driving, 48
water regulator – for high pressure, 52
WD-40 – do not use on rubber, 82

weather patterns, 109
weather radio, 109
weigh scales location, 177
weigh your RV – don't overload, 176
winter camping, 19, 89
winter living in an RV, 85
winter travel, 62
winterizing an RV, 85
wireless technology for the Internet, 262
working on the road adds to the cash flow, 225, 266

About the Author

Peggi McDonald and her husband John are approaching their 20-year mark of living and travelling in their RV. As a fulltiming RVer with close to two decades on the road, Peggi's wealth of experience is shared through her writing. As well as being the author of the best-selling *Spirit of the Open Road*, Peggi is a featured columnist for many RV publications, has made a number of TV appearances, guest-hosted radio talk shows and is a featured seminar presenter at many of the RV shows, dealer open houses and RV lifestyle schools in both Canada and the U.S. She is also the author of two e-books and the host of www.rvliving.net – one of most-visited Internet sites by fellow RVers.

Printed in the United States
118070LV00002B/234/A